You're Welcome

A Dog Lovers Novel

By

A.J. Arentz

Edited by: Meghan Largent

Cover Design: Rae Matthews

Formatting: A.J. Arentz & Rae Matthews

Dedication

Ludo:

Thank you for your amazing companionship and all you taught me over the years!

You will forever be ultimate in my eyes and in my heart!

Chapter 1: Ejected

Changes in life come in many forms; often, they are hardest when the change is more drastic. I recently learned that I have two choices when change arises: I can roll over and submit, or I can stand and conquer it. Regardless, change seems to always be coming for me. I have found one only weapon capable of battling change, and that is choice. *Brace yourself now, boy. Here comes another flurry of change.*

"Stop crowding me!" squeals Big Girl.

"Yeah, no kidding. Back off," agrees the smallest male. He is the most squished out of all of us as he doesn't have the strength to push any of us back. We call him Runt.

POP... WUSSSHHHH!

"Who kicked me? Come on, now, fess up so I can kick your butt. I know it was him!" Challenger threatens as he points to Portly Boy. Challenger is the second largest male and he challenges everyone constantly, hence his ever-so-fitting name.

"Wait, did anyone else hear that pop?" I inquire, trying to solve our new dilemma.

"You mean that deafening noise just before this

1

strange suction force around us started? Yeah, I think everyone heard it! Why? What do you make of it?" Big Girl asks. "Should we be worried?"

"Why is everyone crowding me? Back off already! For crying out loud, a guy needs room to think." I try to calm everyone down and earn myself some extra space at the same time. As the biggest boy of our recently established tribe, I am more than aware of the small space we inhabit. I noticed that our environment started shrinking a few weeks ago on a steady and consistent basis. I have been working to figure out this new predicament for the past few days, but I haven't come up with anything substantial yet. The one thing I know for sure is that we all seem to get larger every time we wake from a nap. I can only assume that there is some kind of grow juice being pumped into us through these cords that tether us to the bubble we inhabit.

I redirect my focus back to the source of the recent explosion. *What caused it?* Just as I start to investigate the noise further, a tremendous amount of suction-like pressure pulls everyone down. *Now I know how Runt feels all the time.* The fluid that once filled our blissful bubble and allowed us to float freely drains hastily away. *Great, now our space is getting even smaller!*

Cords tether us to this bubble, and it's impossible to break free of them. I know this because I have tried everything from chewing to non-stop spinning myself around and around. Much to my dismay, the cord does not break. I only end up getting very dizzy as the cord untwists itself back to its original state. By spinning at a rapid speed, I proved to everyone that our cords are simply unbreakable.

None of us know where we came from or how we got here. I'm just thrilled we all get along and seem to agree on most matters ninety percent of the time. Our most recent debate before today's loud pop regarded the angle of the dangle. We all agree that there are two different genders amongst us. Somehow, we know that this makes some of us male and others female. We came to this conclusion because some of us have a smaller third leg if you will that hangs between our back legs, on others this little jewel is absent altogether.

It is strange how we all seem to come equipped with a vast amount of knowledge, and yet none of us seem to have any real experience to back up what we claim to know. We all speak the same language, and after our first week together, referring to one another by our characteristics became everyone's natural habit. No one took offense. I am Big Guy.

"Get your butt out of my face!" Feisty Female chimes in.

"What is going on? Anyone else feel like they are being squeezed to death?" asks Lazy Guy. I know things are about to get interesting since he is awake. That and the fact he rarely talks is a definite cause for concern. I can feel worry gradually growing inside me. I know if my worry gets much bigger, it will become a monster of sorts, giving me no choice but to battle it.

I find it fascinating how life can change in the same amount of time it takes my heart to complete one full beat. It seems only a few beats earlier, I was just a blip floating in a vast bubble. Several beats later there were fifteen of us populating this bubble. We thought this was Utopia. We lazily floated around as best we could in our small space, picking on each other or engaging in small talk as we drifted past one another. Eventually, the indestructible cords secured to our bellies always pulled us back to our initial positions.

The days of somersaults and backflips to entertain one another ended a while ago. We are all too big to completely turn around anymore. The temperature and lighting we all share has always been delicately soft and toasty warm, also, until this point, the noise level was always serene. This perfect little bubble had been our reality for the past sixty days.

Oh, I forgot to mention that we know how to count, too. Usually the only time Lazy Guy talks, if he talks at all, is just before we all drift to sleep. Lazy Guy counts us all repeatedly. Maybe he is scared we won't be here when he wakes up. He should know me better than that. If we ever leave this bubble, assuming it's even possible, I wouldn't leave any of them behind. I have grown attached to them all. Even the ones who annoy me, like Challenger.

I have found that each member of our little tribe brings a special element to the group that I would not want to be without. I have learned something from each of them. That being said, if we ever left, we would travel at the pace of our slowest member: Lazy Guy. I fear it would make for an excruciatingly slow journey. We have all peacefully shared this Heaven-like place, and I have never planned on leaving. Today, however, is much different. I learn a big lesson today. It seems that one of the best or worst parts about life, depending on how you want to look at it, is that just when you think you have finally figured it all out and know how to live, it makes a three-hundred-and-sixty-degree flip-flop and changes entirely. *Things were much less complicated as a tiny blip.*

Suddenly, the top of our paradise falls smashing us together violently. Our once balmy temperature plummets down to a chilling level. Cold air and intense light come rushing in from what appears to be a vast and quickly forming tunnel. *Our eyes have only ever encountered light in the form of soft glows.* We all battle to keep our eyes open as the new, garish light rushes in through the opening.

I keep being shoved closer to the hole of uncertainty; my tethered cord is unfortunately secured closest to the events unfolding. My eyes close, resisting the unwelcomed change to our environment. I rack my brain, trying to come up with a solution, when the tribe begs me. Each of them speaks frantically and without waiting their turn to be heard. Generally, we always respect one another and wait our turn to talk. Not today, though. Chaos is consuming us all. Everyone is frantic as they try to figure out what in the blazes is going on. I'm terrified and can only assume that everyone else is, too.

Unwelcomed feelings well up within me. I have no time to sort out these new emotions, so for now I will refer to these unwanted feelings of mine as my little Monster. Monster is wasting no time feeding and growing himself into a powerful beast that demands my full attention. He seems to feast on all these uncertain feelings swirling within me as if they are sort of steroid. I fear Monster is rapidly accumulating power and in the process, diminishing mine. *Okay Monster you asked for it. This is war!*

Something tells me that none of us is braver than the one who stands beside us at this point. I'm contemplating giving in to Monster and the panic he seems to have seized my chest cavity with. It is getting increasingly harder to breathe. Anxiety is the only word screaming itself from a faraway place in my brain. Is that the name of these feelings that are feeding Monster? Whatever it is, I don't have time for it. This rising anxiety level of mine is quickly depleting my hope reserves. I must free myself both internally and externally. My lungs need to find air soon! *Think now, focus!* I need a plan. Black spots appear before my eyes. *Come on lungs, in and out!*

Finally, I decide that I will push Challenger in front of me to peer through the new hole that is ripping our peaceful environment apart. Hopefully, I can then get a handle on Monster. If I can cross dealing with the large gaping hole before me off my list I can focus all my efforts on him. Challenger's cord has always been closest to mine. *Come out, come out wherever you are, little Challenger!* Honestly, I am in disbelief that he's not already trying to get ahead of me in some fashion. Go figure? The one time I am hoping he will challenge me, Challenger's off somewhere hiding. I search frantically for him. *That little rascal.* Somehow, Challenger had squirmed his way back to fourth in line, intertwining his cord with others along his way to further secure his safety.

Crap, plan Shove Challenger to the front of the line has been completely foiled. With my size, there is no physical way I can reposition myself behind him now. So much for letting Challenger deal with the hole. I look around to see who remains closest. I only spy Runt. It appears everyone else had the same idea as Challenger. Poor Runt is being repeatedly shoved forward because he is too scrawny to fight back. Something inside me tells me that it would be wrong to copy the others and do the same. I know the little fella looks up to me, and this would be a cowardly move on my part.

Oh, what to do now? I close my eyes and silently ask, or at least I thought I did. *Did I say that out loud?* Either way Big Girl squeals my answer. "You must go first! You are the biggest and the strongest. You are our leader!"

Dang. How had she known I was actively forming a plan to abort my post? Big Girl's words stroke my ego. I feel pride course through my veins. *I am the leader!* I was unaware that an election had even occurred, but I will gladly accept this title. I like the way it sounds; it makes me feel important, respected. When this is over, I will make them call me Leader instead of Big Guy.

I puff out my chest to make myself look as intimidating and powerful as possible. I need to appear fearless, like a force to be reckoned with. I do the best I can to fulfill the role I have just obtained. I decide there is no harm in taking a peek out the hole. Besides, I have the fourteen of them behind me as a backup if something goes wrong. Part of me fears that my only true backup will be Feisty Female and Runt. It's backup, nonetheless. *Okay, here goes nothing. I've got this!* Nothing a little self-pep talk can't get me through.

I swallow loudly—more of a gulp, really. I hope none of them can sense my apprehension. I inch closer to the opening of the windy tunnel and the eye-searing light. My pupils instantly shrink as light pours into them. I have also now waged a full-on war against my Monster as he seems to have joined forces with my negative psyche. As my eyes try to retreat further from the light my anxiety level increases again along with the decibel level of Monster.

"This is a suicide mission!" shouts my Monster.

"Man up and lead! You've got this," my positive inner self counters. Monster does not give in easily. Somehow, I know this negative part of my psyche only wants to take me down the easy path of defeat.

Neither Monster nor me will be declared the winner today. I find that it is instead my inquisitive side that seems to take over. It overtakes even my hair-standing-on-edge, scared-enough-to-pee-myself side, so I advance forward to embrace the new journey that lies ahead of me. *Here goes nothing!* I steel myself, gathering up one last ounce of courage. I am one step away from exiting the tunnel.

I step forward. Tremendous pressure seizes and detains me, a significant squeezing force that holds me securely where I stand. The tunnel is caving in around me. I still have not seen what is on the other side. I will not fail! *I will win this battle if it's the last thing I do!* Aside from the fact that there is no way I can live cooped up like this any longer, the time has come to move on. Time to embrace Change.

Determination fills me, causing every fiber of

my being to stand at attention and await my next command. I heave my body back and forth trying to resolve the skirmish between me and free myself from the collapsing tunnel. *I've got this. I can overcome this. This is nothing!* I silently chant to myself in an effort to fight the pressure from the tunnel and Monster. The two are trying desperately to win the battle and force me to retreat. Determination drives me forward. *I must see what lies beyond the breach.* I dig deep within myself. Finally, my strength prevails, and I find liberation.

"Victory is mine!" I shout in celebration towards the others behind me. I inhale deeply as the tunnel releases its pressure. A sigh of relief escapes me as I regain my confidence and realign myself to complete my mission. I gather my wits and prepared to take the last step. Then suddenly, instead of stepping out as planned, I am instead ejected out like a cannonball with extra gunpowder loaded behind it. I shoot out of my warm, safe bubble and into the great unknown.

"Brace for impact!" I yell. I'm trying to both warn the others and prepare myself. For what? I'm not sure.

Chapter 2: What's This?

Ouch, my eyes. Something has burned them shut! Wait what's going on now? Something has a hold of me again. Large, spindly objects wrap around me. These then hand me off to smaller, colder rod-like structures that encapsulate me momentarily. I try to open my eyes, but I can't. I am not sure if it is the temperature or the bright light out in this vast open that keeps my eyes shut tightly. Thankfully, my ears still seem to be in working order.

I hear a voice that seems female. "Look at him. What a fine specimen for the pick of the litter!"

I assume the voice came from a female as it reminds me of the girls inside the peaceful bubble with me. *What is this great unknown unfolding all around me? What happened to my vision?* I sniff at the air and listen, intently gathering information with my other senses. *Where is everyone?*

A stern male voice answers my last unspoken question. "Get ready. I think old mom here has a full litter inside her. They are coming fast, now!"

Chaos envelops me a little longer. I fumble around blindly in my new environment. Now I am contained in a structure with inescapable sides and soft material. I feel, hear, and smell the others being plunked down all around me. One by one they are now joining me on the outside. "Can any of you see?" I inquire over and over as each of them softly lands next to me.

Everyone replies at once with "No," or "We are blind, help us!"

Crap. I had hoped that at least one of them could act as our eyes. "Calm down," I command. "We will get to the bottom of this shortly. We have to work together. Everyone come to the sound of my voice. We must make a plan to..." I didn't even get to finish my last sentence because Challenger felt the need to rudely interrupt me.

"Oh yeah, come to your voice. Look at how great your last plan worked, Big Guy. Epic fail! You made us all blind, for crying out loud. Everyone come to the sound of my voice. I will take the lead for now," Challenger said dryly. He is clearly butt-hurt by the whole me being elected leader situation, but this is no time to argue. We must work together to conquer our current state of affairs. I am about to shame him by pointing out that Challenger had pushed Runt in front of him and retreated from the great opening when a new voice interjects.

"Children, calm down. None of you are blind." The voice is female and seems incredibly familiar, very mature, safe, and calming. I find myself drawn to it immediately as are the others. Everyone shifts around me, and we all migrate in the new voice's direction.

"Stop arguing and listen to your Mother." This voice is deeper and more commanding. Shivers run through us all. Now that is a leader's voice. How do I sound more like that? We all stop exactly where we stand and listen. Fear of some sort of wrath if we failed to obey this voice hangs in the air.

The more inviting female timbre begins again. "You will get your eyes back in a few days. First, you must adjust to your new conditions. It is a test of sorts, and it helps to build and tune your other senses. Take advantage of this time. Now, come to the sound of my voice. I will feed you. Everyone must keep up their strength for the events to come."

I assume this softer voice is the one that the commanding voice referred to as Mother. I do as instructed. *Talk about a struggle.* Previously, I moved about by swimming freely in warm fluid. This is not the case in this outside world. I stand on unsteady legs and shakily make my way to Mother's voice. Out here, my legs barely bear my body's weight. Each step tests muscles I did not know existed. Though unable to see, I force myself to move faster. I am determined to reach our mother first. I am extremely competitive, and my inflated ego from my new title and the recent threat from Challenger fuels my internal fire.

I succeed in reaching Mother first. As I do, she thrusts a soft, warm, tubular structure with a round nub at the end into my mouth. I quickly close my lips around it and suck. The sweetest and most satisfying substance I have ever tasted flows into my mouth and warms my belly. I drink my fill. As we eat, the commanding voice continues to talk. He introduces himself as our Father. He explains all the events that had occurred today. I only half listen, as I am lost in sweet, creamy euphoria.

Father says something about today being the

sixteenth in a month that the humans call April. *What are humans?* He says our eyes will hurt more today because it is clear and sunny outside. He makes the sun sound like it should warm us. *Personally, I feel the temperature is a bit chilly.* Mother's next statement contradicts Father and confirms that my thoughts on the temperature are more accurate. She says something about it only being sixty degrees outside. *Not sure what degrees are, but it sixty sounds like a lot.*

Mother then says, "Gather around, children. Then pile on top of one another. We call this a dogpile. It will help to keep you all warm."

I, of course, go straight to the top of the pile. I have to maintain my leadership role. Plus, this position allows me to stay alert and attuned to everything. For whatever reason, the top seems the most natural choice for a leader. I refuse to give up my role. However, as I sit on top, I question the logic of my decision. On top of the pile, half my body remains exposed and cold. I have nobody to help trap my heat. Even so, I hold my position. I don't want to look weak or appear to be second-guessing myself. The warmest spot is probably somewhere in the middle of the pile. I will aim for a different spot after our next feeding.

Our parents continue to inform us that what we had just gone through is what they call being born. The whole birth thing is a very harsh and drastic climate change for any living creature. When we were inside our Mother, it was a constant one hundred and one degrees with perfect lighting. Not to mention the fact that we could see. The lighting in our new environment has somehow seared our eyes shut. This outside world will take some getting used to.

Mother and Father then explain what we are. It turns out we are angelic, mystical creatures otherwise known as Great White German Shepherds. *I added in the Great part. Perhaps it's the leader role talking, but somehow, I know that I am truly great!* My father says he tips the scales to just over one hundred fifty pounds, and Mother comes in at a solid one hundred twenty. We are a family of large, proud, strong, and, of course, brilliant animals.

Chapter 3: The First Piece

Seven days and lots of listening later, my eyes are the first to open. I get to discover what exactly our journey to the great unknown was. Apparently, it was all of my brothers and sisters and me being expelled from our Mother's backside into the human hands of very pleasant people that my siblings and I call Marsha and Al. It turns out that this was our fate, whether or not we wanted it, thanks to something Father calls biology. Father explained how all the biology stuff works. Most of my siblings thought his description was disgusting. I found it all pretty intriguing. Father also explained that the order we came out of Mother tells them a lot about us and helps to determine our fate.

It seems the discovery of fate will be yet another of my slow-going quest, though I have learned one thing for sure. If one is going to born, then they want to come out first. I got lucky in this instance. Since I decided not to push Runt out in front of me, I earned major points. I had no idea at the time that this minor detail would determine a significant portion of my life's journey. *Note to self: I must remember to watch for these tiny decisions in the future. They seem to make the largest impact when it comes to moving forward.* As it turns out, this decision of mine made me look like the toughest and strongest.

I can't say I am upset by this small fact, as Father told us this is something we will all strive for in life.

Father explains that long ago, our ancestors established a hierarchy for all pack animals, such as ourselves. Alphas are the leaders; all packs have them. There are two Alpha roles and two different ways to become one. The first role is simply that of a basic Alpha. The second role is that of the Alpha One. The Alpha One role is the highest achievement one can obtain in life. One must earn this spot through blood, sweat, and tears. A significant amount of time, research, planning, and action are required to become one. An Alpha One leaves a legacy and changes the world. *Now that is what I am talking about! Where do I sign up?*

The basic Alpha, on the other hand, is a title awarded by circumstance. Like me, for example, in the case of our birth. I am only an Alpha because I just so happened to be ejected out of our Mother first. One becomes a basic Alpha in one of three ways. One, he or she takes a chance from courage fueled by ego. This would be me. I will never tell Big Girl that her calling me the Leader was what lead me to my newly acquired Alpha power as she more than fueled my ego with her words—a secret I will take to my grave. Two, they act in ignorance. It is true, one can become a basic Alpha with zero clue as to what they are doing. Father explains this as 'happenstance': they just happen to be in the right place at the right time. Runt would have obtained the basic Alpha role had I decided to be weak and push him in front of me. The number three way one becomes a basic Alpha is by looking for an adrenaline rush. I guess some are what they call 'adrenaline junkies.'

There seem to be no such junkies in our group, at least not yet. I can see the Feisty Female becoming a basic Alpha in this way in the near future, though. Nothing in this outside world really seems to scare her. I can't help but wonder if she somehow managed to leave her negativity monster inside Mother when she was born. *Perhaps she lacks one altogether. Lucky dog!* Regardless, I will never seek an adrenaline rush, as I have found that I hate surprises and the unknown. Being born and blind for a week was more than enough excitement for this dog.

There are major differences between the two Alpha roles. The basic Alpha is awarded only a fraction of the power that an Alpha One retains. One does not have to work very hard to be become a basic Alpha. An Alpha One on the other hand, must earn the upmost spot and show the rest of the pack that they are the best dog for the job and deserve to have such power. Only one similarity is shared between the two Alpha roles, and that is that both types of Alpha's must work hard to maintain the power they are given. If an Alpha chooses to act as a bully, his or her power is stripped away in short order and awarded to someone more deserving. No matter what Alpha role one has, they must always act in a positive manner and keep the pack moving forward towards better things.

Our parents conclude today's history lesson by telling us that we choose our path in life. They say that we are actively creating our futures every day through our choices. I call bull crap! Well, at least partial bull. I do not agree that we get to choose our path in life. I think we all have a pre-determined path. Birth is a prime example of this. We did not choose to be born; our womb simply decided it was time for us to go and evicted us. No one asked us what we wanted. I can agree with my parents, however, on the fact that as the path of life unfolds before us, we are given the luxury to then map out our journeys through our choices.

This map—or maybe better said, this life of ours—is built by the pieces of knowledge we collect and the events we overcome along the way. The way to where we are all going, will be revealed one scenario at a time. Father always says that "If we are not challenged, nothing will ever change. Amazing things come if we weather and face our challenges."

Regardless, each time we are faced with a fork in the road, we have the power of choice. It is our choices that determine our future and lead us on our own personal journeys. It is up to all of us to build our legacies the way we want them to be. The life chosen for me inserted a fork in the road on the day of our birth. If I had gone left, I would have pushed Runt in front of me. Thankfully, I went right. It appears that I have some sort of protect-the-weaker-amongst-us instincts. *Well, that and the fact that my sister called me a leader and inflated my ego.* I took the reins from there and was born—or should I say ejected into life with the daunting role of a basic Alpha male. *What does it mean to be an Alpha?* This new position of mine seems to have given me a thirst for power and a legacy I can call my own. I need to figure out how to become an Alpha One. Clearly, my

Father has achieved this title. I hope he will give me a few tips.

Over the next two weeks, we continue to learn more. The human female that cares for us, Marsha, spends some of her free time doing things she calls puzzles. She spends countless hours searching for pieces and placing them together. *Life is a lot like a puzzle.* With a little hard work and effort, one can acquire all the right pieces and then fit them together perfectly. Once the puzzle is complete, the most breathtaking and beautiful picture is finally unveiled. I wish my life puzzle came in a box with a picture on the front of it like all of Marsha's. *Is it too much to ask for more concise directions?*

I sit in the sun by an open window after one of our learning sessions with Mother and Father, wallowing in a little self-pity. Life doesn't seem fair. My puzzle lacks a box, and instead appears to be some sort of free-for-all. *How will I ever become an Alpha One?* Father approaches me after seeing disappointment and frustration painted upon my brow. He assures me that if life were not this way, it would not be a life worth living.

Father says, "Son, if your life came in a box like a puzzle, that would be too easy. There is no reward, discovery, or legacy in easy."

Wait, did he just say legacy? I for sure want a legacy like him one day. I adjust my attitude and listen intently as Father further explains that obtaining an Alpha One role is no walk in the park. The mystical mountain peak comes at a price which is why this title and power is not handed out freely unlike the basic Alpha role. Laughter, tears, and blood will mark the chosen path and pave the not-so-yellow brick road.

Father's next words make my blood pump faster as excitement dances in the air between us in the form of static electricity. My hair is literally standing on edge! Father continues, "Every one of life's painful seconds is an insignificant price to pay along the way for what comes at the end! Some events may seem like mountains at the time son, but in reality, they are only small bumps in your journeys road. In the end, it will be worth it! The highest peak beyond the clouds is one hundred and ten percent worth it!" As Father ends our dramatic conversation, a shock zaps my nose and I yelp with surprise. *Does Father really have that much power? Can he really send electricity through the air at will? What else can an Alpha One do?* I find our conversation very inspiring, and will play these exact words over and over in my head whenever a challenge in life rises to face me from now on.

My Father is worldly, so he must be right. These little bits of information give me new light and hope. Now, I look forward to the future challenges that will one day rise to face me. *Bring it on, world! Legacy, here I come!* I sit for the rest of the day and ponder all the information we had been given. As I do so, I also visualize the empire I will someday create. As I bounce back and forth from reality to daydreams, I realize that there are some unknown factors that give rise to new concerns. *What does Father mean by pain and blood? Also, what are tears?*

I glance around our whelping room, also known as Marsha's laundry room. Everything comes to us so easily. We cry for food and Mother lies down to feed us. We ask questions and Father answers them. If we need extra warmth and snuggling, we whine and Marsha or Al come quickly to aid us by picking us up and enfold us in warm blankets from the dryer. The only remnant of possible pain I have encountered occurred when Mother ejected us and our eyes rejected the light. Life so far only seems to be one big easy mystery after another. Nothing has been impossible or very challenging yet. *I rise to this so-called challenge of life and I say to its face, "Prepare to be conquered, because I am the next Alpha One!"*

Chapter 4: Adjusting to the Climate

The first seven weeks of my life streak by lightning fast. We are learning and being trained by our mother, whose name is Macy, and our Father, Snow King. Father is addressed as King by the humans of our house. *Even they know he is an impressive royal force!* Today our parents tell us we will soon leave to lead packs and run houses of our own. *Must we really leave?* The thought of leaving gives me anxiety so I make a mental note: when life inserts a new fork in the road and left is leaving and right is staying, choose right.

Due to our parents' royal nature, each one of us is given a prodigious name today. Mother and Father sit in the middle of our backyard and one by one each of us pups run two laps around them. During our laps, we are to jump, roll over, belly crawl, and demonstrate various types of barks and growls. Once our laps are complete, we are to bow before Mother and Father, I mean the King and Queen, by assuming the downward dog position before them. We all seem to struggle with addressing Mother and Father as King and Queen so it is a relief when Mother, I mean the Queen informs us we only have to do it for the duration of the naming ceremony, at the end we can resume using Mother and Father.

Once one has assumed their downward dog position after finishing their laps they are not allowed to rise until the following occurs. Father, I mean the King, announces our name. As the King says our name Mother, I mean the Queen, simultaneously licks her tongue up the bridge of our nose and between our eyes branding us with our name. It is now that one may finally stand and as we do so our surrounding brothers and sisters erupt in cheerful howling and loudly chant the name that has just given to one of us. I am a little sad that all the former Big Girl, and Big Guy names we previously had are put to rest today, however, I love all our new names, so this is a change I have decided to embrace.

After the naming ceremony is complete, Father explains, "One of the most challenging and rewarding things you will learn is solid communication with your sole human. I will explain the communication part in a moment. First, I want to elaborate on what a sole human is. There is a special human out in this world that is waiting for each of you to find them. Al is mine, and Marsha is your Mothers. Once you meet this person, both of your lives will change for the better. You will both immediately grow stronger and start accomplishing great things in this world once this connection is established. That being said, in order to accomplish great things, you must be able to communicate and understand one another. This brings me to the solid communication part I spoke of in the beginning. To help you build this communication with your human, Mother and I are issuing each of you the task of getting your sole human to call

23

you by the name you were just given at today's ceremony."

Several of us let out sighs of dread. I say what everyone is thinking out loud. "But Father, humans don't understand us. They only hear our words as barks, growls, and grumbles. How is this even possible?"

He replies, "Children, we can't give you all the answers. That would be easy, and you know what the easy way of life yields. I promise you will find a way. Many of you will find that your human seems to stumble blindly onto your name. Just trust us on this one. When the time comes and your human says your name, make sure you pay attention to how communication was achieved. No life lesson is ever too small." *Great, another you-must-figure-it-out-on-your-own puzzle piece. The hits just keep on coming.*

Our training session moves on quickly after Father makes it clear that no more questions regarding our names will be answered today. I try to move forward and follow along with today's lecture, but it's proving to be a real struggle for me. I am sitting by one of my sisters, pondering our new name conundrum, when Mother says something that gets my full attention: we are closely related to wolves! *Wolves? Did I hear her right? I love wolves.*

Wolves are the most mystical of creatures, and they hold the highest standing in the dog community! There is a few breeds that stand before German Shepherds in the relative-to-the-wolf lineup, a *trivial detail*. The fact that we are closely related to wolves at all excites and intrigues me. Wolves are responsible for the creation of the Alpha roles that guide us all. Long ago, the wolves determined the standards, rules, and classifications for each type of Alpha. They paved the way for all dogs to be able to make their mark on this world. I am not just talking about little marks like lifting a leg on a mailbox here either, these are serious big marks that get recorded in dog history so others may learn and study them long after they are gone. Wolves have created an amazing world of opportunity that we as dogs are blessed to have access to. *I am destined to be an Alpha One now. I have wolf power in my blood!*

German Shepherds are in the top three for most intelligent dog breeds. These rankings are populated from about one million other breeds. You heard correctly; I said one million, if you factor in all the hybrids and mixes of dogs out in this world there may even be more than that. It's funny how some humans talk ill of mixed breeds and call them mutts. Mutts are some of the strongest most amazing dogs on this planet. Technically all wolves are mutts as they walk the earth freely and breed as the need comes to further their lines and build their packs. As German Shepherds, we are already awesome, but now with the added wolf power we are indeed mind-blowing creatures. *I feel that the words 'awe-inspiring' and 'astonishing' will best describe me one day.* Mark my words: if they redo the list after my family's existence, we will no doubt be number one for most intelligent. Wolves will run to claim us as their closest relatives!

During a break between lessons, my siblings and I conclude that we live in a castle. It sounds more aristocratic than a house. The humans of our house, Marsha and Al, dote on us. Al is Marsha's husband, and he works a lot so he isn't around as much as Marsha. Last week I heard him say something about almost having all his medical bills paid off and being able to take time off soon. I am not really sure what he means by all the talk he sometimes does, but I do know that whenever Al is around he goes above and beyond to give us his full attention and extra treats. Marsha and Al not only feed us and pick up after us, but they also make sure we have every comfort. Nice plush beds and fresh blankets surround us in abundance. *This is the life!* As my siblings and I stand around our food dishes and talk further, we also decide that we are likely princes and princesses. It makes sense. After all, Father is King.

My sister Aada, formerly known as Big Girl, tries to argue the statements we have been declaring. I immediately prove her wrong. "Father has the AKC papers to prove it, Aada." *Don't ask me what those letters stand for.* Nonetheless, he and Mother are royalty. "Since we are their descendants and we have servants, this confirms that we are princes and princesses! Come, I will further solidify this thought process." I herd my bantering siblings towards the large glass trophy case in the front room. "If you don't believe me, you can see for yourself." I point my nose up and to the right of the towering case. There Mother's and Father's royalty declaration papers hang in shiny gold frames. Next to the frames, all kinds of ribbons and trophies that advertise our parents' achievements rest under bright lights. "See, I told you. Our parents are not only noble but also well titled! Besides, Father is an Alpha One. It only makes sense that he would be a King."

Aada replies as she lies down and rolls onto her back. "Alright, I submit. You are right again, great leader of ours. But don't get too cocky, you are only a basic level Alpha, you know." She smiles as she taunts me, signifying she is only joking and not challenging me.

We all sit and gaze up at my parent's trophy case. As we do, my brothers and I daydream out loud about having castles and servants of our own one day. Just as I am basking in the glory of all the trophies I will obtain and how my future legacy will look one day, Aada says something that quickly deflates my bubble. "You are aware that for that to actually happen, we have to leave here one day, right?"

Crap, she has a point. Maybe Father will want to share Al and his legacy with me, perhaps I can take it over for him one day? I can't seem to come up with another reason one would ever really want to leave here, except to create legacies of our own. I ponder this conundrum for quite a while, ignoring Aada's question. There must be a way to create my own legacy while staying here. Perhaps this is yet another piece of my life puzzle that I must gain to move forward. *Fear not, world you will still be blessed with my great legacy. I am determined to find this foundational piece, so long as I don't have to leave here.*

Most of our accumulated knowledge at this point comes from assumptions we have made thus far in life. *How right are we on how this whole royal thing really works?* We formed our judgments and ideas from watching an episode of *Game of Thrones* one night with Marsha and Al in the den room. Not all of

27

our conclusions may be accurate, and I am especially terrified that the show may not hold any truth. In *Game of Thrones*, if one is royal, they have to spend a good portion of their time watching their backs, as it seems everyone is out to steal their power. Our lives are much less stressful and uneventful than theirs. The day-to-day business and goings-on that those poor people on *Thrones* go through is pure insanity. Also, I have not heard of any upcoming dragon battles we need to prepare for. My instincts tell me that dragons no longer exist. I am sure Mother and Father would have given fair warning if dragons were something we needed to worry about.

We all have a strong fascination with *Thrones*. Why wouldn't we? Look at the star of the show. Everyone knows the true star is the dire wolf, Ghost. *Why doesn't he get more screen time?* I know Ghost will conquer all in the end. I have no doubt that he will show us how it is done as each episode is released. Ghost is clearly an Alpha One, so he will save the world! I find it hilarious that *Thrones* mainly seems to be a battle amongst women so far. They all will be blindsided when Ghost steps in and saves them all from their demise! *Alphas always act for the greatest good of the pack, even if it kills them.* The women in the show only seek power, yet have somehow obtained basic Alpha positions. The only woman on the show worthy of an Alpha title is Daenerys. She puts the best interest of humanity above herself. *Who knew humans could be Alphas, too? Do all species have them?*

My siblings and I wander from the trophy case back to our feeding stations. We continue to elaborate on what is to come of our royal lives. Blissful visions are dancing about in the atmosphere like holograms. It doesn't last long though, Mother comes around the corner and interrupts us by saying: it is time for more life lessons. She and Father need to prepare us for our futures.

Mother and Father laugh at us as we all continue to talk as if it were medieval times. We address them as King and Queen instead of Mother and Father as they enter the room. Mother quickly informs us that if we do not listen to all that she and Father have to say, we will be fools in our new castles to come. *I am no fool. I am an Alpha One and a prince.* I award my parents my full attention.

Chapter 5: Picking Pack-mates

Today's big lesson covers how to pick out good human members for our packs. Mother explains that we will meet good humans and bad humans throughout our lives. She teaches us how to use and trust our instincts. If we utilize our senses, we will be able to detect the different feelings and intentions of humans. I find myself struggling to quiet all the racing thoughts in my head as Mother continues. Surely if I wait long enough, the answers I seek will come.

I can't seem to focus, though. *Do we really have to have humans in our packs? Why not just dogs? Wolves stay with wolves. Can we have wolves in our packs?* Lately, I have heard Marsha and Al talk about genetics and pedigrees a lot on an object they call a smart phone. *I haven't discovered what makes it smart yet.* Getting back to genetics and biology, a wolf would beef up our lines. *Ugh, get to the answers already!*

I lack a small thing called patience. I think this concept may be comparable to what Yoda was trying to teach his human in one of Al's favorite movies, *Star Wars.* What people don't know about Yoda is that he is a hybrid German Shepherd. His ears and brilliance gave it away the first time I saw him on the big screen. Now that I think of it, I should probably refer to him as a Jedi Shepherd to be politically correct. *Yes, Jedi Shepherd!* I want to be just like Yoda when I grow up. He is another Alpha One! *Okay, Jedi, focus on what Mother is saying or you will be eaten by Jabba the Hutt for sure.* I force myself to stare directly at Mother's lips as she talks. I need to make myself actively listen so I don't miss anything.

"When humans are happy, they smell like a dewy spring morning on a field filled with forget-me-nots. When a human is sick, they smell like rotting flesh, probably because some part of them is literally rotting with illness," Mother explains. *Gross, rotting flesh! Okay, so sick is bad.* "When humans are sad, they will smell faintly of salt. You can taste it on their cheeks if you are close enough to give them a lick." *Sad... Well, I like salt.* Mother then furthers her lecture on salt by informing us that humans will also smell of salt if they have been exerting themselves.

Father interjects with a chuckle. "Humans will have a much stronger salty scent if exercise is the cause. Human pack-mates do not sweat the same way we do." *What? I thought everything sweats through their feet!* Father continues, "Humans sometimes smell horrifically, and you can even see the salt accumulate on their skin due to their lack of hair. A little salt on the face is sad. More than that means they were exerting themselves or they are stressed."

Mother and Father list off various scenarios to confirm that we understand the differences between sad and stressed. It's humorous to me that some people think dogs smell poorly. Humans take baths daily and use perfumed soaps. Dogs only need infrequent baths because our hair is equipped with special oils that keep us clean. One would think that would be enough of a sign that humans are wrong on this matter. Denial must keep them from seeing that they are, in fact, the stinky ones.

Once we finish the who-smells-worse debate, we learn about the two most dangerous human emotions: anger and fear. We are told to avoid both when at all possible. If we encounter a human with a pungent smell like algae-ridden marshland, it's fear—so steer clear! Basically, if a human smells sick or rotten, pass them by and do not add them to your pack. *Got it. Next lesson, please.*

As our day continues, I find myself starving for all the knowledge Mother and Father are sharing. Father says it is best to study others who have already obtained what you are trying to achieve. Father says we are to respect our history and learn from it. If we find something in our history we don't like or agree with we can make it part of our life's mission to change that as part of own legacy. This simple realization helps me to put all my unanswered questions to bed. Now, I can just focus and absorb the information handed down from the masters.

Our next topic is learning how to smell and identify human habits. Mother says, "Humans will smell like their work and their obsessions. If one works as a nurse, they will smell of hand sanitizer, antiseptics, and cleaners, like Marsha. If they work on cars or airplanes, they will smell of oil, like Al. Farmers... Well, they smell like dirt, mainly, or whatever animals they raise. Steer clear of pigs, if you can."

"But aren't pigs where bacon comes from?" I call out. *I like bacon.* Al snuck me a piece under the table the other day during breakfast. *I think I am his favorite.* He has to hide his actions from Marsha, though, because she is very particular about what we get to eat and drink. Al seems to be the laxer one when it comes to our diets. *It is safe to say that he is my favorite in return.*

My bacon question is ignored. The purpose of the warning is due to pigs' smelly, destructive nature. It is harder to smell a threat coming to a farm filled with pigs than it is on one filled with sheep or cows. I guess if we get a human with a farm, our lives will be out-of-this-world amazing. Mother and Father go to visit Father's brother, King Thompson, on a farm once a year. They describe it like a prize-winning lottery ticket. The farm has a pond and miles of fields to run. There are all kinds of new things to sniff and pee on.

I get the feeling that a farm is the equivalent of a human staying at the Ritz. Marsha talks about these establishments often. She says they are where all the beautiful people stay. Marsha's always begging Al to take her to one of these places. *Humans beg far more and far worse than dogs.* The conversations Al and Marsha have about these places never seem to hold my attention long. I am not sure what all the hype is about. As far as pretty people go, I think Marsha and Al are fine-looking humans. *May-*

be it is because they are the only two I have ever seen. Getting back to what really matters today, I hope to at least visit a farm one day. *Better yet, I think I would like to own one.* A farm sounds like the perfect place for my outstanding Alpha One legacy to live on.

"Focus, kids. I can see the daydreams in your eyes!" Father chastises us. Then he warns us of bad-smelling habits. "If a human smells strongly of beer and fried food, stay away from them. Humans who smell of these substances will probably leave you home alone for long hours. Beer can make some of them violent, too."

Father's last statement sparks my memory. Two weeks ago, Mother taught us about the road of no return for dogs. *In the case Mother shared with us, the dog in the story was justified.* Mother had told us about a sister of hers who used to live down the street. Long story short, the man living with them loved his beer. When the man had too much to drink, he would get mean and toss his wife around. One dark, fatal evening, the man had intoxicated himself far beyond the limits of any normal thinking. He began to savagely beat his wife. My mother's sister, our brave Aunt Matilda, tried to save the wife by biting and attacking the man so he would refocus his attention on her. Matilda's dog instincts told her that if she did not intervene, the man would kill the wife. The wife was Aunt Matilda's sole human, because of this Matilda was left with no choice. She had never liked the man, anyway. She only tolerated him because the wife liked him, for reasons I will never understand.

Even though biting a human leads to the road of no return for almost all dogs. *Our aunt was a hero.* The story ends tragically: the man exploded in anger after Matilda bit his arm. He retreated to the bedroom afterwards, and our aunt thought she had won the battle. *Never underestimate your competition or celebrate early.* Minutes later, the man returned with a shotgun just as our Aunt was running over to console the wife. Our Aunt saw victory and let her guard down, a costly mistake. The man shot his wife, and then Matilda. Mother said he did it in that order to be even more ruthless and cruel. The man had known his wife was Matilda's world. The man wanted to completely crush our Aunt's soul before he killed her as well. *Some people are pure evil.*

The story's ending is the worst. The man only got a life sentence in jail. I hope our Aunt at least got to disfigure the horrible man before she died. Mother explained to us that in cases like those, the courts often decide a dog's fate. She said the courts are prejudiced. Mother wasn't sure if Aunt Matilda would have lived even if she hadn't been shot. I think that is garbage. The courts should give dogs like my Aunt medals of honor for their actions. She was a true Alpha! Matilda was fierce and acted in the best interest of her pack. By wolf laws, she would have at least gotten a celebration dinner in the form of a deer or antelope. I hear humans are awarded a purple heart for such acts of bravery. Had my Aunt been human, surely she would have been given one.

As I am recalling the sad story of my Aunt's demise Father's voice brings me back to the present, and he continues our lecture. "Oh, and kids be sure to steer clear of humans who smell heavily of cigarettes." We must stay away from humans who smoke heavily because that ruins one of our greatest gifts: our sniffers! We must preserve our noses because that is how we get most of our information on all the humans and situations we encounter. "Keep a strong nose, sharp ears, and clear eyes, and stay in tip-top shape. If you do these things, you will always be King of your castles." *Whoop, whoop! King of the castle!* When Father talks, I feel he is directing everything towards me, like I am the only dog in the room. I think he knows I will be his best successor.

Chapter 6: Dogs Have Super Powers

Mother clears her throat and comes to the front of the kitchen where my siblings and I all stand like sponges, ready to soak up information. "We have saved the greatest lesson of all for last. We will end our teaching early today so you will have time to take this final lesson in. You must gather around and take this seriously."

Father's eyes are stern, and the looks on his and Mother's faces are intense. We gather in a circle around them and listen as they explain that all dogs are given the gift to perform miracles. *Wait, did I hear right? Come again?*

"You are capable of directing all of your energy towards a specific, pressing demand—a manifesting of sorts. When you do this with immense focus and control, you can persuade the universe to perform a miracle." Mother's words just blew my mind!

Mother and Father continue to explain something about an energy frequency we can tap into. They say we will understand it more when the time comes, and a miracle is truly needed. To be honest, most of what is said after the miracle part is lost in an eruption of noise as my siblings and I rejoice at our amazing gift. We triumphantly dance in circles, jumping and wagging our tails and barking excitedly. Thayer, formerly known as Challenger, shouts elatedly, "It just keeps getting better!"

I suppose he is right. Not only am I royalty, but I have super powers! Watch out, wolves, I may create a new level of Alpha—perhaps an Ultimate Alpha! I will leave the level of Alpha One in the dirt! Today, my Alpha quest has changed. I will need to do a little more planning and research but I will align myself with a new set of Alpha goals. Time for me to establish my own personal mission and vision of life. *Out with the old and in with the Ultimate!* Change can be a very good and empowering thing. *That must have been what Father meant the other day.*

Today has been the best day of my life so far. It is right next to playing in the fish guts that our sisters spilled when they knocked over the garbage can in the yard. The divine smell had drifted over to the big oak tree where my brothers and I were playing. We could not let the girls have all the fun, so we immediately ran over and joined them in rolling around in the guts. I can't say Marsha and Al were overly thrilled, but we enjoyed ourselves.

Father vociferates and shuts down the miracle celebration and my reminiscing. "This is not a joke, nor is it to be taken lightly. We have been given this gift to help our humans. We may only use this ability if it is *absolutely* necessary!" *Wait, why do we need humans again? We have superpowers. Let's just take over the world already!*

Father continues. "If you ever use this gift, know it comes at a tremendous price." *What could the price*

38

be? It's not like we have much to give besides our bravery and intelligence. "The human must be worth your miracle and they must be able to repay the debt back to you via an incredibly spoiled highlife. They must be able to carry on your legacy."

"Legacy? But only Alpha One's get those. How can a human continue our legacy? Don't we have to name another dog as our successor? Don't you have to be a wolf or a dog to even have one?" I can't keep myself from interrupting him. I have an Ultimate legacy on the brain and I need answers.

Mother interjects "It is indeed the steepest price you will ever pay. The exact cost of each successful miracle is one year of your life! You will feel this miracle's toll as a formidable force that will rob your body and spirit of energy for the next few days."

We only feel like crap for a few days? I could have sworn she said one year. Now I'm confused. Silence overtakes the group as the reality of these facts settle into our brains. We are astounded by the power we hold within us and the price to use it. We all ask several more questions throughout the rest of the day. Our parents tell us we can learn more by reading the book on Marsha's nightstand: *The Power of Choice and the Universe* by Kitty... *What's her last name?* I get lost at Kitty and can't help but shout my concerns. "We are supposed to trust something that was written by a cat? Cats have been known to do the devil's work. They have strange powers, like always landing on their feet after unnaturally high falls. Are you sure this book is safe? If there is a cat involved, it could contain black magic!"

"Don't worry, son. The human who wrote the

book is named Kitty. She is not a cat." Father eases my worries. I feel bad for the poor human though. I can't imagine being named after such a dreadful animal. Father explains that he and Mother learned of these powers we hold and how to use them from this special book.

I run over to Marsha's nightstand to gaze at the book and the powerful knowledge it contains. I never took Marsha for the magical type—or cat-loving, for that matter. I guess I should be grateful that she did not let the author's name deter her from bringing the book home. I would have passed it by as soon as I saw the author's name. *'Kitty' makes my skin crawl.* I have heard rumors that these creatures are always plotting death and destruction. I saw the neighbor's cat eat a beautiful songbird the other day after stalking it. I was enjoying the happy tweeting, and then the atmosphere erupted into horrific noises. If that ever happens, you can bet a cat is behind it.

I return my thoughts to Marsha. I know she is into crystals and oils for healing, but I have never seen her perform a miracle. *How did I miss this? Are miracles happening right under our noses? I must pay more attention to Marsha and read that book immediately!*

Dogs are much more intelligent than people want to give us credit for. We are born with the knowledge to read and have been doing so for centuries. It is part of our hard-wiring, not some privileged knowledge we have to learn ourselves. *An inherited blessing that makes us even greater!* One thing I find particularly funny is that humans have the audacity to claim the dog ear page marking technique as their own invention. They truly think they came up with this brilliant idea to hold their place in a book. *Come on, people, it's in the name. Dog ear, hello!*

Years ago, some handsome—or gorgeous, more than likely—German Shepherd was reading one day when their humans came home from work early. The dog hastily marked his or her place in the book by folding the top corner of the page down. This would allow him or her to pick up where they left off later so they could finish their reading once the humans left again. All dogs like to read in privacy so it is mostly done when the rest of the house's occupants are gone. This dogs hasty action and brilliance birthed the greatest bookmarking technique ever. *The Dog Ear!* However, later that day, the dog's owner picked up the book and thought that was where he or she had left off the last time they were reading. They then saw the brilliance in the technique of spot holding and claimed it as their own. *Thief!* If we steal something that is not ours, we are kenneled with no treats. Thayer learned this the hard way after stealing a pair of Al's socks from the laundry basket yesterday. This bookmark stealing human was not punished at all. *Life isn't always fair.*

Getting back on the miracle train, Father tells us of a time he had to use a miracle to help Al. Al had gotten sick with something they call colon cancer. Mother and Father thought it was the end for Al. Father decided to read the book that Marsha had been feverishly reading for days since Al had gotten the diagnosis. He then put his newfound knowledge to work and channeled his energy and focus.

Mother explains that the miracle itself took two days to perform. Al had gone away to what the humans call a hospital for treatment two weeks before. Marsha came home daily to let Mother and Father outside for bathroom breaks. She would then feed my parents while she showered and grabbed things for herself and Al. Then, Mother and Father would get let out one last time for the day. *Sounds like a lot of alone time.* Mother and Father say they could sense in Marsha that Al's situation was terrible. Father says he was sure that if he hadn't acted when he did, they would have lost Al. Al is the one who will carry out Father's legacy. Father describes Al as his one true human. *This 'one true human' thing seems to be a reoccurring theme. I can't quite put my paw on the concept yet though. If we have this power why do we need humans at all?*

Mother unveils the facts of Father's miracle. "Your Father sat by the window in the front room and used his newfound knowledge. He did not eat or sleep for two days. Then, on the third day, Al came home cured! Your father, however, was drained of energy, and it took a few days for him to recover. He looked and felt another year older after the miracle had taken place. This is how we know a miracle's price is steep!"

"Couldn't Father have been tired from not eating or sleeping for two days?" I ask. If I don't eat, I get hangry! At least, that is what similar behavior is called on *Snickers* commercials. We don't call it 'hangry' in our house—we call it 'going Thompson.' Our parents told us another story a while back about our Uncle King Thompson. He is known to become a monstrous beast if he does not eat frequently. Sometimes, he stops right in the middle of his farm chores to go eat. He must do this or he becomes intolerable. *By eating frequently, can he ward off the evil little monster that lives inside him? Maybe I should try this.* Perhaps everyone has one of these dreadful things. I haven't asked Mother and Father this question because I don't want to single myself out. *What if I am the only one with this fault?*

The term 'going Thompson' was derived from one bad day on the farm. King Thompson's humans did not allow him to go get dog food when he needed it. Hunger set in and transformed him into an angry volcano on the verge of blowing its top. A poor, unsuspecting chicken crossed our Uncle's path and clucked too loudly. This chicken did not get to the other side of the road. It did, however, make it to the other side of the universe as it passed on.

Uncle Thompson was reprimanded for the chicken situation, but it really wasn't his fault. Now, his humans let him eat whenever he shows signs of going Thompson. More than likely, it was due to low blood sugar, but what do I know? I'm no doctor. I've made this assumption from an article I saw as I peed on it. The page had been ripped from a magazine and placed into our whelping room. Marsha is always spreading papers and magazines out on the floor in this room that she calls ours. *In reality, it's her laundry room.* We are allowed out of it during the day, but at night, we have to stay in there. None of us can quite make it through the night yet without having to take a leak. I think Marsha likes to leave us things to read on the floor because she knows people like to read while going to the bathroom. Al always reads on the toilet. I can't believe how long he takes to get his business done. Perhaps the colon cancer made things more difficult for him in that department.

Either way, back to the topic at hand. How can Mother and Father be so sure of the one year miracle price? My siblings and I sit in awe of my parents and our new powers. We then launch questions at my parents like a firing squad unleashing bullets on a range. We are filled with all the hows, whens, and whys one could imagine. My parents' replies, which I find to be vague and almost secretive, annoy and frustrate me. Apparently, we have to figure this part of life out on our own. *Great, add that to the list of puzzle pieces I need to acquire.* All I know for sure is that there must be no other way out of a situation in order to use a miracle. Oh, and our one true sole human—whatever that means—must be worth the miracle's price. Our human must be capable of repaying us by helping other humans and dogs in need. Thus, our positive legacies live on.

I'd better read this book later to fully understand this business. I am sure it will be vital, considering my new Ultimate Alpha quest. I am just starting to really enjoy life. Why would I want to give away a year of it? *I like Marsha and Al, but are they worth that? How are they paying it forward? Can we really trust a book written by someone named after a cat?* My mind is exhausted from firing like a pinball machine with all these new facts. Yet, somehow, I am restless. *Maybe it is due to all my unanswered questions.* Mother must sense my unease as I lie down by her to sleep for the night because she tries to explain one more time. "Humans need us more than we need them. I promise you will understand this when you have your own one day. Now, rest yourself, son."

"But I don't even think I want my own human. I haven't found a need for one. Humans seem like a lot of unnecessary work," I retort. I ask Mother why several more times. She is explaining in what seemed to be a vicious circle, and it only confuses me more. *What am I missing?* Finally, my agitation earns me an annoyed response from Father.

"You all have a purpose which you must figure out on your own. It will all come in good time. Good night!" Father says curtly and with a don't-speak-again finality, indicating that it is time to say no more and go to bed.

When Father says enough, he means it. You never challenge an Alpha unless you are sure you can take him down. If you celebrate early and an Alpha gets back up, you're toast. My mental state is disturbed by all this. *What does it take to get certainty around here?* I like to get answers right away. If something smells funny in the yard, I sniff it out until I get my answer. I have a slight problem with patience and control. *How long is 'in good time,' anyway? Days seem endless. What is time, exactly? How do I tell it? When will this all happen? How will I know? What's a 'one true human'?* Eventually, I drift into a fitful sleep. The only good thing felines ever invented, the catnap, is all I will be receiving tonight.

Chapter 7: The 8th Week

As we approach the eighth week of our lives, new humans come to the house, and we get our first whiff of cigarette smoke. These people smell like a hundred-year-old chimney mixed with a dirty grill. Personally, I do not mind the grill smell—I even lick my lips as their scent blows past my nose, entangled in the wind. Once the humans get closer and the grill part dissipates, the scent of burnt tobacco and ash permeates the air. My nostrils clench, conflicted.

Mother and Father act unruly. Father snarls, showing them his pearly whites as he lets a low growl escape from deep in his gut. Mother runs around the yard, yipping like one of those teacup-sized dogs and acting as if someone had lit her tail on fire. This is erratic behavior for them. Evidently, it startles the humans and serves as a major deterrent. They waste no time aborting whatever mission they had come here on once they see our bizarre parents. Turning tail the new humans get back in their vehicles and return to wherever they had come from. One thing is clear: none of us will leave with them.

I abandon my command post by the open window from which I had watched the people. I'm bummed that they left so fast and we didn't get a chance to meet them. I had wanted to put my newly

46

acquired skills to the test. Father sees my disappointment and explains that those humans are not suitable pack members for any of us. "Remember, we only do things that support the greatest good of the pack. Don't worry, kids. Your time will come. Your Mother and I will help all of you to judge your first pack member—or members, if they come as a family. We will decide who gets through the gates to see you. After that, though, who they leave with is up to you pups. Oh, to be young again..." Father finishes with a laugh.

Our parents encourage us all to watch them and take mental notes. They will evaluate and judge any new humans that come to the house. They also inform us that many more people will come over the next few weeks. As they come and go, Mother and Father will give us quizzes. We need to show them we understand why certain people are or are not allowed through the gate into our yard. Who knew that a puppy is prime for picking between eight and twelve weeks old? It reminds me of the avocados Marsha keeps on the counter. She checks them each day by squeezing them. *Perhaps they are ready to eat when they finally squeeze back.* Human actions are often peculiar to me.

The thought of being squeezed like an avocado and picked by a person gives me anxiety, which feeds my little monster. I decide to flip the situation and view it as a game of me picking people. I love games, so looking at my situation like this has allowed me to welcome this situation instead. This will at least put me one step closer to becoming an Ultimate Alpha and help start my legacy. The only thing I have left to figure out is how to squeeze the people without hands. The other thing that adds to my anxiety, is the fact that once I choose a person or family, I will have to leave here. Leaving is the only way my own personal jigsaw puzzle of life will slowly start to assemble itself.

My parents will no longer hold my paw and help me. I will have to seek out my own wisdom and advice from other sources. *Surely this will be a major challenge in particular circumstances.* I like the way things are done now. For the most part, if I ask a question, it gets answered. I am no dummy and have not taken any of this for granted. *Again, more unknown. Ugh, it's everywhere!* Perhaps I should just behave poorly and stay here with Mother and Father a bit longer. *Forever sounds good.* Okay, maybe not forever, but at least until I have all the knowledge I need. I like it here. Life is easy. *Why would anyone want to leave easy?* I need more information on these secret powers of choice and miracles. With that knowledge, I can advance to the Ultimate Alpha level much faster. If I leave now and have to seek out the rest of this knowledge on my own, things will take twice as long. S*taying is certainly the smartest thing to do.*

Today marks the third day of our eighth week of life. Perhaps it should be some sort of holiday. Anyway, a human finally meets Mother and Father's standards and is allowed to enter the gates of our kingdom. As the single woman walks deeper into our backyard, Mother commands us, "Now children, when you are released to greet the woman out in the yard, just be yourselves. If, for some reason, you get a weird vibe, follow your instincts. Remember that you can bite the woman as hard as you can and create a great commotion until she leaves!"

Okay, so if she shows interest in me, I just bite her. Then, I can stay here. *Wait a second, did you say to bite a human?* "But Mother, I thought biting a human was going down the path of no return!" I exclaim.

Mother laughs. "Yes, it typically is, but not when you are a puppy. People like puppy teeth and puppy breath! You can't bite them once you are of age. You will be fine so long as you stop this behavior around six months old. At that point, it is no longer considered cute. You must also remember never to draw blood unless it is a life or death situation. Now, outside you go, and good luck." Mother ushers us towards the door to the backyard where the woman stands petting Father and talking with Al.

I quickly blurt out one more question as we near the door. "Mother, you said if we bite her she will want to leave and won't take us. But you also said she will think that us biting her is cute. I don't get it!" Confused, I stand staring out the door Marsha is now holding open for us, awaiting my mother's answer. All I get is Mother's nose under my rear end as she propels me forward. She noses us all out the door one by one without answering. *Crap, I hate the unknown.*

I struggle to maintain my basic Alpha role and run for the front of the line. My siblings are shoved out the door in rapid succession and stagger out towards the woman. *I must be the first one out. I am the leader.* Thayer has been gunning for my spot lately, and he isn't standing down today. The little turd nearly beats me out to the middle of the yard where the woman waits with Father and Al. I nip at Thayer as I sprint past him, indicating that he needs to fall back in line behind me where he belongs, or there will be a scuffle. Thayer backs off, and I take a galloping lap around the woman.

I give her a wide berth as I prance around her. *You can never be too cautious.* Excitement fills me. It is finally time to assess my first potential human. Being our pack's basic Alpha has worked out well for me so far. So, I do my best to fulfill my role. Mother gave us instructions, and as the basic Alpha, I should lead the rest by example. I will oblige Mother and do as told. *Well, almost.* I have a few minor modifications planned since I have no desire to leave here today. Pretty woman or not, I told myself before coming into the yard that this was not the human for me.

It doesn't feel like it is, as Father has said lately, 'my time.' I have important business to finish here before moving on. I need to read that book on Marsha's nightstand, for starters. Plus, I have so many questions for Mother and Father that have yet to be answered. I will uncover these truths a lot easier and faster if I remain with them. Curiosity has me in its grips, when it comes to human-picking, so I decide to at least play around with my newly gained knowledge. I need to put some of my new sensing skills to work. It's wolf law, after all: use it or lose it. *I'm totally an Ultimate Alpha. Wait until I tell Father my revelation. Wolf law. I'm brilliant!*

Practice makes perfect. That is what Mother has

told us over and over again, every day. It is a little redundant, I know, but my parents aren't the kind to tell us something that's not true. I need to work my senses and get the hang of things, so I decide to play along. *Halfheartedly. Remember, don't be extra cuddly and cute. That will keep the woman from picking you.* Recently, I have watched a few movies with puppies starring in them. The most recent one was called *Marley and Me.* Anyhow, my point is the cute, cuddly one always gets picked first, so in an effort to secure my spot here at home, I am going for the starring role of 'least desirable pup.'

Chapter 8: The Woman

I start my assessment of the woman. *How do I judge without squeezing?* The first thing I note about her is her voice. She has a low-pitched, soothing timbre as she talks to Al. *Very calming.*

Al is the main human male in our pack. *He also thinks he is the Alpha One, but only because Father allows him to believe that.* My Father is the true Alpha One of our pack. *Sorry, Al.* Father says it is easiest to let the humans think they are in control and hold the highest-ranking spot. He claims humans would be insulted if they ever knew the truth. Apparently, we let the humans believe they hold the upmost spot to make life easier and keep everyone happy. It is one of those out of mind, out of sight tricks. The humans think they hold the highest role because they are unaware that an Alpha One level even exists. Humans have only heard one story about Alphas, and through that, they have assumed they know everything. *We must always seek knowledge and we can never truly know everything, silly humans!*

From what I have learned so far, humans assume a lot. *You know what they say about assuming...* I can't remember how the saying goes exactly. What I do know, is that when it comes to humans, they think they are the big cheese. In reality, humans are just the crackers. They are not privy to the knowledge and rules that the great wolves established long before humans ever existed. We dogs continue to keep them in the dark on this matter so we don't have to deal with any future uprisings that might occur if they find out about the higher spot. Humans can be power-hungry, greedy, and materialistic. Dogs never act in such ill-mannered ways. This is the exact reason humans are kept in the dark about the Alpha One role. Humans jump to conclusions and don't listen to the entire story. Often, humans only hear what they want to. This can create dangerous situations. The humans hear only what they want, then they grasp for the basic Alpha power and run with it. Humans believe the basic Alpha position they hold is cream of the crop. They have passed this belief on for generations. The problem with this is that once one thinks there is nothing else, they stop searching and learning. This is detrimental and backfires by selling them short and robbing them of potential new discoveries.

Another emotion humans sometimes suffer from is pride. Excessive pride can harm them because they react without all the necessary information and then blame someone else for their mistake if the situation goes poorly. They just aren't Alpha One material. Alpha Ones accept responsibility for everything they do, including failures and mistakes, and then use them to learn and grow.

I am going to sound like a hypocrite here because I am about to 'assume' and I just said that is something one should never do. However, I assume that this life lesson is a challenging one for everyone.

I say this because we spent one whole day with Mother and Father identifying what fault and responsibility are, and what to do with them. I am told very few humans understand the difference between the two. Everyone will be a victim of fault at some point in their lives, but the thing that matters most is how they choose to deal with it. It is how we take responsibility for the matter at hand that defines us. Wolves and dogs understand responsibility and what it truly means. We must learn from all failures and faults and act appropriately. It is because we are capable of this that we are even in the know when it comes to the Alpha One role. *Knowledge is power. Failure and fault lead to knowledge. Accepting responsibility is key!*

Perhaps we should count our blessings though. Thanks to the humans' greed, they are blinded by their beliefs. Humans think they have it all, and have since moved on to other things. So while greed is their downfall, it is our benefit. The true Alpha hierarchy with all its power and integrity remains safe! One day, when I take a human, I will show them their faults and teach them why taking responsibility is the higher way of life. I will let them in on the Alpha One secret as my human will need to become one in order to carry out my Ultimate Alpha legacy. *Together, we will change the world.*

The woman speaks again, bringing me back from my daydream. Her voice hangs in the air like a song from a bird. "Can I see only the males, please?"

I really must work on this whole attention span thing. I am worse than a gnat sometimes. It seems the woman has just as many questions about us as we do about her. My sisters are led back into the house with Mother, and I find myself becoming more intrigued by the woman and her curiosity. *Very dog-like and investigative of her, and not reactive at all.* My brothers and I remain outside in the backyard with her. Al excuses himself to join the others inside for a few minutes, giving the woman time to check us all out in private. Several of my brothers' approach and sniff her feet. They remind me of cats as they rub against her legs and jump playfully at her knees. *Don't you boys see how ridiculously you are acting? Who will be the first to go? Perhaps I should start a betting pool. I love a good gamble.* I keep my distance as I watch my brothers make fools of themselves.

I am taking mental notes of what not to do when I am finally ready to leave here when my nose catches the woman's scent. Her essence drifts through the air like the cotton tops of dandelions. *Delicious!* Dang it, my thoughts have been hijacked again. How long was that? Two seconds? Tomorrow, I will start a new daily habit to work on training my focusing abilities. Anyway, the woman smells sweet, almost candy-like. I turn my head from side to side and inhale deeply to really assess her. I key in on the heaviest parts of her natural odor and decide that it mainly consists of coconut and driftwood, an odd but captivating combination.

The more I sniff at her, the more entranced and relaxed I become. Perhaps the smell and the sound of her voice are what a day at the beach is like. My experience of beaches is limited. My only knowledge comes from what I have seen on the television and read in travel magazines. Marsha often places travel magazines next to the toilet in Al's bathroom as not-so-subtle hints. She marks the pages she wants Al to focus on by using the brilliant dog-ear technique. *Al spends a disturbing amount of time in the bathroom.* The other day, he read a whole magazine front to back while sitting on the pot! Marsha is a genius for using this tactic. I wonder what else she does that Al hasn't caught on to.

Lost in thought again. Get a grip or Thayer will take your spot before the day's end. I remind myself of what Mother told us moments earlier: be yourself. After making myself swear I would not get distracted from the task at hand again, I had decided to do just that. *Time to just be myself.*

It had rained an hour prior to the enchanting woman's arrival, leaving a large, untainted mud puddle in the yard. I need to refocus and break my entrancement with the woman, so I do the most obvious thing to do whenever one sees a stagnant mud puddle: I run straight over to it and jump in head first!

If you are going to be an Ultimate Alpha, go all in. Make a plan and follow it. Do not allow yourself to be disrupted by mere distractions. Be strong and always maintain your focus. Also, if you are going to jump into a puddle, do it like an Alpha. Only cowards dip their toes in. An Alpha dives head first!

Sploosh! I submerge myself in the dirty water and start to play. I splash and paw furiously at the water, creating mini tidal waves all around me. This makes a mess of my white fur. *Good. Lessen my desirability: check.* I am in line with my stay-here plan. I am secretly keeping a tally of events as they occur.

I award myself points in the getting-to-stay-here column due to the mud that now stains my white coat. I like to turn all situations into some sort of game. It not only keeps me focused, but it also takes some of the seriousness out of situations.

Little games like this aid me immensely when it comes to battling my evil little anxiety monster. I do all I can to keep from feeding that dreadful creature. I mustn't allow him to grow on potential milestone days such as this. *My monster will not taint my future pack judgments.* I must say, I am pleasantly surprised that I have not had to beat my monster down into submission since I was born. That experience alone was enough to keep me from wanting to do battle with him again. *Life's darkness can be powerful, and not in a good way.*

I shove thoughts of my monster aside, as I know they are just his way of trying to sneak into the present moment. Monster hates peace and happiness, so I make him retreat by having what feels like the time of my life playing in this puddle and acting like a fool. Sure, I am intrigued by this woman, but one of my brothers can have her. *I will know when it is my time. I am an Alpha.* Alphas can see events like this coming days before they arrive. Today I woke and saw only the beautiful sun. Nothing indicated to me that today should be any different from yesterday.

I roll onto my back in the puddle to really get myself covered in the mud. As I do, I notice that everything has gone quiet. Not a single sound wave is vibrating through the atmosphere. Suddenly, I can feel the eyes of all my brothers on me. I look up, a little perplexed by the sudden loss of volume and my newfound popularity when, moments ago, no one was paying me any attention. Suddenly, I have a strange feeling from deep inside that what is going to happen next will not be in alignment with my stay-here plan. I realize why my brothers are staring at me, and my nerves begin firing rapidly like a thousand tiny lightning bolts. The woman is headed my way.

My paws begin to sweat and my heartbeat quickens. The lady seems to be floating towards me like a beautiful dream. She wears a forest green silk blouse over dark denim pants that are tucked into knee-high gray boots. She has mahogany-colored hair and full pink lips that begin curling into a brilliant smile to show white teeth as she approaches me. I have never really paid attention to humans' teeth until now. Perhaps it is because hers are so white. Hers are similar to mine, only not nearly as sharp. *How does she eat with those?* They seem a bit dull. Only two of them have a pointed edge.

Forget her teeth. Focus! The distance lessens even more between us. The tension in the atmosphere has become palpable—or maybe that is just my pulse going haywire. Surely the entire world can hear my heart thumping against my chest as if it is trying to escape, especially as the woman kneels beside me. She is assessing me further. Now, only inches separate us. *Breathe!* I have stopped breathing; I cough and gasp for air before I can pass out. I must regain control of the situation. To calm myself, I decide to take this opportunity to further assess the woman kneeling before me. *That's it, boy. Turn the tables on her. Make it a game.* A tennis match. I can focus on a tennis match. I whack the metaphorical fuzzy yellow ball back to her side of the court with a muddy whip of my tail. Now I have my game of distraction in place and enough mud on me to be considered a black and tan German Shepherd, surely, she will knock off this nonsense and go check out one of my brothers.

Wrong again. I am not doing well at this whole seeing-the-future thing today. Movies make it look so easy. Maybe I will try looking into one of Marsha's crystals before the next human comes. *Couldn't hurt.* I notice my breathing shallowing once again as a stillness gradually overtakes my body. I am scared to look up at the woman. *An Alpha must show no fear.* I gather my courage and cast my eyes upward.

Our eyes meet, and I think the world stops turning. The woman's bright blue eyes, like a clear, sunny sky, are rimmed with a bewitching grey. They immediately capture my chocolate brown ones, and I can't look away. I am completely enthralled by her. She must have put a spell on me! *Is she a witch?* No, wait. There is something about her I can't quite put my paw on. This woman has a purity about her, an ultimate goodness of sorts that radiates through her. I couldn't see this part of her at first because it is hidden behind a curtain of deep pain and sadness.

What could hurt this beautiful, kind woman? She needs my help! I'm trying to figure out what caused this woman's darkness when she picks me up and hugs my wet, filthy body against hers. Even though I am the dirtiest I have ever been, she holds me up to her face and inhales my scent deeply. She follows that with a kiss on the top of my head. This immediately transforms me. I am overtaken by a great compulsion to be the cutest, cuddliest puppy ever. Before I know it, I am licking her face as if it is covered in peanut butter. *Dogs love peanut butter, especially the crunchy kind!* Her skin tastes as sweet as she smells, and I cannot get enough. I also find comfort in knowing that I am not the only one in this world with a dark monster hibernating inside me. *Maybe everyone has one? I at least know she does.*

My eyes lock with the woman's once again as I take a second to catch my breath before resuming her complementary face washing. That's when I notice for the first time that the pain in her eyes has lessened significantly. The answer to this situation dawns on me like the bright sun rising over the mountaintops: I can lick away her sadness and pain. I can free this woman and help her slay her evil monster. Then, the woman's ultimate goodness will be revealed—not just to me, but to the world. With this woman, I can reach the level of Ultimate Alpha. She is how I will build my legacy!

I nonchalantly look above my head to see if there is a flashing lightbulb to indicate that I have just figured a good portion of my life out. On Sunday mornings, we get to watch cartoons. These lightbulb moments happen to the cartoon characters often. This moment seems so bright that I am a little sad there isn't one above my head for my brothers to see.

I understand now what Mother and Father meant by finding my purpose. I want nothing more than to rid this beautiful woman of all that is holding her down and keeping her away from an amazing life. I know I can reveal the real her that lies underneath it all. She is like an onion: she needs the first few crusty layers removed. Marsha cooks with onions all the time. Once she removes the dismal dry outer parts, a sweet flesh is revealed. Then, Marsha adds the onion to the entrée of the evening, and the onion enhances it. Onions are magical and bring new flavor and life to otherwise boring dishes. This woman and I could have the same effect on the world. *Together, we are an Ultimate Onion.* My overall plan is much larger than just making a simple meal. This woman and I will add our purity to the world to enhance it for everyone.

This woman and I will be epic, the thing that books are written about and legacies are made of. I will help her find her light, and then she will teach others to do the same! Together, we will rid the world of pesky monsters, just like the *Ghost Busters!* We will act as ripples on the water's surface. She and I will start in the middle and will keep growing until we have reached and helped everyone. Life's dark monsters will lose their food source and become extinct in no time. The power of light and happiness will win!

My daydream bursts abruptly. I come back to the present moment with a thud from the clouds I had allowed myself to float in for the last few minutes. *What have I done?* I am filthy. I destroyed my coat and acted like a fool. Panic sets in and feeds Monster. I hope that the woman holding me won't put me down and look at one of my brothers the way she had looked at me. Jealousy and passion are stirring deep within me now. I want this woman to be mine. *She needs to be part of my pack. She needs my help. She is how I will become Ultimate!*

My monster feasts upon this new emotion I have never felt before. I struggle to see beyond the curtains of anxiety that act as my monster's dessert. Finally, reason finds me in my unnerved state, and I know exactly what to do. *I will pee on her!* After all, that is how we mark our territory so no one else touches it. I am sure my brothers will receive the message, especially since I hold the basic Alpha role. If I pee on this woman, my brothers will be forced to stand down. The only one here who can urinate over me is Father, and I know he has no intentions of leaving Marsha, Al, or Mother.

Last week, Father taught us how to mark our territory out in the yard. He explained what the action meant and how the whole system works. By marking our territory, it keeps other dogs away from what is ours. The scent of our urine serves as a billboard to the area, showing other dogs who the boss is. The only time you pee where the boss has already gone is if you want to challenge him to a battle. The winner of the battle is the leader, and the loser is usually dead or exiled. Father always gets the last squirt in our yard. No other dog has ever dared to challenge him. We have seen dogs walk past on leashes with their humans, and they always wait until they are at least ten feet from our property lines before letting a drop hit the ground. *Now that's respect.*

Father told us that one day, we will pee in the yards we own and command the same respect from those around us. *Does this work on humans, too?* I am the leader of our puppy pack, so if I pee on this woman, that will make her mine. I am overwhelmed with emotion and the desire to make her the first member of my pack. I can feel the deep need we have for one another in my bones. I am not entirely sure what these feelings are. All I know is that I want and need more of them, and nothing will stop me from getting them now that I have had a taste.

I hope with every hair on my body that this woman needs me as badly as I need her. It is as if we are two different ends of a magnet being strongly drawn to one another. One of my brothers' barks, and panic shoots through me as I fear she will move her attention to him. *That's it, I'm going to pee on her. Desperate times call for desperate measures.* Just as I am about to let the yellow river flow all over her silky green blouse, she walks with me over to Al. *Huh?* I hadn't even realized he had come back outside to join us. *Hold it, wait and see what she is going to do next.* I decide I will give her sixty seconds before I let loose. After all, she has not put me down yet. *That's a good sign.*

The woman's gentle voice says, "Hey Al, I will take this one!" Relief instantly floods my system. I can breathe more deeply again.

The only problem now is that I really have to pee. The sixty seconds I was going to hold off for is up. My bladder has started to force urine towards its exit point like a waterfall about to go over the edge of a cliff. Just in the nick of time, she sets me down on the ground by her feet. I immediately assume a squat like one of my sisters. I have waited far too long to even contemplate lifting a leg at this point. Truth be told, urine started trickling out as she lowered me down. I no longer have control of the bladder matter. I hear Thayer call out, "You pee like a girl!" He is always taunting me. The rest of my brothers erupt into a fit of laughter at my expense.

"You all sound like a pack of ignorant hyenas. You will be in the same situation one day. There is a thing called karma, you know," I retort. Then, I ignore them. This conversation isn't worth the air I had already spent on it, so I switch tactics. *An Alpha does not allow the opinions of others to dictate their feelings and actions.* I am slowly regaining control of the situation. To be honest, I can't blame my brothers for reacting to the spectacle that had just taken place. I don't think they have ever seen me almost lose my composure until now. I can't imagine the amount of snickering that would have been roaring out of them had I lost it and peed all over the woman!

I refocus and watch her as I continue my business. Sometimes, I am amazed by how much urine I have in there. *It just keeps flowing.* The woman removes odd-smelling green paper stuff from her pocket. I wrinkle my nose at its unfamiliarity. The material looks like fresh leaves, makes noises like old leaves, and yet it doesn't smell like leaves at all. I have not seen any of it around the yard. Perhaps this is one of the many new discoveries she and I will make together as we change the world. I cannot fully investigate the odd green paper because I am still going. *Longest pee ever... This may be a record!* Maybe I will get to this new substance later today. Either way, it doesn't seem to be a pressing matter. Whatever it is, it does not overly excite her. I find it odd how much it excites Al, though, as he takes it from her and puts it in his back pocket with a large grin of satisfaction. Maybe humans are simpler than I had thought. *The leafy green paper makes them happy. Easy to please, I guess.* I must remember that and bring it to my new human whenever I find some.

Once I have finished relieving myself, the woman shakes Al's hand, waves at Marsha, and then scoops me back up into her warm embrace. *This feels like home.* The woman then carries me over to where two other women stand by the gate to our yard. The older of the two crinkles up her nose and says, "Really, that one? You couldn't have picked one of the clean ones? He is filthy and smells like a wet dog!"

The woman holding me does not seem offended in the slightest by the older woman's comments. Instead, she holds me up with a proud smile on her face. My human has skipped the introduction and transitioned straight to the showing-me-off part. She doesn't care at all what these other two women think. My body temperature grows warmer with slight embarrassment at first, but then I solidify my human's choice by holding my head high and puffing out my chest high with pride. I don't want her to regret her decision. *Yes! She realizes how great I am, too! This is going to be awesome!* The two other ladies quickly concede, realizing that there is nothing they can say to change my human's mind. They then greet me with coos and rubs as we make our way to the car.

Chapter 9: My Castle

I reflect on all the events that had transpired as the car shifts into gear to drive away from the only family I have known. I find it fitting that I am the first to take a human. I was, after all, the first to venture into the world through the tunnel Mother provided us with, and our former puppy pack leader. I am sure Thayer will take over in my absence. I lean out of the open window and bark once to say goodbye to my old pack, then another time to congratulate Thayer on his new position. Then, I watch as my first family gradually disappears into the background.

I am saddened that my first pack will now become a memory, but excitement and this new feeling I have not yet named confirms that I have made the right choice. Even though I did not go in the direction, I had originally intended when the road forked; I know I am headed in the right way. "Just because something is easy does not mean it is right." I replay Father's words of wisdom in my head. I have just secured the first real piece of my life's puzzle.

A smile finds my lips as I think about my brothers and sisters and how, once they pick their first human, they will start piecing together their life puzzles. I am eager for them to experience the same amazing high of starting their own pack I have right now. I wonder if they, too, feel that they are lost in the dark. I know I did while trying to figure out the true meaning of Mother and Father's words. I had not expected such a strong lightbulb moment, but it sure was nice to catch a break. This woman and I are meant for each other. I have no idea what adventures this lady and I will go on, but I know that I cannot imagine going on them with anyone but her. Sure, she is a slight wrinkle in my original plan, but somehow I know that she is a key part to my legacy. *Besides, she needs me.* The Alpha in me has to help her.

Excitement and anticipation bubble inside me for the rest of the car ride. Father goes on lots of car trips with Al, and he says every one of them is remarkable! During the ride, I am allowed to put my face out the window while the older of the two ladies holds onto me. I want desperately to be back in the arms of the lady in the green blouse, but she seems to be controlling the vehicle at the moment, so I figure it's best if she is left undisturbed for the time being. This older woman smells like her, so she must be a good human too. *Maybe they are from the same pack? My siblings and I have a similar scent.*

Father was right all along: car rides are exhilarating. My lips are forced apart by the wind, exposing my teeth and gums in a grin that I can't control. My ears are pushed back by the rush of air, creating all kinds of half up and down variations. My ears have only just begun to stand upright, so it's not like it is a major feat for the rushing air to pin them down. Amazing new smells enter my nose all at once as we advance down the road. I struggle to keep up with all the new aromas that pour into the open windows. I need more practice; I can't identify them all.

Finally, after about an hour, we arrive at my new home in Bee Town Illinois. Boy, am I happy that we dropped one of the other women off along the way. There was not anything wrong with her, per se, but she was a little too intense for my taste. I would describe her as very kind, but a little too excitable and overwhelming. Had this lady come into the yard to get me, I would have bit and run for sure. She must have just been a friend since she didn't come home with us. Marsha always has friends stopping over to play with her oils and crystals. They were fun for a while, but we were always happiest when they would leave and things would return to normal.

On the ride home, I got acquainted with my two new companions. The older lady remained with us. I now refer to her as Grandma. I like her a lot. She has spoiled me already and reminds me in a lot of ways of my favorite pack member: the lady in the green blouse. I must admit, the Grandma title throws me a little since she is not a dog. Grandma is what she told me to call her, though. She also referred to me as her first grandpuppy, whatever that is. Grandma looked over at the lady in green, I believe she is my sole human and she said, "He can't come in the house until he gets bath!" I admit I am filthy, but beyond that, it was clear that Grandma had accepted me fully. So I, too, accepted her.

My dazzling green-shirted beauty calls Grandma, Mom. Perhaps this warrants the Grandma title since my lady in green calls herself my mom. Honestly, I will call her whatever she wants. I can't get enough of all the extra endorphins that surge through my body when she is in my presence. Nonetheless, no matter what her true name is, I am pleased to claim her as mine. *Human Mom it is. And I didn't even have to pee on her!*

After listening to a lengthy conversation between Grandma and Mom, I finally learned that her real name is Melody. *I know, I know. Even her name is perfect. Music to my ears...* I feel that her real name is much better than the title of human Mom, so that is what I have decided to call her. All I can think is that we will be an inseparable pair, happy forever. *Just me and my Melody.*

Upon our arrival to what the two call 'our house,' Melody comes around to the passenger side of the car to get me from where I sit waiting on Grandma's lap. She then carries me over to a large, plush, and excellently manicured yard that is four times the size of the yard I previously played in with my siblings. I jump with joy and delightedly bark in approval of my new home as I chase Melody around the yard. She laughs as I playfully nip at her heels. Her laugh is delectable, and I love that I'm the one who caused it. It seems that the more joyous she is, the more this unnamed emotion courses through my veins. I think I am addicted to her and to this feeling.

Once I have received a bath and finally exhaust myself by playing in the yard, Melody guides me to the front door of the house. A large maroon door encased by sandy brown siding stands behind three large white pillars. This is indeed a castle. *My brothers and sisters had it right after all.* I follow Melody into the house, where I am introduced to a few more people. I had no idea I would be getting so many human pack-mates all at once. I hope they will all be as good as Melody and Grandma. However, I don't think anything can go wrong as long as Melody and I are together.

First, I am introduced to a large, towering man who calls himself Grandpa. He reminds me a lot of Al. I have identified him as the basic Alpha of this house, as he seems to be the one in command. I suppose he is until I take over. He smiles at me, and in his gentle voice, he says, "He looks like he will grow to be a big pup. Look at the size of those paws!"

I then meet two other ladies. The first I refer to as Kassandra. She resides here with us. The second I call Bailey. She does not live with us because she owns a house nearby. I assume these women are my aunts because they are Melody's sisters. This is really a lot to take in on my first day. It makes sense that they are all related as they all have similar characteristics and smell the same. I feel that my brothers and sisters and I look more alike than these girls do, but we are like twins on steroids or something. These women have many of the same mannerisms and gestures, which I find adorable, but beyond that, they look and act nothing alike.

Fascinating. It appears I have four full-time pack members and one part-timer. I will have my work cut out for me here. The first few hours with my new pack have been wondrously intoxicating. Positive emotions fill me from my toenails to the tops of my ears. This, however, seems to also be making me tired as I finally take it all in.

It has been hours since I last snoozed. If I don't get my eight, I am a bear. The perfection of my situation astounds me as I revisit the events of the day while drifting off to dreamland. Adventures that Melody and I will go on play like a movie behind my closed eyelids as I rest on top of a giant, round, taupe-colored pillow in the corner of my new living room. This family has rolled out the red carpet to welcome me. The fuzz on my dog bed tickles my nose as the steady respirations of sleep find me. The sides of the pillow consume me in what feels like a constant hug. This must be what Heaven is like. My dreams transition to fond memories of snuggling amongst all my brothers and sisters back home.

Chapter 10: Say My Name

The first week of my new life passes by incredibly fast. The humans of my castle all cater to my every need, and everyone thinks everything I do is adorable. *Except peeing on the floor!* Urinating in the house seems to be a serious no-no! At least, that is what they say whenever I can't hold it any longer. My humans get all charged up every time I sprinkle a tinkle in the house. First, I get a firm, but not painful, tap on the backside. This is followed by them ringing a bell at the door as they carry me out of the house by the scruff of my neck. I am then placed in the grass and told sternly to "go out, go potty!" I think they are trying to teach me something, but there is some sort of communication barrier we all seem to be transitioning through. *Don't worry, my humans. I will understand you yet!*

Speaking of communication barriers, my humans are starting to agitate me with their name-calling. The women of the house call me Puppy, Puppers, or Doggie. *Don't they know my parents gave me a name of greatness?* At least Grandpa's nickname for me is bearable. He calls me Big Guy, which is more masculine and Alpha-worthy than Puppers. I can deal with Big Guy for a while longer. After all, it is the name I had while living in Mother's womb.

You're Welcome

I have a true leader's name, though, and I must figure out how to get my humans to say it. I know this frustrating conundrum is part of the next piece of my puzzle. Communication is a foundational piece of all great relationships. How can I possibly focus on not peeing in the house and ringing a bell at the door when I am trying to communicate my name and am constantly referred to as Puppers? I move the problem to the top of my to-do list for tomorrow. This has become an unacceptable issue.

The next day arrives, and the warm, buttery light of the sunrise fingers its way in through the blinds and onto the bed where I sleep next to Melody. I am already awake, but I remain curled up next to my sleeping beauty, pondering my name quandary. I need to find a way to amend this dilemma immediately. I can't possibly bear another day of being called insignificant and derogatory names. I love my humans, but this has gotten out of hand. I am deep in thought when I hear the front door open and the voice of Aunt Bailey chirping away. "Morning, family! I brought doughnuts and that movie Kassandra wanted to watch."

Perhaps I can put the name thing on hold for a few minutes longer while I beg for some doughnut pieces. *Yes, definitely a valid reason to postpone my naming.* Melody and I emerge from our bedroom to greet Bailey. Kassandra pads out of her bedroom shortly after us. Melody lets me outside to do my business, and I make sure not to dawdle. *There is pastry-begging to do inside.* When they let me back in the house, I trot over to join them in the kitchen.

My pretty ladies all congregate around the

73

kitchen island, and the aroma of coffee fills the air as they wait for it to finish brewing. I put on my most adorable face and wag my tail enthusiastically. Unfortunately, the only one who refocuses her attention on me is Melody. "Come on, bud, your breakfast is over here." She leads me over to my feeding station, and I follow, disappointed. *The morning is not over yet.* I refuse to be discouraged. These girls are always working out together and talking about healthy stuff. There is no way they will eat all those tasty desserts. *There's still a chance. Alphas never give up!*

As I finish my breakfast, the girls fill their mugs with the steaming bean brew and load doughnuts onto small dessert plates. Once everyone is equipped with goodies, they head towards the living room. *Follow those doughnuts... I mean, girls.* This has to be heaven. Where else is it acceptable to eat dessert for breakfast? I can't think of anywhere else where this would ever be an acceptable practice for the first meal of the day.

Bailey loads the movie she brought into the DVD player. It is a strange movie called *The Labyrinth*. At the start of the movie, a peculiar human male that Kassandra calls David Bowie dances around in tights and sings. *A lot!* This David Bowie is not a bad singer by any means; I am just not interested in what he is singing about. He seems to think a tiny little infant has some kind of magical power. *Nothing about the kid looks too impressive.*

I refocus my attention back on the pastries. I name my new mission "Operation Choker Hole." I decide to be discreet and use the name loggers and lumberjacks use for doughnuts. This way, the girls won't catch on easily. *Go ahead, applaud my brilliance!* I need to pretend like I have no interest in the scrumptious delicacies on their plates. I divert my attention to one of my favorite toys for a while, a small orange alligator. That's right, make the girls think I don't want anything to do with those doughnuts. Then, they will force me to eat one.

This tactic has worked well lately, allowing me to get what I am after on several other occasions. *Don't fail me now!* After a good play session with Gator, I realize it doesn't seem to be working as well today. I am ready to degrade myself and try the full-on begging thing again. Operation Choker Hole is starting to look like a bust. The girls are all talking about the movie and therefore eating slowly. Annoyed, I leave the room to get a drink of water and regroup. It is time for Plan B. *'B' is for begging.*

I hide around the corner and stare at the girls, re-evaluating the situation. I decide that making a grand entrance back into the room would be best. This will allow me to reclaim their attention. I wait for a spell, and then, like a lion stalking its prey, I put Plan B into action. I bound into the living room where the girls are still ogling the odd movie. It seems this Bowie fella on the big screen is serious competition. I try to be the most adorable and goofy thing the girls have ever seen by chasing my tail, but even that doesn't work. *Kill them with cuteness, and victory will be mine in the form of a doughnut hole!*

Plan B is slowly turning into plan 'B-F-F,' or 'big fat fail.' *Or is it?* I halt mid-tail chase right in front of the big screen. My timing and my entrance could not have been more impeccable. My original plan had gotten slightly derailed as I had been doughnut distracted. *Imagine that. Me, distracted. I have really got to work on my Jedi skills.* When I had barged back into the room to make my cute, unscheduled interruption and began to chase my tail, I overheard the girls conversing about what I should be named. *Could they really come up with my name?* I hope with all my heart they somehow will come across my name of greatness.

Why can't I speak human? That would be so much easier. I change tactics yet again. I must capitalize on this moment. *Make it count, boy!* I abort Operation Choker Hole and sit in front of them, trying to mastermind a way to communicate my name. I decide it is best to give up on the glaze-covered delicacies, as my name is a much more pressing matter.

Either one of three things occurs next. Number one, I am a genius. Number two, I have figured out a way to control the universe without having to use one of my miracles. *Did I find a loophole?* Or number three, I just plain got lucky! The conversation between the girls continues, and suddenly, this big, furry, half-human half-dog creature comes onto the television screen. This creature is a magnificent specimen, insanely large and able to walk on his hind legs! I sit at attention, staring up at the screen, mesmerized by the creature.

I want to be like him. At least, the walking-on-two-legs part. I, of course, am far better-looking than that creature. I am, however, ridiculously envious of his upright walking talent. Then, it happens. I am guessing 'it' is the universe feeling bad for me and literally throwing me a bone. The amazing creature on the big screen howls his glorious name, a wondrous name that just so happens to also be mine. *"Ludo!"* the creature bellows.

Okay, I admit it: I want to walk and talk like this character. *Hello, he speaks human too. How cool is he?* Filled with jealousy and awe, I stare at the large screen with the magnificent creature that shares my name of greatness. I bark and jump circles in front of the television, hoping the girls will receive the message. Maybe they will at least see my delight with the hairy creature and connect the dots that way. "That's it! Call me that. Ludo is my name!" Bark, bark, bark! *What I wouldn't give for a tongue that speaks human words.*

Nerves course through me and turn my stomach. Will the girls figure it out? I am better-looking than this creature. They may not make the connection. Then, it happens. My brilliant, beautiful, and receptive Aunt Kassandra looks at Melody and says, "I think he is trying to tell you his name is Ludo!"

My excitement is so profound I shoot into the air like a space rocket and end up flipping over tail over head style in an ungraceful and unsuccessful backflip like manner. Once I regather my equilibrium and right myself to a standing position, I leap into the oversized chair to join Melody where she sits nestled next to Kassandra under a blanket. I am doing my best to signify my approval of the name. Melody responds to my actions with laughter. "Okay, Ludo it is. Relax, boy!"

Elated, I continue to jump and lick the girls profusely. I now get to celebrate not just my name, but our communication breakthrough. I will need to figure out what exactly occurred so I can utilize the same tactics again in the future. More than anything, though, I am most excited about the death of the name Puppers! Long live the great King Ludo! I sing as I lick their faces and prance around on their laps as if they are a part of the chair they sit on. Maybe I should be more careful, but I am overwhelmed with joy!

As things calm down and I compose myself, and receive a sweet double bonus. Kassandra reward me with some glazed doughy goodness. *Operation Choker Hole is back on. I repeat: mission is a go!* I gobble it up quickly and gratefully. Then, as I go back to basking in the glory of my name, Melody then hands me the last piece on her plate as well! Do I dare run over to Aunt Bailey to try for a third? *Nah, best not to be gluttonous.*

The name Ludo is a great German name—which is fitting because I am possibly one of the greatest German Shepherds of all time. The other reason I love it so much is because of its meaning: famous fighter. I am not aggressive by any means, but I am a fierce protector and will protect my pack to the death if I must. Never will anything ever get to my Melody so long as I am around!

Dogs are, in a sense, knights, sworn to protect and add value to the lives of their humans. This is not a chore for us; it is a delight and an honor because we fall increasingly in love with our humans with each passing day. I decide that the weird emotion I keep feeling for Melody is love. This is what I have gathered from watching a sappy TV station called Life something or other recently. *What was the name of that again?*

Anyway, between the TV station and the various chick flicks I have recently watched with girls, I have formulated this assumption. This feeling inside me seems strongest with Melody. However, I find I am always happy to spend time and get attention from any of my other pack members in her absence.

Ah, they all finally know my wonderful name! Relief and calmness fills me as my adrenaline starts to taper off. Must be time for another nap, or is it merely the sugar high dissipating? The girls always talk about how sugar is bad for them, yet they always seem to sneak it in and treat themselves with it often.

My dog Mother always said, "Everything happens for a reason. Sometimes it takes time." She also told me that, "All the good things in life take hard work and special attention. They are not just handed to you. The good things in life are not always easy, but they are always worth it."

I guess I should work hard and focus on the things I want. Then, somehow, they might manifest themselves. I wonder if that is what I did today to get the delightfully furry creature to say my name. *That wasn't so hard!* This running-a-castle thing may be a breeze after all. I am not sure why Mother and Father wanted us to think it was hard. *Alpha One, I here I come. Then, the creation of my Ultimate Alpha! Legacy!*

I inflate my chest and take a stance in my best power pose. I am proud of my first pack accomplishment and our communication breakthrough! I wish my dog family was here to see me, but somehow, I know they are all smiling from afar at this very moment. I, too, smile at the thought of them having their own similar accomplishments. I settle down for my nap and dream of my brothers and sisters and how they are getting their new families to say their names.

Chapter 11: Time, History, & Goals

Four weeks have passed and we are all adjusting just fine. I am growing rapidly, honing my knowledge, and learning a lot about my pack. One of the things that pleases me the most about my first month here is the headway I have made on Melody's wall of pain. Melody spent her years prior to finding me building a wall around her that is similar in size to The Great Wall of China. She tells herself that this wall of hers is there to protect her. *It does more harm than good.*

Melody's wall gives shelter to all her negative beliefs: all the I cant's, I am not good enough, or skinny enough, or smart enoughs—you name it enough—remain untouchable. This wall does not protect Melody; it protects the evil little monster inside her. One day, I will turn this wall to dust with doggy dynamite, and Melody will embrace her whole self and see that life is better outside these walls. I may not have found a way to destroy it just yet, but I have located its weak spots. I have even dismantled a few of its bricks. *It's a start.* There is no such thing as a small win. If you or your pack are moving in the right direction, each metaphorical stepping stone deserves a celebration. *One brick at a time.*

Four weeks is much longer for dogs than it is for humans. Dog's age significantly differently. The first year of a dog's life is equal to about fifteen human years. Each month that passes during our first year, ages us by one-and-a-quarter years. This simple fact derails my train of thought. *Me, sidetracked? Imagine that.* Anyway, the new thoughts that encroach on my mind cause me to giggle. If humans aged the same way as dogs, I can't imagine how much wrinkle cream they would have on hand trying to combat Father Time. *Now that would be a business to buy stock in.* Aside from fitness and weight loss-related topics, anti-aging is another hot topic amongst the girls in my castle. *Why women are so obsessed with these things is beyond me.*

In the short time I have lived here, I have concluded that Melody and her sisters need more than a few lessons in this area. One of the things I plan to teach these girls is that they are already perfect. We are all made exactly the way we are supposed to be. I will show these girls how to embrace all parts of themselves, including the bad and the ugly. They need to learn to see that there is good in the parts they feel are bad. Together all their parts make them whole. The sooner my girls—specifically Melody—realize this and finally see their worth, the sooner they can share it with the rest of the world. My girls will make this world a better place by helping others see their worth. *Open your eyes, ladies. I have a legacy to build!*

People assume that one human year is equivalent to seven dog years. *Wrong. That is a myth.* Actual dog years are determined by size and breed. If you are a king or giant in your breed, like my parents and I are, you age much faster. Take Great Danes, for example. When they make it to age sixteen in human years, they are actually one hundred and twenty years old, not the presumed one hundred and twelve. Either way, when we reach ten, eleven, twelve, you name a double digit, as a large breed dog, we have long surpassed the average human's lifespan. Retirement doesn't worry me though as I still have plenty of time for planning in the years to come. *Yes, we do that. Or at least, we should.* Everyone wants to maintain their dignity all the way to the end, and that takes planning. Perhaps I should put away a few extra treats for the future. *Never hurts to have a rainy day stash.*

A dog's job with humans is very similar to the role of the 'king's hand' back in the old days. At least, that is how dog's like to refer to it. Our roles are a lot harder and more involved than humans think. Often, I am irritated by the thought that people just think we eat, play, and sleep all day. Managing a human takes a tremendous amount of work. Stay-at-home moms are the only ones that come even close to understanding this. I watched my mother and father do a significant amount of work behind the scenes at Al and Marsha's place. My parents made the lives of their human pack members much better. Not an easy task.

Before my departure from Al and Marsha's, Mother explained to my siblings and me that our first year of life is our knowledge-building year. I fully intend to extract and absorb every scrap of knowledge this year has to offer me. I will be an impeccable leader once I am ready for full command.

By then, I hopefully will have destroyed Melody's wall of pain and will unleash all these great girls in my pack to the world like the Charlie's Angels they truly are.

I finally understand what Mother and Father meant that night when Father told me to go to sleep. I hate to admit it, but they were correct when telling me I need to figure it out on my own. Everyone respects and sees things more clearly if they have to earn and discover it on their own. What I have learned thus far means so much more to me now that I have put in all this work.

Through the absence of words that night, my parents were trying to tell me that I need to figure out what my objective for living this life is. *Basically, I need a goal.* I need to define how I want to make my mark on this world. Without a goal, I have no direction and am only a wanderer. My father told us that there are two ways to navigate the mountain of life: one can hike it, or one can climb it. If one hikes it, they walk around and explore but never advance to anything new or undiscovered. Hikers follow other people and stay on the trails that have been pre-established. To hike is to take the easy road. Hikers lack a purpose and are therefore destined to wander. The other way to navigate the mountain of life is to climb. Climbers step off the trail, take chances, and forge their own way. They are propelled by their goals to make new discoveries at the top. *I am a climber.*

During my first month with my new pack, I find my reason to climb. Melody is my purpose and will one day be the successor of my legacy. I realize now I can't waste precious time chasing my tail and second-guessing myself. Big goals are obtained by making smaller ones. I will plot the smaller ones out like places on a map. Then, once my map is made, I will commit to going to each place, no matter the outcome. Some of the plot points in my plan will bring success, and some will bring failure. Before, I was worried about the outcome of my plan, but now I realize that that doesn't matter. What matters is the knowledge I gain from the situation and what I do with it next—like sharing it and adding value to Melody's life!

Sure, I could have picked a different human—one with a smaller wall, perhaps—but that would have been easy, making for a small, insignificant legacy. My dreams and goals are bigger than that. Melody's are, too. She is a climber, she just doesn't know it yet. *Life brought us together because she needs me to help her climb, and because I believe Melody and I were made for each other!* I must admit that I was shocked at first when, on the day I stood in the mud puddle, the world seemed to stop spinning as we locked eyes. Amazing things happen when you find your soulmate and realize your purpose. *Everything is clear now.*

I will enrich Melody's life to the fullest. If I can do that and change the way she thinks and lives, then she can do the same for others in need. Like ripples on the water's surface, I will start with her; then, my knowledge and message will reach others. Nothing makes me happier than making her lips curl into that dazzling smile, or getting her to throw her head back with joyous laughter. Melody holds the key to my heart. One thing I know for sure is that happiness is contagious. If I can give it to Melody, then the others around her will catch it. *This must be how my legacy will live on.*

Today is going to be a scorcher for July. Thankfully, it is still early morning when Melody and I work on basic commands like 'sit' and 'stay' in the yard. I play the games as Mother and Father had instructed me to do. Father told us that it, "Allows your human pack members to feel like they are in control."

I am following the rules and letting the humans of my house believe they are the true Alphas. I have done well in this department as Melody thinks she wears the pants in this union. *In reality, it is the one without pants who is always in control.* This should be common knowledge, but I will explain for any who disagree. If two people are giving commands, and one is wearing pants, and the other is not, who gets all the attention with no hesitation or thought? *Think about it.* All eyes drift immediately to the one without pants every time. The person wearing pants just fades into the background. *See, I told you: pantsless is where the power is.*

During a dog's first year of life, they learn the most effective way to train their people. Everyone learns differently. At least, that is what I gathered from Father's lectures. I can again hear the doubters from afar, so I will elaborate. This family not only feeds me on a set schedule, but they also let me outside whenever I ring a bell, and even pick up after me when I go to the bathroom. If I had hands, this would be done at the snap of my fingers, but I implement other methods that work just as well. Ring,

ring goes the bell, and a "Yes, master, how can I help you?" follows shortly after! I am still working on communicating some of my commands, but for the most part, if I sigh, groan, or bark, I get exactly what I want! *You can call me the pantsless master.*

Recently, I have discovered a new power, one that really excites me. I have named it my "puppy-dog eyes" power. If this family knew all the things it has allowed me to get away with so far, they would be astounded. Of course, I have no intention of stopping any time soon. Of course, being the alpha I am, I will only use this power of mine for good.

I think all dogs may have it. At least, that is the consensus my new dog friends and I came to while Melody and I were out at the park for a playdate. My dog friends are all a little older than me, so they gave me a few pointers on how to truly master my puppy-dog eyes. *Why didn't Mother and Father didn't tell us about this power? Did my brothers and sisters get it as well? Surely they did.* Anyhow, when I put my power into play, I give my victim a look that could melt even the maddest of men. This then turns him or her into a mushy pile of I-will-give-you-whatever-you-want. I think if I do a little more work honing this power, I may rule the world one day, not just this house. *Watch out, White House. Melody and I are coming for you!* Why the dogs at the park have not attempted to take over the White House yet is beyond me. Perhaps they are not as ambitious as I am. *Are leaders born, or do they evolve over time?* Maybe there is something to the whole nature-versus-nurture argument, or maybe my power has just accelerated faster than most. Either way, Mother always said it best: "You will find out in good time, son."

I love history and have dedicated some of my learning time to researching some of the most acclaimed dogs. I look up to them as role models and have learned from their mistakes. I have been practicing some of the methods they once implemented. So far, I have had excellent results. When I first came to my new castle Grandma had a no dogs allowed in certain rooms of the house rule. With my power knowledge of the past, I have since destroyed the segregation laws of this house and am free to roam anywhere they do. I have no doubt that Melody and I can do great things in this world just like that, but on a much larger scale. I feel I may be much more efficient than some dogs of the past. I may have a slight advantage, though, since I have history to learn from. *Or maybe it is because I am a closer relative to the wolves than some of my predecessors were.*

The great George Washington needed a whole team of dogs to help him run the country. Good old George had strong, brilliant American Staghounds named Sweetlips, Scentwell, and Vulcan to help him out. He also had Drunkard, Taster, Tripler, and Tipsy, who were black and tan Coonhounds. I think he may have needed more handlers because the IQ level of these dogs is not known to be at the top of the charts. However, these dogs were the true pioneers. Our power has clearly evolved. Now, it only takes one or two dogs to get the job done and command the human of the ultimate White House.

Want to know who is at the top of my list of idols? You'll never guess, so I will tell you. It's the first German Shepherd that ruled in the White House! His name was King Cole. *All Shepherds must be Kings.* Old King Cole was not just a merry old soul—he managed Calvin Coolidge. He may have gotten the short end of the stick with his human, but I have no doubt that he did the best job he could managing him. They did not have a long run in office, but he got our paws through the gates and has since opened the doors for the rest of us to follow. *I love a good history lesson.* These examples are the ripple effect at its best. Through one person, these dogs managed to reach a whole country. My legacy will do the same.

Chapter 12: School

Lately, there has been lots of talk about Melody going back to college. *What's college?* Whatever it is, I am going with her. *Where she goes, I go.* All this talk of Melody and I leaving to go somewhere else makes me anxious, so I put finding out what college is and means for Melody's and my future close to the top of my mental to-do list. First, I have to go bury a bone out in the yard for a later day's consumption. I admit I have been on the naughtier side more recently and have been using my puppy dog eyes on everyone in the house. This behavior of mine has treats coming out of all their hands around every corner in the house it seems. By no means does this disappoint me, but if I eat all the treats I am receiving I will be out of shape in no time.

Finally, after burying my bone I catch a break on my 'what is college' investigation as it gets elaborated on as the dinner table for this evening is being set. I am laying under the dining table while Grandma and Melody walk laps around it getting all the places set for the family, including mine. I too eat at the table with the family. Thank you puppy dog eyes! The conversation between the two of them makes college out to be a seasonal thing where people go away to learn more. I wonder if this is partly why a human has so many more life conundrums? Why do they only learn at certain times of the year?

Dogs are always learning. We never stop to take breaks. We take our knowledge with us and build on it every chance we get. Sure, we are born with a vast amount of knowledge for reasons unknown. Don't worry, that is also on my to-do list as I plan to one day discover where dogs get all their vast knowledge from. *But for now, I only know we all have it.* I need a few more resources before I can dive deeper into that investigation. Resources being other dogs in my pack to help me work the many theories and leads that could be the answer to that question. I am pretty sure I know the answer though. I just don't want to say it out loud yet because it's slightly bizarre. Dogs are known for these astounding life concepts, and we are always right. That's because we never release a theory to the world as fact until we have taken the time to learn and research the original hypothesis. We would never make these great discoveries if we only learned at certain times of the year.

Dogs brains are highly adaptable, and we never turn them off. Unlike humans, we take in all elements of our surroundings and situations. We are constantly learning without even trying. It has become evident to me that humans shut their brains down—or set them on vacation mode from time to time. This most recent brain vacation of Melody's is called summer break. *I can't find the sense in this.* I see it as a lack of respect for the things around us. I will need to address this problem with Melody later on so she too becomes an always learner. Melody will need to put her brain vacations on a permanent vacation when we start to build my legacy.

People miss out on so much in this world. They miss at least part of each interaction by not using all their senses. People seem to be selective. They only see and hear the things they want to, or that they think will benefit them in some way. People enter interactions with closed minds. Often, one of their senses is occupied by some sort of electronic device. I just make sure I have my collar on when I leave the house so I have a link back to Melody in case an emergency arises, then out the door I go to take in everything the world and universe are offering for the day. *Another one for the to-do list: teach Melody how to live a minimalist life. Or at least, a more simplistic one.* Once I re-frame Melody's life, she will be able to fully enjoy this great world we live in. I will train her to leave electronic gadgets behind when interacting with other living things. I feel like this should be a given; we should show all living things the same respect we expect in return.

People need to remember that they see things through their own lenses. Humans place their past experiences and perceptions overtop of what is happening before their eyes and then decide if it is a positive or negative experience. The exact same event is very different for each person. I have concluded that this is what causes so many communication issues amongst people. If humans could all decide to be more open-minded, they would have an easier time understanding one another. Just because you view a situation as a negative one does not mean your neighbor feels the same way. If people would talk about their feelings instead of holding them all in, they could grow from each situation. Once Melody grasps this concept I will be well on my way to an Ultimate Legacy. Hopefully, they will help me teach her this in college.

Take failure, for example. Some people view it as the worst possible outcome. To them, failure equals shame and embarrassment. When people believe this, they stop trying because they now live in fear. Other people embrace failure. These people learn from it, and then use their newfound knowledge to try again. Einstein failed repeatedly, but because he chose to learn from each failure, he created amazing things we all use today! Did you know he is the reason we have refrigerators? I am most thankful for that invention of his because that is where bacon comes from. *Uncharted territory mapped out by many failures creates legacies!*

I plan to improve Melody's life in this way. I want her to stop missing out on the miraculous things going on around her. The other day, I watched a butterfly as it emerged from its cocoon. It was wondrous. I looked at Melody's face to share my joy with her, but all I got was disappointment. Melody and her friends were talking about who is dating who now. They were oblivious to the rebirth of the caterpillar. At the end of the conversation, Melody only seemed irritated. Her thoughts were only on her no-boyfriend situation. She failed to embrace the miraculous gift that life had shared with us. *Personally, I am glad she is manless. It gives her more time for me and our mission in life.* Melody's wall of pain is a lot like that cocoon the butterfly sprang from. I am bummed that she missed such a symbolic moment. I must get her to emerge from those walls of hers. *She has so much to learn.* I wonder if I can shorten summer break and get Melody back to college sooner? If this is where humans do most of their learning than I think we should live there for at least a few years. Lucky for her I an abundance of time on my paws, so I can teach and train her until we can get her back to college to start learning again!

Chapter 13: Setbacks

The inky sky battles with the sunrise for longer than usual this morning. When the sun finally wins the battle and Melody and I rise to begin the day, I have an unsettled feeling in my stomach. We start with our normal morning routine. First, we empty our bladders and refill them with a long drink of water. Second, we go outside for our daily workout and training session. Melody and I always wait to eat breakfast until our workout is complete. If we gobble food before running and jumping about, our stomachs get upset. One time, Melody and I shared a peanut butter protein bar before going for our daily run. I'll just say, it didn't stay where it was supposed to. I will spare you all the nasty details.

My apprehension from earlier in the morning finally starts to dissipate when we return to the house for breakfast. *Perhaps all I needed was a good cardio session. I hope I am not coming down with a cold!* The neighbor kids came over to play with me the other day. One of the little germ boxes kept trying to feed me boogers. I personally find small children a little gross. Supposedly, if the child is yours, this kind of behavior is funny and cute. I doubt I will ever want to eat anyone's boogers though, my child or not.

As Melody and I enter the house, we are met with dead air. This is highly suspicious for a normal morning at the castle. Usually, we are met with an eruption of noise, and I get an immediate rub down from Grandpa or Grandma while they ask how our run was. That's not the case today, though. Something significant must have happened that caused Grandpa and Grandma to take a sudden leave with no goodbye. *They always say goodbye.*

I trot through the house in search of my pack. I only discover mute rooms. *My castle has no servants.* Melody is obviously just as concerned as I am; she has already started her own investigation. Finally, we solve the mystery when Melody finds a piece of paper on the kitchen counter and reads it out loud.

Girls,

Aunt Ciara has unexpectedly passed away. We got the call at six this morning and packed up immediately. We are headed south to make arrangements for the funeral. We did not think it would be practical for you girls to come at this point. Your mother and I will call you when we get to your Aunt Juliana's house. We will be staying there the next few days.

Love,

Mom & Dad

Someone in the family passed away. *I assume this means she died.* This is tragic. I feel terrible for Grandma as I believe Ciara was her sister. Neither me nor the girls have ever met her though so I could be wrong. Losing a sister would be a trying time for anyone though, family is family. I find that I am slightly relieved because I don't know who this person is, and because my initial gut feeling as we walked in the house was wrong. My first thought upon entering our castle was that something horrifying had happened to one of my pack-mates. I was worried that I had in some way failed to protect them by being out with my Melody instead of on duty at home. I read in the paper yesterday about a recent robbery in town that took place only five miles away from our castle. Because of this, I have been on high alert ever since. If a mouse were to fart at night inside the walls of our house, I would know about it. I am glad I didn't fail to protect my pack, but my heart goes out to Grandma.

Melody assures me that either Grandpa and Grandma will be back in a week, or we will head south to join them. The news mollifies my concerns. Anxiety installs itself inside me as my monster starts to feed upon it. In the interim, I will have to assume the Alpha role of the house. Melody, Kassandra, and our castle will need to be looked after while Alpha Pa is away. I like to call Grandpa 'Alpha Pa' when he is in command. *Everyone in our house has nicknamed me in various ways, so I am only returning the favor.*

Regardless, there must always be an Alpha in charge. My father, the amazing King that he is, made sure we were all well aware of that fact. Father even told my sisters they could rule for a period of time—but at some point, they would need to get a male pack member to take over. Females have to relinquish their Alpha role so they can move on to their motherly duties and continue our existence. By no means does this make them any less of an Alpha in my eyes. The fact that they can create smaller versions of us inside themselves and then bring them to life is astonishing.

I think the females may hold more power than males within them. Without them, our breed would cease to exist, and we could never rule the world. I am glad I was born a male and built to lead though. I don't have the patience for motherly duties. My mother always looked uncomfortable and exhausted as she cared for us in the early stages of our lives, especially when we were all incessantly biting at her nipples for food. It is a wonder she never bit us back.

Grandpa's unexpected absence was not at all in my plans. I had originally planned to take over midway through my second year of life. Mother and Father said it is best not to take the Alpha role until you are older than the main humans in your pack. Older is wiser, and since we age faster and never stop learning, we gain access to wisdom much more quickly than one would assume. I will surpass Melody in the age department by the time I am two-and-a-half human years old. Since she is my main pack member, I decided that then will be a good time to take over. Until then, Alpha Pa will continue to manage the residence and our castle.

I like to think of it like the *"Don't break something that isn't broken"* saying that is often tossed around. Luckily for humans, we dogs are nice enough to take over the Alpha role when we are ready for it. It is a blessing to them more than to us. I assume this to be part of making our human's lives better—though, as I learn more, I feel it may go both ways. I think humans improve our lives just as much as we do theirs. Melody has a way of making

98

the sun shine brighter than it ever did before I met her. *I'd be lost without her.*

Due to the urgency of this situation at hand, I decide I will make an exception and assume a brief command as the lead Alpha. I am not overly thrilled at accepting this high-stress position so soon, but someone has to do it. Melody and Aunt Kassandra will need protection while Grandpa is away. I will use this opportunity as a trial run until Grandpa returns. Upon his arrival, I will give him back command until I reach the correct age and obtain the proper knowledge. *And so it begins. Watch out, world. There is a new head Alpha in town.* Perhaps if all goes well, I will earn the Alpha One spot earlier than expected.

This morning's upset makes the day more dismal than usual. Melody is extra fidgety and seems slightly distressed. Surely she, too, is saddened by the death in the family. However, I can't shake the feeling that there may be something more going on in that mind of hers. I spend most of the day trying to be silly in an effort to cheer her up. For the most part, I succeed. She grins here and there, along with an occasional giggle. However, I am disappointed that Melody's happiness seems to dissipate just as rapidly as it finds her. *I mustn't let her rebuild the parts of the wall we have already dismantled.*

Finally, our seemingly endless day meets its demise. Melody and I lie in bed next to one another, pretending to sleep. Eventually, Melody's breathing slows and true sleep claims her. Shock finds me a few hours later when the morning sunrise appears, casting a warm, golden light onto the bed where I rest next to her. Apparently, at some point in the night, sleep had overtaken me too. *Deep sleep, at that.*

Perhaps all the light sleeping I have been doing lately had finally caught up with me. I haven't had a choice in the matter lately. I need to be alert in case the fugitive robbers come our way; they have yet to be apprehended. I am disappointed in myself for sleeping so deeply, but I am happy that no one had tried to come into our castle while I was off duty. After re-evaluating the night's events, I let myself off the hook for my lack of consciousness and focus on the day ahead. I am determined to make today better than yesterday. One of my favorite things about a new day is that if you did not like the one before it, you have the power within you to change the next one.

Melody is already up. I must have really been out cold. The fact that she had gotten out of bed without waking me boggles my mind. She seems anxious as she quickly dresses. She calls saying, "Hurry up, Lu, you need to go out and eat. We are going to be late!"

Late for what? Melody picks me up and carries me outside so I can do my business. Apparently I'm not moving fast enough for her liking. We go back in the house, and she tells me to eat up. Confused, I saunter over to my feeding station. *We aren't going for our normal workout and play session?* I barely finish my kibbles when Melody shoves me back out into the yard for my second order of business. *You know, the one everyone normally does after eating.* Humans hate to talk about it, so they often pretend no one does it. If some of you are still claiming ignorance, I will just say it: poop!

See, that wasn't so bad. *Poop.* I often laugh at how the girls in my pack dance around the subject. Bowel movements are natural. Everyone has them. There is no reason one should be ashamed of them. *Better out than in, or else we become toxic.* Maybe that is what makes some people so crabby around here. One day, when I rule as Ultimate Alpha, I will address the turd crisis of the world. I will teach the next generation how to live the life of a free pooper. No one will ever be ashamed or laughed at. Everyone will simply go the way they were meant to. I sit in the grass, envisioning my glorious triumph and a world of regular people free from hostility, as I scan the yard for just the right spot to get the deed done myself. Melody's voice interrupts my process: "Come on, Lu. Just do it already."

Um, hello, Melody, they call it taking a picture for a reason! To say 'taking a picture' in reference to a dog taking a crap stems from our unique position. We get all hunched over, and a serious look consumes our faces. Once we find the right spot—the right spot being one with proper scenery to gratify our eyes and mind during said event—we relax and our bowels let loose. For hundreds of years, we have assumed this position. Evidently, someone along the way decided that we reminded them of a photographer all hunched over and serious. I guess this is how photographers look as they gaze through their camera lens before snapping the picture. It makes sense to me. At our castle, the women don't say they are going to take a poop. They instead say that they "have to go take a picture." Maybe they are making fun of me. I don't know, and I really don't care. I am not shy, nor do I have a problem with the word 'poop.' I am just thrilled that my girls don't hold it in. There are some seriously angry people in this world who would probably be a lot more pleasant if they pooped!

I do as I am told and pick a less-than-optimal place for a peaceful dump. I get it over with as quickly as I can. When I finish, I trot over to Melody, who is standing impatiently in the driveway. *Jeepers, what's got her panties so far up her butt?* Melody often gets crabby if we have to shorten the distance of our morning run, so I anticipate that she is a little more agitated than normal since we had skipped it altogether. Still, this is a little ridiculous. *Do you need to poop, Mel?* I head towards our car since we are late—for what, I am still not sure. Melody walks swiftly over to meet me and picks me up. "Not today. We are running too far behind to take my car. I forgot to fill my tank on the way home last night. We will take Dad's truck." *Oh, good. At least we are still going on a car ride.* She had me worried for a second there.

Chapter 14: The Green Machine

I love Grandpa's truck. I call it the Green Machine. It is a massive beast of a vehicle with a large chrome ram on the front. It is by far my favorite vehicle to ride in. Its motor rumbles and roars, and it has massive tires that I love to pee on when no one is looking. I am secretly trying to make it my own. The truck is powered by diesel fuel, and I find the aroma intoxicating. Lastly, I really like the ram in the middle of the grill. The truck is tough, powerful, and very Alpha-like. I get a little embarrassed when Grandma gives me rides in her little, girly blue car.

Melody places me in the passenger seat. *Yes, shotgun position!* This is my usual position unless someone else rides with us. Somehow, I get demoted to the back seat when company comes along. I must amend this predicament as I am clearly a front seat dog. Melody climbs in on the driver's side and buckles in. *Houston, we are ready for takeoff!* I have been obsessed with space ever since I read one of Grandpa's airplane magazine articles last week. I decide to pretend that Melody and I are on a spaceship and not in Grandpa's truck as we begin our journey. Melody breaks my concentration when she says, "I am sorry, bud. We are going to the vet for your twelve-week shots."

Wipe that sad, worried look off your face! I have no idea why Melody looks so concerned. She is not the one getting shots today. I will let everyone in on a little doggy secret: when dogs get shots, they don't hurt. Dogs of the past simply fabricated this myth. As dogs of the present, we play along to continue the myth's existence. We put on a show sometimes, pulling back on the leash and pretending we do not want to go in to the big, bad vet. The reality is, we love going to the vet because afterward, our humans feel bad and spoil us the rest of the day. *Who wouldn't play along?* Don't worry, Melody. We can go to the vet every day if you would like. I have yet to meet a dog who would turn down this opportunity. We have to endure a small bee sting in exchange for a day of over-the-top pampering. *Oh, my—it's almost unbearable! Yes, if you give us an inch, we will most certainly take more than a mile.*

Melody is clearly feeling poorly about my vet situation. She tries to lighten the somber mood by turning on the radio and belting out some Tim McGraw song called "Don't Take the Girl." At least, that is what the display on the radio says. This makes her laugh. Through a chortle, Melody says, "I am sorry, Lu. Your mom is not much of a singer. It's only acceptable because we are in the car where no one else can hear me."

My sweet girl, you are a hundred percent right on that one! I love my Melody, but her singing voice is definitely not that of an angel. This is a particularly funny fact, as her name means music, at least in part. Despite her name though, Melody's singing voice is far from acceptable to human ears. However, I am grateful Melody is having fun and her mood has lifted significantly when compared to yesterday. I do not want my girl to be saddened by taking me to the vet. *Pampering, here I come! I'm shaking in my seat over here because of the shots that are headed my way. Or not!* Realistically, I should probably pretend to sulk right now to strengthen my case and earn a higher level of pampering. I decide against that though. Instead, I join Melody in her sing-along. At least my howling is an acceptable noise to any listening ears. *I can't let her give a good song a bad reputation!*

The sing-along helps me relax after our rushed morning, and I finally begin to enjoy the truck ride. The windows are cracked open, and the warm July air blows through the truck and combs through my hair like thousands of tiny fingers. I take pleasure in the invigorating ride and the passing scenery. As I scan the road ahead, I notice that we are approaching a stop sign. I can hear a clicking noise in the background, signaling we will make a turn soon. At least, that is what I think the noise means. I always hear it before the vehicle makes a left or right turn. The stop sign is about two miles ahead.

I don't know if I fully understand stop signs. I know I don't typically like the word 'stop' or 'no,' probably because I am usually doing something fun whenever it is squawked at me. I wonder why people have placed these signs all over the roadways. Dogs are positive creatures; we never dwell on the negative. Personally, I find 'stop' to be negative. Perhaps if humans put up more positive signs on the roadways, there would be less rage amongst the drivers.

Speaking of negative things in our world, people wonder why all dogs seem to have a fetish for destroying newspapers. Newspapers are full of negative stories that no one should read. People shouldn't watch the news, either, as it's even worse. *Now that would be a great place for a big red stop sign.* Please refrain from reading newspapers—at least, most of them. There are only three good sections: the comics, the sports section, and the classifieds. The comics should be obvious. There are multiple sayings that have been said for years that support this, my favorite is, "A laugh a day keeps the doctor away!" The sports section is also awesome because dogs absolutely love balls and anything that involves them. Maybe you saw that one coming. Now for the last good section of the paper, the classified ads. This is where we find new dog pack-mates and cars. *I love a good muscle car!* Dogs typically leave these sections of the paper untouched. *There you have it, folks— mystery solved!*

I personally find it humorous that people assume they had the great idea to get another dog to accompany their poor, 'lonely' dog. If people would stop and think back to the day they found that classified ad advertising the 'new dog,' they would see that the actual events that led them to that great idea of theirs wasn't really theirs at all. Think about it. Was the paper magically opened to that exact spot when you sat down for your morning cup of coffee? Or was that the only section of the paper not ripped to shreds when your dog was left unattended?

My father said that when he found Mother in the classifieds, he strategically placed a muddy paw print next to her ad. While pretending to chase a bee through the house, Father jumped onto the dining table where Al sat reading the paper, knocked over Al's coffee—which soaked the worthless parts of the paper—and left the only two parts worth reading intact. Of course, they were the sports section, for his later pleasure, and the classified ad he had just drawn attention to with his pawprint of approval. Father had essentially highlighted the ad to grab Al's attention and draw his eyes there. After Al scolded Father and cleaned up the ruined parts of the paper, he looked down and read Mother's ad. After a moment of silence, Al got the great idea. He then walked over to the phone and called to arrange an appointment to see Mother's litter immediately. Later that day, Mother rode home with Al and Father. *Mission accomplished!* My Father is like a brilliant puppet master with Al and Marsha dangling at the end of his strings!

I plan to do something equally as brilliant when I am ready for a new pack-mate one day. We dogs are so smart and so good at our jobs that our humans give themselves all the credit. They pat themselves on the back for the genius moments we create. We don't mind—after all, we are only making both of our lives better. We especially love making our people feel smarter. The easiest way to do that is to let them think they have just had some brilliant idea.

I like to think of us dogs like the wizard in *The Wizard of Oz,* always orchestrating events and outcomes from behind the curtain. That's one of Grandma's favorite movies. I feel it could have been better had Toto been a German Shepherd. However, I must give the Scottish breeds credit for their tremendous bravery. One would think their small size would cause them to run and hide, but that is never the case with them. Truth be told, there is not much in this world that can deter a Scotty once he or she is determined to something.

I suppose that is enough bragging and day-dreaming for one day. I rejoin the present moment with Melody as we ride along in the Green Machine. *Hi-ho, hi-ho, to the vet I go.* I am finally settling in and taking in the day. The sky is a brilliant azure tone. I lean my face farther out the window, into the wind and the warm fluorescent glow of the sun. Then, I notice the dreaded sign growing bigger as Melody applies the breaks to stop before it. Aside from the STOP sign's negativity, I embrace this peaceful moment of sing-along in the car and completely shrink the evil monster inside me that tried to grow off this morning's anxiety.

I sit, silently praising myself for beating my little monster back into submission. *Take that! Won't be long before you are gone for good.* I am getting stronger in the mental department with each passing day. I only need to figure out how to get rid of it entirely, and then my life will be perfect. I proudly puff my chest out in the passenger seat. Then, I am abruptly torn from the peaceful moment. Melody lets out a shriek: "Crap!"

Instantly I see what had caused Melody to scream. A quick side note: I am often amazed by Melody's ability to not curse. I think this situation warrants a bad word or two, yet she still takes the high road. I peer past Melody out the driver's side window and see a navy blue Buick barreling toward us at well above the speed limit. The intersection we are stopped at is considered a blind intersection due to a farmhouse and a lumberyard obscuring the view of its entirety. I am not sure what makes them blind exactly, as the intersections themselves don't have eyes as far as I can tell. Anyway, due to the intersection Melody had had no choice but to pull out past the stop sign in order to fully see if there was any oncoming traffic. *Unlucky us—oncoming traffic coming right up!* The other driver is on a direct route to connect with Melody's door in three, two, one! *Houston, we have contact!*

Just before the bone-crushing impact overtakes us, Melody makes what seems like two smooth, simultaneous, brilliant movements: she jerks the wheel of the truck hard to the right while unlatching her seatbelt. Before I know it, Melody has slid over to my side of the truck and scooped me up into her arms. Had she done so a moment later, I would have slid to the floor. The next thirty seconds are a blur of insanely loud crunching metal, an avalanche of shattered glass, and an explosion of large white bags with chemical clouds that encompass and blind us. Melody secures me against her chest with incredible strength. *I can't breathe! Is it the chemical dust or Melody's tight hold on me? Come on, Mel, loosen up a little, it almost feels like I am being born again.*

We tumble around in the truck like rocks in a polisher. Grass and dirt pour into new openings, and the things inside the truck like Melody's purse and my leash bounce like rubber balls on concrete inside, trying to escape. Objects from the inside desperately want out, and objects on the outside are forcing their way in. Pure chaos! *On second thought, hold tighter,*

Melody. Stay close, I will keep us safe! The Green Machine spirals out of control and rolls head over tail numerous times. A fence post pierces through the roof of the truck and impales the driver's seat. Thank goodness Melody had unbuckled. *Everything happens for a reason!*

Finally, after what seems like an eternity, the truck comes to a halt in the middle of a cornfield. Melody and I lie outside near the rear of the truck now. *Probably more accurate to say what is left of the truck.* The once glorious Green Machine now looks like Godzilla had tossed it around like a cheap children's toy, and then stepped on it to show his displeasure. *Total destruction.* I wiggle out of Melody's grasp to assess the situation further. I notice a crushed beer can lying next to us in the field. I find the can a little ironic as it and Grandpa's Green Machine both share the same fate now at the recycling center. I stretch and shake myself to check that I have no injuries. Once I confirm that I am unharmed, I gallop back over to Melody.

I begin to further assess the scene and find myself in a state of disbelief. By the looks of things, it is miraculous that I am uninjured. I glance around the disheveled field. Corn stalks lie everywhere, ripped from the earth like a tornado had gone through. Wire and fenceposts are strewn about in every direction. *Where are we?* I turn to look at Melody for reassurance, but get none. Melody is lying silently on the ground, her body bent in ways that could not possibly be comfortable. I quickly key in on a heavy metallic scent permeating in the air. I take a closer look at Melody and realize that large portions of her body are oozing dark red blood that tries to hide itself in the dirt. *How did I miss that?*

Consciousness begins to find Melody. It is evident to me that she is in a tremendous amount of pain; her face contorts into all kinds of snarls and grimaces. Garbled sounds escape her lips. I struggle to still myself and think. My body trembles at the sight of my sweet Melody laying on broken corn stalks with her arms and legs in impossible angels. *Get a grip, boy. She needs you! Do something!* But what? I need to be like a little ankle-biting dog and just react already, now is not the time to be the thorough thinker I normally am.

I fail to regain control of my thoughts. My system is being held hostage by fear. *Melody needs my help.* She closes her eyes between moans, drifting in and out of consciousness. Something in my gut tells me that if she goes to sleep, things will only get worse for her. *This is not our bed, sweet girl. We only nap in our bed. Come on, now, get up. It's time to go.* I lick Melody's face fiercely every time she shuts her eyes. I only allow myself breaks when her eyes are open wide. *Oh, no you don't. I will not allow you to drift away from me. Not today!* "Ludo, no," Melody weakly grumbles at me. She tries to reach me with one of her arms, but I keep at her and dodge her grasp. *I am doing this for your own good. Trust me. Now, I command you to stay awake. Don't you shut those baby blues*! Licking and barking. Barking and licking. *If only I could use human words.*

Chapter 15: Help from a Stranger

After a few minutes that feel like hours, I see a lady on her phone running towards us. Once she gets to where she can see Melody and me, her jaw momentarily drops to the ground. I watch her with great envy as she quickly gathers herself and then takes command of the ugly situation. I am not at ease giving up control to this stranger, but she seems to have some sort of plan guiding her actions. *She is helping Melody, which is more than you are doing right now. Let it go for a minute. Give the lady room to work.* I step back as the lady bends down to check me over. "Don't look at me! Look at Melody!" I bark at the lady. Once the lady confirms that I am as good as any dog could be after being thrown from a vehicle, she turns her attention to Melody. I find myself wanting to take back control from the lady. I am annoyed by the fact that she is still on her phone. "Is that thing attached to the side of your face? Put the phone down and help me, for crying out loud. Can't you see we are in crisis mode?" Bark, bark, bark! I attempt to tell the lady what to do, even though I know she can't understand. *Melody is the only one who seems to understand me most times.*

The lady still has the phone mashed to her face. It protrudes from her cheek like some weird growth.

She doesn't even have a hand securing it to her ear like Melody does whenever she talks on one. The lady's head is cocked to the side; I assume her shoulder is keeping the phone pinned to her face while she works. "I am sure you could work more efficiently if you would just put the darn thing down. What are you doing? Clearly, this is no time to talk!" I continue to bark at her as she fumbles around Melody. I fear that if I don't micromanage her, she will lose interest and leave us for her more interesting phone conversation.

I am not sure why, but as I look around the field, I become dizzy. I try desperately to steady myself, but my environment has started spinning all around me like I am on a fast-moving merry-go-round. Hysteria is stampeding in like a herd of chased zebras on the desert plains with a lion hot on their heels. I sense that my monster is out for blood. The phone-faced lady speaks again, and the sound of her high-pitched voice brings me back to the present as she tells whoever is on the other end of the line, "It is bad, she is really bad! Come quick!" Finally, the lady turns off the phone and slides it into her back pocket.

Fully focused at last! The lady tends to Melody. First, she rubs her knuckles over Melody's breast plate, trying to help keep her awake. This trick of hers works well, or at least causes Melody a lot of discomfort. Melody makes a lot of noise to indicate her displeasure. I am more than a little scared now. *Perhaps I should work a miracle? But how? I am not ready yet. I have not yet learned that amazing art. I know Melody is worth it, but how do I do it? Come on, universe—throw a dog a bone, here!* I howl up to

113

the clouds, hoping something or someone will hear me. I need more than a strange lady!

I pace anxiously back and forth behind the lady, waiting for her to fix Melody. *What is taking her so long? What are the rules on the miracles again? Think, Ludo, think!* I sit next to them, silently scolding myself for not paying more attention to Mother and Father on lesson days. I am disappointed that I never got to read the book on Marsha's nightstand before leaving. I cannot, and will not, lose my Melody. We are destined to do great things in this world, along with the rest of our pack. *I can't do this alone. Come on, my girl, just sit up already. Get up now, and we will walk home.* All I can do is whine. *I just want to go home. Sit, my sweet girl, sit!* Melody is my number one pack member. Melody is who I live for! This is not an acceptable situation. This can't be happening.

I rack my brain as I supervise this strange lady who is caring for Melody. As I do this, loud sirens begin blaring in the background. *Is the universe answering my call?* I tip my head back and howl. "Over here! We are over here!" I howl and pray that the humans will understand. Somehow, I know they are coming to help. Large box-shaped vehicles with flashing blue and red lights appear along the horizon and pull up to us one by one.

The lights on the vehicles remind me of the Fourth of July party we had for Grandma a few weeks earlier. If only we could go back in time... There never seems to be a time travel machine around when you need one. *Why didn't I hurry this morning when Melody asked me to? If only we had gotten to the stop sign earlier, we could have avoided this.* Sheer terror is consuming me. My monster is massive now, his mouth agape, sharp teeth gleaming in the light and all his intentions set on burying them in my throat. I focus on the task at hand and run to meet the new people. I feel as though I am now starring in some *Lassie* movie, guiding the rescuers to Timmy. *If only this whole scenario was fictional.* The men push a bed on wheels while carrying black bags with red and white patches. *Those bags had better contain miracles. I need all the help I can get!* "This way, men! One of you had better be a miracle-working Alpha!" I bark and run as fast as my paws will carry me to guide them to my distressed damsel.

The men gather around Melody and begin working on her. Honestly, it reminds me of one of those sci-fi movies where someone gets abducted by aliens. You know, the one where the aliens strap the person to a table and probe them incessantly. The men cut off Melody's clothes with scissors. "What are you doing to her? I thought you were here to help. Stop at once! She would never be okay with being naked outside. Put her clothes back together immediately!" I bark and run circles around them, trying to see what they are doing to my girl. Maybe these men are aliens, and those boxy, lighted vehicles are their spaceships. The men's backs are an impassable mountain as they hover around her, steadily working. I cannot find a way through or over them to my Melody. "It is me she needs. Get out of the way. Let me in! Stop at once!" Bark, bark!

One of the men speaks into a radio on his shoulder. "I know this girl. Her name is Melody. She is a friend of my daughter. She doesn't have time to wait for a chopper if it is ten minutes out! I am making the call. We are taking her by ambulance. The woman from the other car can ride in the bird when it gets here. Surprisingly, she is in good shape. Only a little shaken up, with a few broken bones."

That's it? The lady who destroyed the Green Machine with her blue Buick only broke a few bones? The universe is unfair. *This is all her fault. Where is she? Let me at her.* I begin to growl in the direction of the blue Buick. I have some choice words for her. The lady from the blue car has men in uniforms huddled around her as well. *I see you!* I start to stalk over there to give the other driver a piece of my mind.

Suddenly, I am lifted into the air by large, thick arms. A man in a blue and grey uniform has picked me up and is carrying me away from Melody and the other driver. I decide I should put off giving the other lady a piece of my mind so I can get back to my Melody. *Put me down at once. I must be with her, she needs me!* I wiggle in his heavily muscled arms and watch as the men around Melody count to three, then lift her onto the portable bed with wheels. They cover her with a sheet and fasten her tightly to the bed with black straps. Slight relief finds me as they start to push the bed in my direction. I relax a little and take everything in. A man is walking behind the rolling cart, steadily pumping some sort of balloon-like facemask that covers Melody's mouth. Then they do the unthinkable. The men turn the bed on wheels and take Melody away from me. They are now headed in the opposite direction!

You're Welcome

Desperate times call for desperate measures. I relax in the muscle man's arms and lick his face. 'Be cute and cuddly' is the mantra I adhere to. I turn on my puppy-dog eye power and give a little whine. He lets his guard down, just as I had planned. I have played the sympathy card and played it well. I lick his face one last time to force him to release the remaining tension still holding me in place. Then, I use all my strength and push my legs into his hard chest, like one of the cars from *The Fast and the Furious* as I take off. I erupt from his arms like lava from the top of a two hundred-year-old volcano and hit the ground running and barking at the men who have Melody. 'If you are going to take her, at least take me with you. Wait for me!" Bark, bark!

I don't get far. This time, a man in a black uniform with a shiny gold star pinned to his chest captures me with the speed of a superhero. I noticed him and some others emerge from a small, flashy vehicle earlier, but failed to pay any attention to them. This man is bigger and stronger than the last one. *Great. How can I elude him to rejoin my Melody?* I am positive he saw me trick the other guy, so he is aware of my tactics. I try the same maneuver again, hoping he is ignorant to my plan. It is no surprise to me when my tricks do not work. "Nice try," he mumbles. Then, he yells to the others: "What about the dog?" *Yes, what about me? Put me in the back of that box on wheels with Melody! That's what!* "You are a cute little fella," the man says. *Really? Little fella?* He continues, "You would make a great police dog. You are already fiercely protecting your partner! I may have to do some research on where you came from. Maybe you have some brothers and

117

sisters left."

I think this man is trying to comfort me. It isn't working. "Listen here, muscle man. I will be anything you want if you just put me in that spaceship with my girl!" I half growl and half groan at him, but he doesn't understand me. *Melody would have.* One of the many mystical things shared amongst soulmates. Melody has to be okay. I need her.

I hear Stranger Lady squawking away as she walks towards us. "I know the family—Melody used to be on the swim team with my daughter. I will get ahold of them, and will leave my contact information with you if you need it. Also I will take the dog to the vet. He seems okay, but he is covered in blood! I thought Melody had a pillow or a blanket when she came out of the back of the truck. I was behind her when it happened. I had no idea it was a dog until I got to them."

What? Covered in blood? Who, me? No, you are mistaken, lady. That was Melody, and they just took her. Some help you were! You should have put the phone down sooner. I could have gotten Melody out of here before these men arrived to strip and kidnap her! Finally, I stop chastising the lady, as I feel she did try to help us the best she could. I look down at my paws, part of me hopes they will just move me in the direction I need to go to get Melody back. *But how can I get Melody back if I don't know where she is?* Then, I see it. Lots of it! All my white fur has been changed to shades of pink and deep crimson. Due to the circumstances, I had not yet noticed. I was fine, Melody was the one nearly in pieces on the ground. I quickly re-confirm that I have no broken bones. Then, I begin licking at the wet reddish-brown stains that paint my fur and confirm that I am indeed covered in Melody's blood. *If I am wearing this much of it, what is left to course through her veins and keep her alive?*

I start barking at the boxy vehicle as the men close its doors and jump inside. The vehicle then takes off with its sirens screaming. My Melody lies inside as a captured, nearly naked victim. "Where are you going? Take me with you!" I howl after the sirens. I turn to the lady who now holds me in her arms and demand that she follow them. My demand hangs in the air unheard unanswered because the only human in this world who can understand my language is being driven away from me.

The rest of my day passes by in a whirlwind. Stranger lady is taking me to the vet. Once there, she will see to it that I get a thorough checkup. I assume I will also get the shots that Melody had promised earlier. I am now sick with stress and defeat. The knowledge that this was my first attempt as the Alpha One and had not only failed, but now have no idea where my Melody is, haunts me. *What am I going to tell Grandpa and Grandma when they return? What if they don't return?* My monster has won the battle today, all I can do is hope that there is still more to come.

How didn't I see that other car coming? *Ugh, I was too busy enjoying the car ride. I let my guard down.* I vow to myself that if and when—no, wait, definitely when. 'If' is not an option. *When* I get my Melody back, I will never let her down. I will never let anything bad like this happen to her ever again.

119

Next time, I will know how to work my miracles and will waste no time in doing so. We should have been running home long before the boxy alien spaceships arrived. Melody will never again be captured by men in uniforms. *I led them right to her.* Guilt turns my stomach. *What was I thinking?* I thought they were there to help us. My adrenaline leaves my body and I lose control. I throw up on Stranger Lady as she carries me to her purple van. As mean as it is of me, I don't even feel bad. S*erves her right for letting them take Melody away like that. What was she thinking?*

Chapter 16: The Voodoo Doctor

Stranger Lady and I arrive at the veterinary clinic. My new vet is a nice, gray-haired old man whose name tag reads 'Dr. Jerry.' He immediately says something but I am not listening because I am deep in self-pity. What I hear coming from him reminds me of the older lady in *Peanuts. Whamp wha wha wha wha.* Anyhow, as I am ignoring him, Dr. Jerry places a special treat in front of my nose. I eat it, partly out of stress and partly because it was annoyingly shoved in my face. *What can I say? I am like the women I live amongst: I am a stress eater!* To be honest, I also think if I comply quickly with Dr. Jerry's demands, Stranger Lady and I can leave here sooner. I need to resume my mission of finding and saving Melody. Grandpa and I watch a lot of cop shows, and they say the first forty-eight hours are the most critical in finding a missing person.

I chalk the treat up to the pampering that starts after a dog receives his or her shots. After all, it is a known fact that all people feel bad when a dog goes to the vet to get poked by a needle. I assume Dr. Jerry is only giving me a pity treat. He scratches me behind my ears as he talks with Stranger Lady. Then, he speaks a sentence that becomes the driving force behind my forever hatred towards him: "This will help Ludo here relax and will ease any soreness that may be settling in. The poor little guy has had a stressful day. I hope his owner makes it. The accident sounds horrific. I thought Ludo here was a goner, too, when you first walked in with him! I can't believe he doesn't have a scratch on him. Miracles do happen."

"What? Wait, no!" I bark. I need to be sick. Q*uick, throw up.* I must eat grass ASAP! Bark, bark. "This is not the time for me to be sleeping. I have serious business to tend to. Melody needs me!" *What on earth did I eat? Dr. Jerry, you are a true jerk. I can't believe you drugged me!* I bark directly at Stranger Lady this time. "Get me out of here! Get me away from this man!"

Ugh, I wish I had never met this lady. Ever since we met, nothing but bad things have happened. First of all, she called the uniformed men who came and stripped Melody naked and took her away. And now, Stranger Lady has taken me to some sort of witch doctor! *He probably isn't even a real vet!* My relationship with her needs to be terminated immediately. I sit here, barking my disgust, upset at both Stranger Lady and Dr. Jerry. As I do, I notice that my eyelids are straining to stay open. My body starts to sway back and forth on the metal table between the two. I am succumbing to Dr. Jerry's witch craft and his evil drugs. *I'll get you for this! Mark my words.*

Finally, Stanger Lady stops talking to Dr. Jerry and picks me up. *Great, it is about time. Get me out of here. We should have never come!* I am not sure when this occurred, but Stranger Lady had pulled her phone out again. She is already talking to someone on it as we exit the clinic. *Is this what you do all day?* This lady needs a healthier hobby. She should put that thing down already and get a dog of her own!

Stranger Lady carries me outside and begins to load me into the rear of her Barney the Dinosaur-colored Town and Country. Out of the corner of my eye, I see something white and lightning fast flash by. Stranger Lady sets me down in the van, and I see it flash again, this time on my other side. My instincts tell me that the white, fuzzy, fast thing is going to appear on my other side any second now. I sit, waiting to ambush it. I will get it this time, and then I'll figure out what it is and make it stop moving so fast. Whatever it is, it is annoying the crap out of me. The drugs are giving me an epic headache and I am in no mood to tolerate some silly thing that's more than likely a moth flying around without a care in the world. I need to get a head start on whatever this thing is because my reaction time is decreasing rapidly, thanks to the voodoo doctor.

The drugs are almost in full effect now. The edges of objects all blur together, rainbow-like colors streaking behind them. If I were able to actually relax I would probably find this psychedelic light show pretty intriguing and calming. The white thing flashes again; I missed my chance once more. Unluckily for it, I now know its cadence. *That's it—whatever you are, you are about to meet your fate.* I turn my head the other way and wait. This is it! It takes every bit of energy I have left to direct my focus towards the impending doom of the flying white object. I have to end whatever it is. It is irritating me and my pounding head. *Get ready, here it comes again. Now, get it, get it now!* I lurch forward and bite down hard. Pain shoots up through my tail. *What on earth?*

Turns out, the flying white thing was my tail frantically gesticulating back and forth. *Great, these drugs are so strong I can't even control my own body parts!* I catch it, more gently this time, and nuzzle it with my nose. What a boneheaded move that was. I do my best to redirect my focus to the conversation that Stranger Lady is having as she drives us away from the clinic. I must stay alert. *I can beat these drugs. I must save Melody!* I can hear the faint voice of the person on the other end of the phone. *Jeepers, lady, how high do you have the volume on that thing? Perhaps if you didn't talk on it all day, you would have better hearing and you would have understood me earlier.* There is something familiar about the voice on the other end. I'm not sure what makes it familiar yet. The voice is definitely male. *Do I know this man?* I do my best to poke my head over the back seat so I can hear the conversation better. Then, I hear it: it's Grandpa! As the realization hits me, Stranger Lady says, "Do not worry about Ludo. We will take care of him until one of you can come get him. Just take care of your daughter."

Wait, did she just say what I think she said? I have to stay with her? That's no good. We have terrible luck together. I do, however, find a bit of the information I obtained from the conversation reassuring: I am not going to have to live with Stranger Lady forever. Someone will come get me. Also, I now have confirmation that Melody is still alive. The other good thing is that it sounds like Grandpa will be coming home as soon as possible to clean up this giant mess I had made. With Grandpa's help, I will surely get Melody back. However, I fear I will be in trouble for letting him down when he arrives. I hadn't thought of the consequences until now. Perhaps my situation is not as bad as it seems. I hope I am overreacting as my stomach turns itself into knots. Without warning, the lights go out and I pass out into the darkest dreamless sleep I have ever known. *Darn drugs.*

Later that evening, Aunt Bailey picks me up from Stranger Lady's house. I am relieved to see her, and even more relieved when she takes me back to our house. I am still very groggy, but hope fills me as I enter our castle. I run to search for Melody. Perhaps she is already here, waiting for me. I quickly go into every room, but find no trace of Melody. I whine my way back to Bailey. I cannot bring myself to call our house my castle now; without Melody here, it has lost all its magic. The drugs are kicking in again. *What on earth did Dr. Jerry give me?*

I mope around the house, sulking incessantly while trying to eavesdrop into every conversation I can that has Melody's name in it, still fighting the drug's effects. I need information, but no one is giving me any. I am being left in the dark. *Is this punishment for failing to be a true Alpha?* I have heard that if one fails the Alpha role, they either end up dead or exiled. *Is this their way of banishing me?* My negative thoughts consume me, and I fall asleep again by the front door. *How long will these drugs stay in my system?*

While sleeping, I dream of a vast, dark swamp land. I am alone in my dream except for a small white light that seems thousands of miles away. *I must get to that light!* I must have been kicking my legs in my sleep and whimpering because the next thing I know, Bailey is cautiously waking me. She pats me on the head and says, "Don't worry, boy. She will be okay. I promise." I drift back into a more positive resting state. I need to gather my strength and remain optimistic. The look on Bailey's face and the uncertainty in her voice tells me I have great challenges ahead of me.

Chapter 17: Lost and Found

The next two weeks crawl by. Day after day passes without Melody's return. Only one of my human pack-mates comes home at time. They let me out into the yard and try to get me to play ball and eat, but I am too depressed and worried to retrieve anything. The only thing that keeps my spirts up is that when they come home, they smell faintly of Melody. They must be seeing her when they leave here. *Why aren't they taking me with them? Is Melody mad at me for not alerting her to the oncoming car? I would have warned her, but I never saw it coming.*

Apparently, it is Grandma's turn to come home today to shower and clean up. *If I can work my magic on anyone, it's her.* I use my puppy-dog eye power and successfully get my message through to her. Grandma rubs my belly and says, "Okay, Ludo. It's time. We will take you to Melody tomorrow. She is doing better now. Not great, but better."

If Melody cannot come home, then I must go to her. The next twenty-four hours are the longest of my life. I pace through the house and look out the windows every time I hear a car pass. I have had trouble sleeping and eating since my separation from Melody. We need to be together immediately. I know she is still alive, but I don't know where or in what condition. How can I keep my vow to her if we are apart? *I can't protect Melody if I am not with her.* The night hangs endlessly in the air.

Finally, the morning sun rises up above the trees, kissing their tops. The sun's light illuminates the windows in the front room; I must have dozed off by the door. Regardless, I somehow managed to sleep through the night, which means the next day is here. *Finally!* I run and jump into Grandpa's bed to alert him of today's arrival. Grandpa came home late last night to sleep in his own bed for a change. I wake him by bumping my nose under his chin in what I am sure is a rapid and annoying pace.

Once I get Grandpa out of bed, I chase him around the room to get him dressed faster. Grandpa is no lark in the morning. He reminds me of a sloth as he slowly glides around the room, shaking off the night. After what seems like hours, but is only about twenty minutes according to his bedside clock, Grandpa is ready. I waste no time in running right past my feeding station towards the front door. Grandpa has not fed me yet, but I don't want food. I want to see my Melody.

I command Grandpa to load me into our car. Once inside, I settle in the passenger seat as he climbs into the driver's seat next to me. My anticipation is building. Grandpa doesn't have his usual Yeti mug of bean juice, but I pray he will not realize this. Grandpa sits there for a solid minute with a quizzical look on his face, like he is forgetting something.

Actually, he forgot a lot of things this morning, if we are being honest. *Maybe I am being selfish for*

128

not wanting to help him to remember them now. I channel my focus in a new direction and, as hard as I can, begin to will Grandpa to get me to my Melody ASAP. The car shifts into gear and begins to accelerate. *Am I finally starting to figure out this whole directing-the-universe thing?* I watch through the car windows with excitement and anxiety as buildings and people quickly become blurred, forgotten memories as we pass them by. My eyes are constantly scanning the horizon, searching for my girl. *Where is she? Why aren't we there yet? Olly, olly, oxen free. Come out, come out, wherever you are, Melody.* This is no time for a game of hide and seek, though it would be a good game to play once I get her home. I always win, but my nose gives me a large advantage.

Five radio songs later, Grandpa pulls the car into a large parking lot. Hundreds of vehicles of all makes, models, and colors surround us. *Melody is somewhere in this used car lot. Where? Why?* Grandpa took me on a car ride two days before. I thought we were going to see Melody. Imagine my disappointment when we had only gone to a Ford dealership. Grandpa had been on the hunt for a new truck since the Green Machine now has its very own tombstone in a junkyard somewhere. The place Grandpa and I are at now looks like the dealership we were at, only these vehicles appear to be well used.

Grandpa, being the smart man he is, must have keyed in on the confusion that consumes my face. He pats me on the head to soothe me and tells me I have to stay out in the lot with him. This is not the answer I am looking for. I continue to look for Melody. I gaze to the right of all the used cars, and before us stands an incredibly large, grim, gray building with a large red and white cross on the front. I assume it is one of those skyscraper buildings. I saw one on one of Grandpa's *Forbes* magazines recently. This makes a little more sense, at least. *My Melody must be inside that building.* The cross on the building matches the patches on the uniforms of the men who took Melody away from me.

I stare at the big gray tower and will Melody to come out. People start to pour in and out of the building. They are everywhere and it is overwhelming. I observe each person as they exit the large revolving doors at the front of the building to confirm that none of them are my girl. I am spinning circles in my car seat, which clearly is starting to annoy Grandpa. *Maybe I can use this to my advantage?* I whine. Grandpa really hates that. I let out a high-pitched, never-ending squeal. This gets Grandpa's attention. He reaches over and clips on my leash. *Time to get out of the car!*

Now that I am outside of the car, I can use my nose to find Melody. Grandpa refuses to walk any farther than what appears to be a small, grassy island with a brown stone bench in the middle of it. *Come on, Grandpa. We just sat on our butts in the car for a long spell. Let's move. This is no time to rest!* Grandpa sits on the bench. As he does, I notice it has words engraved on it. It really is a pretty bench. I find its placement between the large parking lot and the grim, gray building to be odd. I don't have time to deduce why that is though. I need to find Melody! I guess I should be grateful that Grandpa has at least brought me this far. I figure I had better not irritate him any further. I sit down by

Grandpa's feet and let out one final annoyed groan from deep in my throat. "Calm down, big guy," Grandpa says reassuringly. "Grandma texted and said they are bringing Melody down now. Just be patient."

Easy for you to say, Grandpa. You and the rest of the pack have been seeing Melody on the daily. I haven't seen her in weeks. Finally, a soft breeze comes from the north, and I get a whiff of Melody's scent. It hits me hard in the face, like a baseball bat connecting with a home run hit. I quickly turn to face the breeze. I am sure that the scent belongs to my girl. It has to be her. *My nose is never wrong!*

The strange Melody scent throws me for a loop at first, but then I see her being pushed by Grandma in an odd chair with wheels! My eyes lock with Melody's. *Houston, we have a visual. Prepare for contact!* I jump, barely able to contain my excitement any longer. Relief floods over me as I note that Melody is just as happy to see me as I am her!

I run to her and, once I am a few feet away, crouch down and ready my back legs to pounce into Melody's lap. I am going to give her the greeting of a lifetime. I launch myself high into the air. As I do, my leash tightens and snaps me backwards. *What in the world?* I land on my back on the hard asphalt surface. Grandpa and Grandma help me up, but also continue to hold me back. They tell me to be careful. I proceed this time with a little more caution and a much slower pace. I can't slow all of me, though; my wagging tail maintains the speed of a Shelby Cobra on a straightaway. My energy and excitement has to escape somehow. If my tail were to go much faster, I

would surely lift off the ground like the giant heli-
copter that is currently landing on top of the gray
building. I bark up a warning to chopper: "Keep it
down up there. Can't you see we are finally being
reunited? I can't hear what my girl is saying."

The chopper's loud, spinning blades finally stop.
I am inches from Melody now, assessing her carefully. Aside from the strong chemical odor coming from
her leg, she seems to be doing well. Melody is in
much better condition than she was when we
were separated by the uniformed men. My nose has
not deceived me. I carefully nudge her right hand,
then slowly climb my way up into her lap. Melody
kisses the top of my head between my ears. "I love
you, buddy. I am so glad you are okay. I was so worried."

I softly groan and growl the words I can't say
but want to. "You were worried? I have been sick for
weeks since I lost you! Let's go home. We can sleep
for a week in our bed!" I know Melody understands
me, but she looks drawn. I think the idea of a long
nap in our bed would have excited her. Melody is
like Grandpa in that she, too, loves naps! I bark towards the truck in an effort to get Grandpa and
Grandma to take Melody and me home. Nobody
moves.

After a few minutes, confusion builds as a portly
lady wearing a matching shirt and pants walks over
to us. This woman has a commanding presence due
to her large size and personality. Her outfit reminds
me of ill-fitting pajamas and does nothing to detract
from her size. Her bright red clothes are not a good
color for the size and shape of her body. The woman

reminds me of the giant Kool-Aid Man who jumps through brick walls in bowling alleys and yells "Oh yeah!" on television commercials. The large woman speaks in a gravely chain-smoker's voice: "We should probably get her back inside now. Melody needs her rest."

I growl at the lady. Grandpa gives me a disappointed look. I am baffled that he doesn't take my side but instead seems to be in agreement with the woman dressed in red. He kneels down on the ground and pull me into his chest, as he secures me against himself he whispers in my ear, "Doctor's orders boy. Try not to throw a fit and put on a good face for Melody. I don't like it any more than you do but we don't want to upset her. She will be home soon I promise she just has to get through one more surgery. Once they fix her arm she will be all ours again."

My heart sinks as the infamous word "soon" leaves Grandpa's lips and enters my ears. I hate that word. Soon could be today, tomorrow, or a lifetime from now. Regardless, I receive Grandpa's message loud and clear. We need to be strong for Melody, she needs to concentrate on healing so she can come home. If I cry like I want to, Melody will only think of me and my needs. I refuse to be a distraction that could slow her healing progress and cost me more time with her. I put on my best super happy puppy face and manage to get one more small smile out of Melody before she is wheeled away from me by the woman in red pajamas. Melody and I are separated once again.

Once Melody is out of earshot my strength rushes out of me like air from a balloon with a whole in it. I erupt into a fit of loud high-pitched whimpers and howls while trashing about wildly on my leash. Grandpa doesn't even chastise me as people being to stare at us. I think he lets me throw my embarrassing fit because deep down he wants to do the same.

Chapter 18: An Unhappy Homecoming

After another week of being left home alone a lot, with only occasional visits from the rest of the family, I start to feel discouraged and defeated. However, as I ate my silent supper with Grandpa yesterday, something amazing was confirmed: I will get to see my Melody again. *It's about time!* The news got even better when Grandpa told me it would be at our house, in our yard. Melody is coming home. Grandpa lectured me on being very careful around her. I had already guessed that that would be necessary after my last short visit with Melody. Anyone within a mile of her could tell that she was still badly broken.

The following day, gratitude fills me as I realize that it is already late afternoon. I am waiting with Aunt Kassandra on our front porch when Grandma's electric blue Malibu pulls into the driveway. My body quivers with anticipation; I shake like it's fifty below outside instead of seventy-eight degrees. *This is it. She is finally returning to me. Time to resume our perfect life!* Grandpa gets out of the driver's seat after parking and walks around to the trunk. *Why is Melody riding in the trunk?* Perplexed, I keep my eyes on Grandpa. Then, Grandma gets out of the passenger seat and walks around to the rear door. *Crap, where is she? Grandpa told me today is the day. He never lies.*

Suddenly, I smell her. Grandma opens the rear driver's side door, and my Melody's scent flows out of the car. *Ah, now this makes more sense.* Melody had been lying down, so I did not see her until her head shot up when Grandma opened the back door. She looks a bit sleepy; she had probably been napping back there on the ride home. *Come to me, my sweet girl. Welcome home. Let's go snuggle and nap.* I haven't had a decent night's sleep since our separation. I feel like I am about three weeks behind on true shut-eye.

Grandpa is wrestling with one of those odd chairs attached to wheels. The chair is similar to the one I saw Melody in at that used car lot last week. I'm still not sure why she was there, but since they fixed her enough to get her back to me, I guess it doesn't matter. I assumed that when people got hurt, they went some place similar to the vet, but for humans. Grandma goes to help Grandpa, and together they assemble the chair next to Melody's open car door. I tug against Kassandra's grip on my collar. *Let me at her. I have kisses to give!* High pitch whining flows out of me like water from a steady spring.

Melody emerges from the car, wrapped up in what looks like a lot of colored toilet paper. She reeks of disinfectant, but her sweet coconut and driftwood scent is still there. It soothes me. I stop pulling against Kassandra because I can see that Melody needs Grandpa and Grandma's help to get from place to place. This is something I cannot provide. I stand aside and give them plenty of room while they ready my Melody for transport. *The car place was supposed to fix her.* As happy as I am to see her, I am disappointed by the job they had done. *Grandpa, I think you should have given them more of that green paper stuff. We got shorted!*

Once Grandma and Grandpa load Melody into the chair, I commence my tugging. *Okay, Kassandra. Please, oh please let me go now!* I can no longer control my trembling. Melody is now seated in her chair, beaming at me. "Ludo, you look so much bigger now!" she exclaims. Her previously grim face lights up at the sight of me.

Just seeing one another lights us both up. *It really is the simple things in life that matter.* I tug and whine more forcefully than before, and Kassandra's hold on my collar finally releases. I shoot off the porch like a horse out of the gates at the Kentucky Derby. Grandma and Grandpa give me an "Easy, boy" warning as I approach. I am elated when they allow me to climb up into Melody's outstretched arm. That's right—only one of my girl's arms is reaching for me. Her other arm is bound by hard, colored toilet paper, rendering it useless. Lots of kissing and hugging ensues, and the world around us ceases to exist for several minutes.

As we get reacquainted, I keep alighting on something different that seems to surround Melody. *What am I sensing that no one else seems to acknowledge?* One thing is certain: I seem to be the only one aware of this. I guess that is okay because I now know two things the rest the pack doesn't. Number one: Melody's arrival is also accompanied by a much darker, more threatening force. The elements that had previously built her wall have strengthened and grown in size. Melody's monster is feasting and becoming more menacing by the second. Number two: I am the only one with the power to help her fight this darkness and win this battle. *Don't worry, my girl. I will find a way to get all of you back. I won't settle for less!*

In order to keep the silent vow I had just made to Melody, I need the rest of the family to give me room to work. Melody needs me now more than ever. I welcome the task at hand. This is my time to shine and make up for letting this tragic event happen in the first place. Life handed me the alpha role, and I took it for granted. This time, I will earn it and never lose it again. *I am confident, charming, and aloof—but most of all, I am level-headed and understanding. I am powerful. I am an Alpha One.* This darkness does not stand a chance. *Mark my words: I will find a way to crush your monster, Melody. Your little gremlin should pack its bags and leave now if it knows what's good for it.* I growl at Melody's monster of darkness as it taunts me, a black aura that floats victoriously around her. *Monster, your days are numbered.*

Melody is physically here with me, but she isn't fully present. Part of her is stuck deep in the pit of despair. The sparkle that used to glitter behind her eyes is gone; black holes now sit in their place. I need to get her out of the depths of the nightmare she seems to be trapped in. One thing is clear: if I don't get her out soon, the darkness will win and consume her entirely. The Melody I know and love

You're Welcome

will be gone—and with her, my legacy.

Chapter 19: To Walk Alone

We all have some transitioning to do now that Melody is home. A new, beloved pack member whom I call Grandma Great comes to stay with us and significantly helps my cause. She is Grandpa's mom, a retired nurse. When the others go to work, Grandma Great and I take care of Melody. The three of us play lots of card games and watch soaps and other horrible daytime TV shows. I find daytime television to be very depressing and disturbing.

The three of us also go outside at least twice a day to get exercise and our daily dose of sunlight. *Behold, the powers of vitamin D.* I always aim my chest squarely at the sun and absorb and store every ounce of energy from the powerful rays it blesses the earth with. I hope this method has the same effect as the battery chargers Grandpa sometimes uses out in the garage. I view my sun tanning time as charging myself for the upcoming battle. I have not yet fully uncovered the dark force that holds so tightly onto my Melody, but when I do, I will be ready. *Everything has an Achilles heel. Melody is mine.*

Grandma Great and I have to keep Melody's mind positive with lots of love. We give her goals and things to work towards so she will heal faster. We spend lots of time together, an inseparable pack of three. From listening in on conversations when everyone is home, I find out that some idiot doctor had told Melody she will never walk again. Finally, I have figured out what has dimmed her light and fed her monster the deep depression it yearned for.

Melody believed this villainous doctor. I know the doctor is wrong and that this simply is not true. The chair Melody is currently sitting in will not be her fate. *Our fate.* I can see our future. This chair is nowhere to be found in my visions. I will have Melody on her feet in no time. The time has come to unleash a miracle, and this time, I am ready.

It is Friday night, and I am doing some last-minute miracle research on Melody's laptop while the family sleeps. Luckily for me, Melody has a touchscreen computer and it responds nicely to the commands my wet nose gives. Melody is in our room, lying in bed. She is staring out the open window into the night. I know she is longing to succumb to the silence and darkness her monster keeps offering her. I can tell she hopes it will all end soon. She is losing her will to live. These evil monsters within us fight with the goal of claiming our souls. Sadly, the monsters sometimes win because people do not realize they have the power within them to fight their monsters back. People must make the choice to fight. Fighting is hard and giving up is easy. This is what my Father must have meant all those months ago. Now that I see firsthand that the easy path aches to claim Melody's spirit, I am frightened to my core.

Finally, what I am looking for appears before me, and I know what I need to do. On the computer screen is an image of a white wolf; across the image are printed words. I know this is the ticket to getting my Melody back. The image, created by Fearless Motivation, says, "The hardest walk you can make is the one you make alone, but that is the walk that makes you the strongest." I leave this image on the screen so Melody will be sure to see it when she checks her email in the morning. To my dismay, this has become Melody's new routine since she has dismissed going for a run as ever being a viable option again. Melody has been partaking in too much social media and comparing herself to everyone else. Comparison can be the death of us if used improperly. We must only use comparison to motivate and inspire us. I summon the universe to my cause as I lie down beside Melody to sleep the rest of the night away.

Saturday morning arrives like the true blessing I knew it would to be. Grandma Great has gone home to get her affairs in order. I think it is hard on her living in two different places, but I really enjoy our time together when she is around. She is always positive and very helpful with Melody. She even noticed when Melody was having an allergic reaction to one of the many medications she is currently taking. I am positive she saved her from a more terrible situation by getting her off the medications she had been prescribed. I hope Grandma Great will come back soon. She would be an excellent full-time pack member.

The sun continues to rise and fill the air with the same amount of joy that children have as they approach the tree on Christmas morning. The universe heard me and is aligning and setting up my miracle. I can feel all the positive ions in the air. Melody is particularly depressed and irritated today. What she does not know is that she is in for a much-needed attitude adjustment. Hopefully, I had not let too much time pass us by. With each passing day, Melody's darkness seems to gain strength.

I use my dog telepathy to subliminally urge Melody to check her e-mail and see the image I had left on the screen for her. As she does that, I summon Grandma to come get Melody cleaned up and ready to leave the house. There will be nothing good in Melody's e-mail in-box, only junk mail. I only need enough time for Melody to see that image I had left on the screen for her. I can't help but smile to myself as I look over and see her staring at the laptop's screen with a perplexed look on her face. Through her eyes, I can see her wondering how the image got there in the first place. More than anything, I hope she is reading the words the picture proudly displays. I need her to receive the important message they carry loud and clear. Melody seems to be taking the message in when Grandma enters the room. *Take that, darkness. The light is about to kick your butt!* Today is the day that will change Melody's outlook. I can feel positivity burning deep within me. Today, I will get my Melody back, even if it kills me!

Grandma assists Melody in washing her hair and getting dressed. "We are going out today. You are not living indoors for the rest of your life. It is good for you to get out," she tells Melody, who argues and fights her the whole way.

Melody is in a particularly ripe mood today. I hope this will not ruin all that I have planned. As

Grandma wheels her outside, Melody begs. "I don't want to go out. Can't you just leave me at home? There is nothing out there for me anymore." She is protesting with everything she has. Luckily for Grandma and me, Melody doesn't have much anymore.

Grandma stands her ground. She loads Melody into the car against her will, and then off they go. I call to the universe in the only way I know how: a silent prayer. Then, I thank the universe for the gift it is about to give. We must always remember to show our gratitude, no matter how small the favor. *Humans would be wise to work on this.* I use what I learned from the part of the book I had read at Al and Marsha's. The universe and I have our work cut out for us. I am not worried though. I am fueled with vitamin D and a fierce determination to get my Melody back today. Nothing will stop me; of this, I am sure.

Once I have finished working with the universe to conjure up my miracle, dizziness overtakes me. I have to go rest in my dog bed. It is now the universe's job to place the fork in the road for Melody. I can only cross my paws and hope she will choose the right path. Over the past few weeks, I have been fueling her with as much light as possible for this battle. Hopefully, I have inspired her enough to take the correct side of the fork once it appears before her.

Stress and exhaustion fall over me. My legs weaken, especially my back ones, and I feel older, just as Mother and Father had previously warned. Anxiety propels me to leave the comforts of my dog bed and lie by the window in the front room to await Melody's return. As tired as I am, I cannot sleep while I wait for word of my miracle's success or failure. I find that I am holding my breath, so I inhale deeply as I wait.

Chapter 20: Did it Work?

I wish I could have been there to watch my miracle take place. However, the storm of excitement that rapidly enters the house as Grandma charges in with Melody confirms that I have indeed done it. Melody uses her one good leg to wheel closer to the circle that has formed in the living room. Grandma was so excited as she stormed into the house that she had left Melody by the front door as she ran to gather everyone. *Earth to Grandma—you almost forgot the most important part of this story.*

Melody greets me with excitement as she inches her way towards the group. I immediately notice that her blue eyes are twinkling again. The once-growing black holes are rapidly shrinking before my eyes. *I have done it. I am a good dog. Heck, who am I kidding—I am an Alpha One! Next stop for me is Ultimate Alpha!* I quickly steer myself out of dreamland and back to reality; I can work on that later. Melody and I now have a bright future ahead of us once again. First, I want to hear today's story, the story of my miracle and the current reason for aching hips and legs. *Ouch, cramp.* I stretch out. I now fully understand the meaning of the word 'agonizing.' Hopefully, this new feeling goes away soon.

I assume my position sitting at attention by

Melody's bad leg. I want to take in every detail of the day's events so I can fully enjoy the story. Of course, Grandma takes full credit for my miracle as she recounts the day's events for the rest of the family. I don't even think Melody gets one word in, and it is the story of her success. That is just like Grandma though. Everything always seems to be about her in one way or another. I roll my eyes. This has never really bothered me much. It's just Grandma being her usual self. I won't let it get to me, especially not today. I am elated that my miracle has, in fact, worked! I had needed Grandma to take Melody out of the house. Without her, I could never have completed this miracle. *Give credit where credit is due!* There are times in life we all need help. The strongest thing we can do in those times is ask for and accept it when it is given. The weakest thing we can do is to say no because of our pride, or never ask in the first place. I couldn't have asked for a better person for the job than Grandma today, so she can have as much glory as she wants. The whole family truly is a part of today in one way or another. Together, we are all a true team.

I will relay the shortened version of the day's events. Grandma took Melody to the mall, a public place with lots of people. She pushed a very ticked off Melody around, trying to cheer her up. As they turned a corner, Grandma saw a handicapped man in a wheelchair. *Cue the lightbulb over Grandma's head.* "This is just what you need," she said as she wheeled Melody over to the man, who was waving at them excitedly.

Melody immediately protested—quietly, so she would not offend the man they were nearing. "Mom,

147

what are you doing? Do not take me over there. I do not want to talk to him. Just because I am in a chair doesn't mean I want to hang out with others who are the same way!"

Grandma smiled as she positioned Melody's wheelchair next to the man's electric wheelchair and put on Melody's brakes. "I will be back in a little while. You two enjoy your conversation. I have some shopping to do." Grandma walked away.

Melody said very sternly and as discretely as possible to her mother, "You are not leaving me here. What are you doing? If you do this, I promise I will find a way to leave without you."

Grandma disappeared from Melody's sight. Of course, what Melody didn't know was that Grandma had not gone far. She only went to hide around the corner. Melody was unaware of this. Grandma, like me, would never abandon Melody next to a perfect stranger without being close enough to rescue her if things went sour. The universe had made her do this though. It told Grandma that this was the right thing to do and the right time to do it. *Timing is everything. Often, it is patience that's hardest to muster.* Melody sat next to the man in the electric chair, stewing with anger. *Passion is the key to all motivation. Many things, such as anger, can create passion.*

The man in the chair introduced himself as Dave. Melody was officially stuck and could not go anywhere on her own. She had a broken, severely mangled left foot that was covered with new skin grafts and staples, and she was supposed to keep it constantly elevated so it would heal properly. Melody also had a broken left shoulder. Due to having two broken appendages on the same side of her body, she could not wheel herself away from Dave. If Melody had tried to do so, her chair would have only gone a few feet forward before turning in a circle. I know this because she tries it often at home. I am positive I look just as foolish as she does when I chase my tail but I still occasionally do it.

Since Melody couldn't use her broken arm to control the wheel on the other side of her chair, vicious cycles were the only thing in her future. *Until now*. I must give Grandma more credit since I was not there. After all, it was she who applied the brakes on Melody's chair before walking away. This was a brilliant move on her part since Melody would never be able to get the brakes off with only one good arm. That meant she had to sit and ride out my miracle and talk with Dave. We meet certain people for a reason. We should always be grateful to meet new friends, no matter the length of the relationship.

Melody sat and conversed with Dave for a few minutes. She was saddened by the fact that he had been like this his entire life. He had some mental and physical handicaps, but he communicated well. He never had a choice; he had always been confined to that chair and always would be. They spoke for a few more minutes, and her mood started to shift. Melody was transitioning from sad and ticked off to feelings of admiration.

Since Melody had to wait for Grandma to come back and get her, she had all the time in the world to analyze her mixed feelings towards Dave. Once Melody started to think deeper, she saw things more clearly and settled on admiration. Dave had not let life get him down. He somehow seemed happy and was not upset with the cards life had dealt him. Dave instead embraced them and made the best of his situation. Destined to a life in a chair with bleak circumstances before him, he was still happy. It wasn't just this that got Melody's attention. Dave was sharing kindness, both to her and to the rest of the world. He was an amazing and inspiring person. Life knocked him down and took away his legs. All Melody saw was the choices that Dave had made in life. Legs or no legs, Dave was standing in Melody's eyes.

Suddenly, Melody was hit with fierce jealousy. I am sure her inner negative voice tried to talk her out of what happened next. She was probably telling herself that Dave had never experienced walking, so he did not know the difference. Of course that would make him happy. I am sure her internal monster was saying things like, 'he doesn't know what he is missing' and 'yada yada blah blah.' Dave never had a choice in the matter since he was born that way. This is when the lightbulb went off over Melody's head! *Now, for my favorite part of my miracle. Wait for it...*

Melody realized she too had the power of choice, she realized that she is ultimately responsible for being happy or sad in this life of hers! The fork in the road was laid out before her. When people stop seeing the choices before them, the darkness has won. I realize that this is what my mother and father were trying to tell my siblings and I on one of our lecture learning days long ago. There is always a choice, but sometime people have to look harder to find it. *Or, if they are lucky, they have a dog who is willing to help them out!* Melody is worth more than a miracle's price in my book. I would have happily given my life to put the sparkle back in her blue eyes. Her touch can go further in this world than mine can. Together, though, we will be Ultimate and obtain the farthest reach possible.

Melody contemplated her choices. She could give up and live in a chair the rest of her life, or she could stand fight this challenge of hers with choice and gumption! She thanked Dave, and pushed her wobbly body up into an awkward standing position. Melody had made Grandma a promise, and she intended to keep it. She was going to find a way to leave without her since Grandma had left her there with Dave. Melody was filled with spite for her mom and inspiration from Dave. This was an interesting and very helpful combination for the time being. Melody had lost a lot of muscle over the past several weeks, so just the standing part alone was a battle to be won. Melody stood, shaking as pain and muscle fatigue tried to make her surrender and sit back down, but she didn't give up. This is our dark monster's last resort: physical pain. Melody brushed it off like dust off old books. Excitement and adrenaline propelled her forward as her spirit filled with unstoppable determination. Melody took about nine steps before surrendering to a tremendous amount of pain as she walked on badly broken bones and skin grafts. Melody then fell into a heap on the grimy mall floor, and tears of joy overflowed her eyes. *As well as everyone else's in the living room right now.*

Grandma emerged from the shadows, where she had stood in the mall watching. She wore a massive smile and tears of pure joy streaked her cheeks as she congratulated Melody. "I knew you could do it," Grandma said as she scooped Melody up and helped her back into the chair.

"Thanks. Can we go home now? I need pain meds," Melody said with a half grimace, half ear-to-ear grin. The doctors had had it wrong. Melody would walk again. Not only that, but she was now setting goals for herself to run! *I have my girl back!*

Chapter 21: Anxiety

Now that my miracle has given Melody back her thirst for life and the doctors have given her a new diagnosis, she starts to improve rapidly. As she does, I continue to grow like a weed and absorb more knowledge. I am like a dry sponge placed into a bucket of water, and I am really getting a grasp on all my dog superpowers. There is a cartoon with a dog superhero. I think it is called *Underdog*. I believe it was made for a reason. People laugh at the cartoon because they cannot see the truth. People think they are superior to dogs when they should instead be thanking us for making their lives better. Melody thanks me every day with her endless love and attention. I am glad she realizes I am royalty with super powers! She is indeed capable of paying back the miracle's price—I am living a ridiculously spoiled life now. I thought I was before, but I most certainly was mistaken.

However, with Melody's improvement comes a sad day for me. Grandma Great says it is time for her to officially go home. This means no more returning to spend the week with us after her weekend trips home. I understand that she needs to check back in with her pack. I have a lot of respect for her and her ability to live the double life she has been maintaining until now. She, too, is a miracle worker. Few humans are given that gift, but Grandma Great has it for sure! She has been a blessing in helping me get my Melody back. *I could not have done it without her!*

On one paw, I am okay with this because it is good news! Grandma Great will return home because Melody is strong enough to get though the day with just me. Sure, we get occasional check-ins here and there from our other pack members, but those are only on the phone. It is just Melody and me surviving and thriving by ourselves during the week now while the others go to work. On the other paw, I wish Grandma Great would consider joining our pack full-time. Perhaps she could just bring her pack up here and we could all merge into one big, happy family. *Maybe I should meet them all before extending such a large offer. I can't imagine Grandma Great entertaining any bad company, though.*

The thriving part of my story may not be entirely true. Melody is definitely doing so, but I think I may have a minor problem with our new transition. I have not fully identified it yet, but I have recognized that something is going on with me. I am investigating it so it can be remedied immediately. This new something tries to feed my internal little monster to help him gain strength. I thought I was done with him once and for all when I completed my miracle. I don't have the time or patience to deal with him now, especially with Grandma Great's absence. *Speaking of which, this all seems to have started the first week after Grandma Great left.* Ever since her departure, I can't help but pace around with slight worry and run to the window every time I hear a car go by. I haven't figured out why I am

154

doing this yet. I only know I can't seem to stop.

Perplexed by my new, unwanted behaviors, I snuggle in next to Melody for some crappy daytime TV. Some doctor show comes on. The doctor is trying to help people by asking them all kinds of questions. He is some psychologist named Phil... Or is it Paul? Some sort of 'P' name. Anyway, I normally do not pay a lot of attention to him. The last time I saw him on screen, he was trying to help a lady figure out who the father of her child was. One thing was for sure: the lady on the last episode sure liked sex. She had brought four men on the show because she was "without a doubt" positive that one of them was the father. She, however, was wrong, and they were all 99 percent NOT the father! Each time, the doctor declared the test results so dramatically that it annoyed me. *Just spit it out, already.* It must have annoyed Melody, too, because she changed the channel. Maybe in another life, the woman from that episode will come back as a male dog. Dogs don't shame or judge one another for having sex. It is a natural part of life. We should all just follow our own moral and ethical compasses and not worry or care about what others are doing.

Today's doctor episode is different. There is a young boy center stage with the good doctor. The boy can't be over twelve. *Don't worry, he isn't anyone's father.* This episode differs greatly from the last one. I pay attention and interact with the show by asking myself the same questions the doctor is asking the youngster. I am mainly doing it to keep my eyes open since I am on Melody duty. She isn't much of a handful at the moment since she is nearly drifting off to sleep herself. Suddenly, one of the doctor's questions hits home for me. Dr. P says, "Why do you think you are performing these strange behaviors?"

I ask myself the same questions the doctor is asking his guests and reflect on my answers for a minute. Then it hits me hard, like a bug slamming into the windshield of a moving car. Dogs have a fascination with suicidal bugs. As morbid as it sounds, we find it entertaining to watch bugs fly into the glass at implausible speeds. When dogs sit shotgun, we get to hear the bugs' last words as they come careening into the glass and their splattered deaths. *One of the perks of having superior hearing.* I admit that sometimes it is sad, but most of the time, the things the bugs say are hilarious. The last one I saw shouted, "Crap, I never figured out what happened to Dennis Rodman!" *Splat!*

Getting back to my newfound dilemma. I sit deep in thought, pondering Dr. P's question. I need to figure out my new behavior: why I am constantly running to the window to see if Grandma Great is back. *Why?* Is it the sound of the cars zooming by, is that startling me because of the accident? Maybe I have PTSD like Melody. Grandma Great and her have been talking about that a lot since she came home, one of her doctors said riding and driving in cars may make her extra anxious for a while. I have been in Grandpa and Grandma's vehicles since our accident though and don't seem to struggle with my anxiety monster much unless we come to a stop sign intersection though. I think I can rule out vehicle PTSD. Maybe I am just worried Grandma Great may not come back at all. *But why?* Is it because Melody was gone for so long? I thought I would never see Melody again; I thought I would never get her back. *Lightbulb!* That must be part of it, I think I am performing this strange behavior because I almost lost Melody, and now I am worried that I may have lost Grandma Great! What if she never comes back? She promised she would come back and visit again with the dreaded word 'soon,' but can I trust that when I don't understand it?

My mind is spinning. Then, the good doctor says, "We call this separation anxiety." I, at least, have a diagnosis now. No one wants a problem that's not recognized. Those are kind of like a person with a sugar addiction. People who are supposed to be their friends and family judge them for their actions instead of recognizing the problem and helping them, or worse yet they bring them sugary treats. It is sad, really. I think humans may be some of the cruelest creatures on the planet. How they judge one another and hold grudges is toxic. I work hard to keep Melody from conforming to this pitfall of humanity.

I fear I have no intention of fixing my new problem. For now, I consider it to only be a mild case of separation anxiety. *Hopefully, it won't get worse.* Though, with all the extra time that Melody and I are spending together now, I worry it may. I find it unnatural not to worry at least a little when one of your loved one's leaves for a period of time, no matter the cause. What I am doing is only a natural response. I decide that I will just put my newfound problem on the back burner. I don't see it as a priority now. *I must keep my monster small. Then, I can maintain control. If this problem gets worse and feeds my monster, I will address it then.*

When the other family members take Melody in her wheelchair for appointments, I get stressed out. However, Grandma and Grandpa always say, "We will be back soon." I have learned to trust them, so these events are gradually getting easier. I am not sure exactly how long 'soon' is, though I am starting to hate it a little less. It seems to be different each time, but I have found that whoever uses the awful word 'soon' always comes home eventually, and that is all that matters. Perhaps not understanding this unit of time is a gift just as much as it is a curse.

Chapter 22: Walking

Over the next couple of months, Melody transitions from her wheelchair to walking with things called crutches. Crutches look like armpit murderers. Melody hops around more than anything when she has the armpit-slayers with her. She complains about how they hurt her newly healed arm. I think she overcompensates with her good arm and leg. I am proud of her though. Melody keeps moving forward, and I know nothing can hold her back now. Melody uses her wheeled chair as little as possible, and it makes me smile to watch her push through the pain. It is only strengthening her.

Melody has her determination and thirst for life back again. It warms my heart and fills my soul to see her this way! I must admit, I miss the chair with wheels now and then. Don't get me wrong—I know that for her sake, it needs to be gone as soon as possible, and I know it will be. However, the chair sometimes comes in handy when we are outside playing in the yard and I get tired. I can just jump onto Melody's lap for a free ride to our next destination. It really is a slick device and extra nice on the hot days! *Probably a good thing I don't have my own.* I can't help but wonder from time to time if good old Dave may have been on to something with his electric chair.

Melody and I are starting to go out on new adventures more. *There is nothing like charting new territory with your soulmate!* Since she can leave her chair behind more often, Melody can get around with her friends now. I was worried that I wouldn't like all of her friends at first, but my worries have dissipated quickly. Melody has some truly amazing friends. They always make sure to take me with whenever and wherever they can.

There are times when I can't accompany Melody and her friends, but it doesn't upset me. I generally use my downtime to hang out and reconnect with Grandpa and Grandma. I haven't spent a lot of time with them lately because Melody has been such a priority. I need to be more careful of this. Grandma, Grandpa, and Kassandra are part of my full-time pack, and I should be more diligent about keeping tabs on all my members. Lately, I have sensed a weird distance growing between Grandma and Grandpa. *I don't like it one bit.* Even though I rarely, if ever, am alone, I can still feel my separation anxiety lurking about in the shadows. *This so-called anxiety of mine is conceivably something that grows slowly over time.* It appears to be getting worse, despite my conscious efforts never to be alone. I hoped that by doing this it would keep my monster small, but it may be having the opposite effect.

Of all Melody's friends—and she has many—my favorite is Paige. People are not supposed to pick favorites. Luckily for me, these rules do not apply to dogs. We pick favorite everythings: people, toys, beds, treats, you name it. I get to see a lot more of Paige now since Melody has started to walk on her own. The walking has started to change a lot of things, but I can't say I like them all. The only one I do fancy—or, should I say, love—is our new daily walking routine with Paige.

Paige is a positive, radiant woman. I don't know that I have ever sensed her in anything other than a good mood. *Maybe Paige can't feel anything but happiness.* Whatever the driving force is for her amazing optimism, I hope it rubs off on Melody. *Better yet, the entire world.* Melody is always happier and more motivated after a walk with her. Paige is a woman with an excessive thirst for life, and I can tell that Melody really looks up to her. Paige seems to refuel Melody's fire whenever they spend time together. The two recently set a goal to run a marathon together this October. *Ha, and those doctors told my Melody that she would never walk again.* Another great habit Paige practices is avoiding drama and negativity like the plague. It is remarkable, really. If Paige sees or feels drama coming her way, she gracefully turns the other way and avoids it all together. *If only one part of Paige can rub off on Melody, I hope it's this one.* I really hope that Melody figures it out—and me, too, for that matter. Drama creates anxiety, which feeds pesky, indwelling monsters. *Nobody needs that!* If Paige has an internal monster of her own, it can't be any bigger than a flea! Paige not only inspires Melody, but me as well. She helps drive me to work harder at shrinking my monster to an almost non-existent size.

Melody is branching out a lot more and doing things that do not always involve me. I am trying not to get upset or be a negative influence. I know she needs to get out and be social with her friends. I truly love seeing Melody thrive, but I think I should always be allowed to accompany her. Usually, the only reason I am left behind is because of a sign that says 'No dogs allowed.' *I need to find a way to remove these, along with STOP signs. There is no place for either of these on this green earth.* In an effort to amend my issue, I have decided that I need to somehow be more like Melody's purse. It seems to go everywhere with Melody, however, it doesn't go with her on walks and runs. *There's one thing I have on it.*

My trepidation continues to increase because recently, Melody and I have started skipping our afternoon naps. Now I have to transition from constant play and buddy nap time to time that is scheduled and napping alone. I am being left behind more frequently, and I am not okay with this. I saw on daytime TV that this is a normal way of life for most dogs. I can't say I care for it—and I am not most dogs! I refuse to accept this as my new normal.

I fear that the horrifying monster that tightly grips my chest, that gives me sweaty paws and erratic breathing, is growing due to all these new and unwelcome changes in my life. I have had to deal with my internal monster so often lately that I finally name him Lucifer. I feel this has a great deal to do with the fact I have now graduated to moderate separation anxiety. My lovely Aunt Bailey sometimes calls me Lucifer. Usually, she does it when I am not behaving correctly, but other times she does it because she knows it will get a rise out of Melody. Either way, I can't take credit for the name, but I do feel that Lucifer is a fine name for my mischievous monster! I love watching Melody interact with her siblings, especially Bailey. Those two pick on each other often and for no reason at all. Their playful banter always makes me think of Thayer and how he used to challenge me for the role of Alpha pup.

Speaking of my growing monster... According to the wall clock in the living room, Grandma and Melody went outside to talk to the neighbors in the backyard about ten minutes ago. This is not normally an issue, but today Grandma and Melody left me inside. I always get to go out in the yard with them if I want to. I can't believe they left me inside alone! *Sure, I was napping, but they didn't even ask me if I wanted to join before they went out!* I am especially irritated with this since they are only out in the backyard. I woke to the sounds of them leaving and ran quickly after them to catch up. All I caught was the door on the tip of my nose as Grandma shut it in my face. *What was Grandma thinking? Didn't she see me?* I am not okay with being left indoors while my Melody is outside in our yard. I bark my condemnation: "What if something were to happen? What if Melody needs me? Who will keep her safe? Not you, Grandma. You are too small! Come back, you need me!"

I sit, pouting and rubbing my sore nose by the front door, waiting for one of them to hear my barking and open the door. As I wait, I notice a breeze blowing across the room. With the breeze comes the delicious smell of grilled brats. I inhale my way closer to the scent, and it leads me to the open kitchen window, which faces the backyard. As I lean closer to take in more of the scent, I can hear Grandma and Melody speaking with the neighbors. Everyone seems to be laughing and having a good time. *I need to be a part of this action. After all, you can't have a party without the life of it, and that would be yours truly!*

Suddenly, an idea rockets into my head. *Keep in mind that I didn't say it was one of my best ever ideas.* I make the executive decision to exit the house via the open kitchen window. Since our house has an exposed basement, our kitchen is on the second story. Perhaps this is a minor detail that I should have considered beforehand. I don't, though. No time like the present. I jump up and over the sink, piercing through the screen with one glorious leap. Then, I begin to plummet downward. *Thank you, gravity! Ugh, be a cat, think like a cat, oh please... Let me land like a cat!* Miraculously, I land as cat-like as my one hundred-pound German Shepherd butt can manage: first on my legs, then as my trajectory changes, I fall in a heap on my side with a deafening thud.

Shock hits me immediately, and my chest begins heaving frantically to try and catch the wind I had knocked out of myself. I rise slowly. Not that I have much choice due to my lack of oxygen! *Not one of my best moments.* I feel that I should give cats a little credit here. They are much better jumpers and landers than dogs. Cats have amazing centers of gravity that make me incredibly envious. I refuse to say that their reflexes our better than ours, though. That may forever stay a topic of debate. I am unwilling to give them anything more than a small win on the landing and gravity matter.

I sit chastising myself for my ridiculous behavior and try to gather myself at the same time. I can't believe that I let little Lucifer get the best of me and talk me into something that could have been fatal! *That was careless. If I get hurt, who will take care of Melody?* Speaking of her, I glance over to where she, Grandma, and the neighbors stand in the yard. Their mouths are all gaping open, their faces contorted with shock and horror. *This was not my intention. I refuse to be the source of anything that does not bring Melody joy!* I'm not hurt; I had only lost my air for a few seconds. Other than that, I am okay. *Heck, I am better than okay. Now, I can now see my Melody!* With my girl back in my sight, I am relaxed and filled with delight.

I have to prove to my audience that everything is fine and that I have everything under control. *This is only a small part in my circus act. No worries, folks. If you thought this was a great stunt, just wait for act two!* I need to do this promptly before Melody freaks out. I can see the fear overtaking her face. I eye my favorite Frisbee twenty yards out and run over to grab it. Thank goodness I had left it outside after our earlier play session. I gallop over to Melody to prove I had not hurt myself. Then, I offer the Frisbee to her so she can throw it for me. *Look, Melody, this is all part of the plan. Frisbee is the best game ever!* Did I mention I have a favorite everything? When it comes to Frisbee, I even have a favorite model: the Aerobe. Those are the best Frisbees ever made, for sure. I have found that I prefer the red ones, as they seem to taste better and are easier to see when they are flying through the blue sky!

My fabulous kitchen exit really got the group laughing. Everyone starts petting and loving on me.

As I glance at Melody, I notice that she still carries a startled look on her face. She rubs me all over to make sure I had not broken anything, and the worry in her voice is obvious as she says, "Sorry we forgot you. Don't you ever jump out of a window again, unless the building is on fire!"

Well, I can promise one thing for sure: I will never jump out of a second story window again. They are easy exits when open, but I see Melody's point. The stunt could have ended badly. I can feel a slight soreness settling in, which could make for a stiff tomorrow. As I sit at Melody's feet, I sense that she, too, gets anxiety when we are apart. Somehow, this eases me. Maybe it's because it confirms that Melody and I are in this life together until the end. We will forever be inseparable. I have also decided that this means everyone in this world has their own internal monster to deal with. Everyone's monsters may not feed off the same feelings, but essentially, we are all cut from the same cloth. This realization decreases Lucifer's size today. I know I will never be alone in the fight he puts up. *Strength can be found in numbers.*

Chapter 23: Finders Keepers

More changes come in the next few weeks as well as more escape plans on my part. Melody starts college again. Thank goodness it is a local thing, and she always comes home in the evening. I decide that I need to accept this fact as part of my miracle repayment. Melody needs to better herself at school so she can give more back to me and the world. Melody switched majors and no longer wants to pursue a career in business and advertising. After her accident, and with much thought during her healing time, she decides that she will have a bigger impact if she goes into the medical field. There she can work more closely with people and have a greater impact. In healthcare, Melody will be able to work with patients just as her nurses had worked with her when she was recovering. I have to remind myself that I cannot be selfish I have to share Melody with the world. This is part of the miracle's effects; the universe needs its repayment. *I only wish I could accompany her everywhere she goes, and that 'no dogs allowed' places did not exist.*

Hopefully, when Melody is done with school, I can go with her as a therapy dog sidekick. I love making people smile, especially Melody. If I were to become a therapy dog, Melody wouldn't have to leave me behind anymore, even if the place has one of those dreaded signs! I should find a school for me to go to and suggest this when Melody nears the end of her program. Perhaps I can bypass school altogether and just get one of those shirts that says 'service dog.' *I bet if I get one, I can even go to the grocery store.* I don't understand why we can't go in those anyway. It is not like a dog could eat all the food inside. It would take a pack of five hundred or more dogs to accomplish that. Besides, I only take treats when they are offered and I only beg for doughnuts and cheese. The majority of the food in those places would not even appeal to me.

As much as I hate to watch Melody leave our house every day, it is a necessary evil in our new life. Every day before Melody leaves, she scratches me behind the ears and says, "Love you, Lu. I will be back soon." This helps me because I trust her. I know that if Melody is not planning on coming home for the night, she will say 'in the morning' instead of soon. She has done this a couple times when she goes out with some of her friends who live in the city. I can't say I care for the smell of the stale beer on her when she returns the next day, but I do like the stories she tells me after she and girls have gone out on the town.

I must admit that when the scheduling changes with Melody's school started, I lost my mind for a moment or two. Melody and Grandpa decided it would be best if they put me in these things called kennels whenever they leave for the day. Supposedly, this is to keep me out of trouble and protect me from getting hurt or into something that could make me sick. Melody and Grandpa always make sure these kennels are large, airy spaces. They always have a comfortable bed in them, but there is one factor I can't stand: when I am inside one of these giant boxes, I can't see out the windows of our house. This tiny fact drives me bonkers! I need a reference to tell the time, and for that I need to see the sun. How else am I supposed to keep track of 'soon'? I need to know when the day's end is approaching so I know when to expect my Melody's return. I'm not great with time; I know morning and night, but not soon. *Soon is too general.*

Melody and Grandpa have devised a different plan to keep me contained while the family is either at work or school. Two things led them to this new approach: number one, they know I hate kennels; and number two, I can escape any indoor kennel that Melody or Grandpa puts me in. Over the past two months, I have proved that no metal or plastic in this world stands a chance against my brain, muscles, and teeth. Perhaps in another life, I was an escape artist. I am almost certain that nothing can contain me at this point. Give me ten minutes alone in whatever contraption you can conjure up, and I will show you why it's inadequate. Kennel companies should really consider hiring me for quality assurance testing. I could help them establish a rating system for their products.

The kenneling part of my life has become more of a game lately, and I am excited to see what Grandpa and Melody will try to contain me in next. Today is different as Melody leads me out into our front yard. *What? No kennel?* Once we are out in the

169

yard, Melody kneels and clips a long lead onto my collar. I remember reading about these. Some people call them runs or tie-outs. Melody makes sure the lead and my collar are secure, then goes in the house to see if this will appease me. I sit and evaluate the product's many faults for a minute. I take in the pros and cons of her and Grandpa's newest idea. I like the fact that I am outside, but what I don't like is that Melody is inside and I am not with her. I assume she is spying on me from inside the house to see if this will work. I let a fair amount of time pass before I work on my escape. I decide it will be best to let Melody and Grandpa think I am at least slightly challenged by this new idea of theirs. I do not want them to feel to defeated. I made a new plan over breakfast the other day: if I escape enough times, Melody and Grandpa will be forced to allow me to go everywhere with Melody. I will make this look like the safest option!

Twenty minutes pass, and I have chewed through the braided metal wire and thin plastic coating. *Not much of a challenge. I am now one-hundred percent positive it's impossible to contain me.* Once freed, I walk towards the front door of our castle. The next thing I have on the docket is to bark at our front door so Melody or Grandpa will come let me in with a quizzical look of defeat painted on their face. As I walk towards the door, a gust of wind with the most alluring and tantalizing scent I had ever inhaled makes my nostrils flare. *What could be even better than my Melody's scent? I must investigate this at once.* With my nose to the wind, I venture out of the yard by myself for the first time.

I trot down the road and finally find the source of the aroma that is clearly not food, and is making my loins ache and my belly stir with excitement. I think I am about a half mile from our house in a neighboring subdivision. When I am ready to return home, I will just smell my way back to Melody. I gaze at the source of the scent that lured me away from home. First, I see a group of young men sitting out in their driveway, grilling hotdogs and drinking beer that smells watered down. I prefer beers that have a higher wheat content. *At least, I think I do.* Those are the ones that Grandpa shares with me now and then after we mow the lawn. I especially like it when the beer has hints of orange floating amongst all its bubbles.

I approach the men, and one of them greets me in a friendly manner, "Hey there, big fella. Aren't you a handsome guy? Where are you from?" I ignore the men and the grilled food. Neither of them are the source of the smell that got my attention in the first place. I bypass them all and saunter over to where the most amazing-smelling, golden-hued, glistening-haired Golden Lab I have ever seen sits chewing on a blue rubber bone.

The feelings that are stirring inside me are entirely new. I find myself taken aback by the female dog's scent and beauty. I am in a trance-like state. These feelings bring unspeakable images and events into my mind. I can't even say out loud the things I feel compelled to do to this glistening gold creature before me. All I know is that I desperately ache to climb on top of her and make her mine. Oddly enough, this golden beauty must have had the same

171

feelings awakening within her, too. I still can't believe all the events that take place next as the Golden Lab winks at me and licks her lips after tossing her bone aside. *Is she teasing me?*

I gallop over to Golden Girl with my chest puffed out, presenting myself as the amazing male specimen I am. The men just sit there and watch us, providing only background noise. It seems that this Lab and I are the only two that exist now. Once I have dazzled the paws off of Golden Girl, she turns around and presents me with her backside. *Is she for real? Quick, someone pinch me!* Golden Girl then positions her tail straight out to her right side. I stand for a moment in a state of shock with a ridiculous grin on my face. Golden Girl has just given me the 'I am open for business' sign, if you catch my drift.

It is apparent to everyone around that Golden Girl not only wants me to do the unspeakable things that I had just dreamed about to her, but she is begging me! I waste no time as I am worried she will reconsider. Enthusiastically, I climb onto her back as fast as I can. I am just getting myself into position for some boom-chicka-wow-wow when our encounter is interrupted. I am sternly ripped from Golden Girl's back and scolded by one of the men. "Get off her, and get lost!" It is the man who had been tending the grill. He continues to yell at me as he drags Golden Girl away, shoves her in the house, and slams the door.

Befuddled, I sit down and offer the men my puppy-dog eyes in hopes they will let Golden Girl back out for me to play with. The man who just locked her away walks over and checks my collar. "I am going to call your owner. Time for you to go!"

The sinister man's voice chimes in as he says, "No, don't do that. He is a beautiful purebred. I can take him home when we are done grilling and chilling and make money off him. Finders keepers!"

You're dang right, I am a purebred! Maybe I judged Mr. Sinister too harshly at first. I am a little surprised that it was he who first noticed my greatness. *But what does he mean by make money off me?* Mr. Sinister walks over to me and promptly takes my collar off. Then he throws it in the garbage. His actions make me a little nervous. *What are you doing? That's my emergency link to Melody!* In hindsight, I should have immediately aborted operation Golden Girl and sniffed my way back home at this point. For some stupid, unknown reason, I continue to hang around in hopes that Golden Girl will come back outside. *I will head back home after five minutes. If Golden Girl doesn't come back out again, she probably changed her mind.* I am clinging to hope and the little bit of Golden Girl's scent that still hangs in the air, motivating and corrupting me.

The guy manning the grill speaks again. "You are a sick dude. You know that? What if this dog belongs to a family with a little kid? What if he's the kid's only friend? My son would be devastated if Lady didn't come home."

Mr. Sinister quickly makes his case. "Finders keepers. If the owner is too stupid to contain a well-behaved purebred, I have the right to sell him to someone who will care for him properly. Heck, the way I see it, I am doing this dog a favor. He is neglected."

"Whatever you have to tell yourself to sleep at night, man. But accidents happen. I want no part in this. I think I have seen the dog's owner. There aren't many white Shepherds around here. I always see this dog walking or running with some petite gal early in the mornings. Sometimes, there is another lady with them. I think they are like, fitness freaks or something. I hope she finds out and give you a serious beat down. You aren't right, dude." *At least Lady's owner seemed to be a decent human.*

Mr. Sinister walks over towards me as he talks again. "Oh, stop judging me like you are some saint. We grew up together. I know you better than anyone here. I know every skeleton in your closet. I promise not to tell your wife about any of them if you will keep this one four-legged secret of mine."

The two other men, who haven't moved from their lawn chairs except to get more beer from the cooler, begin laughing as these two argue back and forth. Fear builds within me, and my little monster grows inside my chest. Lucifer is feeding voraciously on my fear as I come to the realization that I have overstayed my welcome and am now in a jam. Mr. Sinister walks past me to his truck, returning with a rope. I am just about to bolt when a small boy opens the front door to the house and Golden Girl, now known as Lady, steps out onto the front step. My fear dissipates immediately as I fall back under her spell.

Mr. Sinister sees my moment of weakness and ties the rope around my neck, securing me to his chair. "Perfect timing, Brady. Thank you. Can you do me a favor? Tie Lady back up over there. I think her lead is by your left foot."

"Don't talk to my son or include him in any of your criminal activities. Brady, you are to pretend Uncle Willy is not here. And Willy, Brady is four and repeats everything like a parrot. If you don't want your secrets told, you may want to consider leaving early. Go back inside, Brady. Daddy will call you back out when the burgers and hotdogs are finished cooking. The big boys are talking right now." The nicer of the two men grabs Lady and leads her back over to where she had been tied up when I arrived earlier.

I sit and stare at Golden Girl from the other side of the driveway. I should be chewing on the rope so I can run back home to my Melody, but I am clearly under some sort of Labrador love spell. I again attempt my puppy-dog eye's power on Mr. Sinister in an attempt to get him to untie me and reunite me with Golden Girl. *Kill them with kindness. Maybe that will work.* I look for the little boy. Surely, I could work my magic on him. *What was his name again? Oh yeah, Brady. Brady, where are you?* I spot Brady and watch as he grabs a monster truck and goes back into the house as his father had instructed. *Crap, now what do I do?* I start chewing on the rope. Mr. Sinister sees this and smacks me hard on top of my nose. "Knock it off, horndog!"

Over the next thirty minutes, Mr. Sinister and

the other men attempt to test my knowledge. They ask me to do things like sit and stay. I start to sit for them when I am suddenly hit by a sense of betrayal. Mr. Sinister says, "I was thinking about keeping him for myself, but clearly he is as dumb as a box of rocks. Or maybe the poor dog has never been trained. I told you he was neglected. I will just sell him. I could use the cash anyway. Rodger over there will require hush money to keep his mouth shut. He never does anything for free!"

I sit, chastising myself for my disloyalty to Melody. *I have got to get out of here, and quick.* If I am understanding correctly, Mr. Sinister plans on giving me to someone else and has no interest in helping me to return home. I look up to take in my surroundings and note what all the men are doing. I need a distraction. I decide to wait until the men are eating and then escape when their attention is no longer on me. I gaze down the driveway toward home. A familiar scent gets my attention. Melody is approaching the end of the driveway. *Thank goodness, Melody! Let's get out of here.* Relief starts to deflate Lucifer, who had inflated to a surprisingly large size during this whole ordeal.

"Excuse me, gentlemen. I believe that is my dog tied to your chair over there," Melody says in a kind tone as she points over to me. "I appreciate that you found him, but I will take him home now." She throws in one of her dazzling smiles for good measure.

Mr. Sinister gives a menacing grin and replies, "He is my dog. What makes you think he is yours?"

The other man stands silently at the grill with a grin on his face and watches the encounter. *I wonder whose side he will take? He seems reasonable enough.*

Melody sets her hands on her hips. Her voice is firmer now. "Yeah, right, because there are so many white German Shepherds around here. He and I run this road every day, and I have never seen another one like him around. Now, give me back my dog!" As she mentions me, I stand at attention. I want to make her proud. I am fairly certain I will be in trouble when we get home. This little gesture is the least I can do for now.

Mr. Sinister's beer breath fills the air around me as he retorts, "I don't see any tags, so unless you can prove it, he is mine! Which he is, anyway. Also, we were just leaving. So you can go look for your dog elsewhere!" He unties the rope from the chair and clasps it firmly.

My eyes nearly bug out of my skull as Mr. Sinister jerks me closer to his side. Lucifer has returned and is now bigger than ever. My anxiety skyrockets, making everything around me spin. *What do I do? Melody is too small to take on this man. If I bite him, I risk going down the road of no return.* I look at Melody, hoping to see some sort of signal. I need her to give me directions. If she commands me to attack, then surely I will not get in trouble for obeying orders.

An intense rage consumes Melody before all of our eyes. I try to jerk myself away from the man and gear up for battle. My Melody is clearly going to take this man down, or at least die trying. I have to be

177

ready to protect her. Melody and I are allies in eve-rything. "I am ready," I bark at Melody to let her know I understand her body language.

Melody begins to speak in short, clipped, and very stern sentences. Oh, these men are in so much trouble. Me, too—but we will sort all that out later. No one survives Hurricane Melody unscathed! If on-ly the men could read Melody as I can. Surely, Mr. Sinister would just drop the rope.

I listen carefully to the words that follow as Melody speaks. "I will prove it. Right here, right now! I am sure you will be more than willing to give my dog back within the next two minutes."

Mr. Sinister sniggers and tugs on the rope around my neck. "Come on, boy. We are going home."

I anchor my feet and don't move. Melody walks over and strikes a power stance right in front of the truck the man is jerking me towards. She holds her chest high and places her hands back on her hips. She is not going to back down. Melody growls with authority, "His name is Ludo. I will show you just how smart, perfect, and mine he really is!" She snaps her fingers as she often does when we train. I award her my full attention. Melody advances her show of ownership with hand signals and com-mands. "Lu, sit!" I sit at attention. "Lay." I do so. "Speak." She holds up two fingers and I bark twice. Then, she holds up four and I give four more sharp barks. "Up," she says. I sit on my back legs with my front legs up in the air like a meercat, awaiting my next command. Melody is almost to my favorite part. I admit, I am a little confused since no one has on a big puffy jacket, and I only attack her or Grandpa when they are padded to the gills. Mr. Sinister is wearing only a t-shirt. I don't think he is going to go down laughing as Melody and Grandpa normally do.

"Have you seen enough, or should I continue? I would be happy to show you his favorite: attack. He only listens to me once he starts. I'll give you three seconds to decide." Melody starts the countdown as if this grown man is a small child.

Sensing Melody's extreme anger and nervousness, I direct a low warning growl towards Mr. Sinister. "Listen to her, buddy. Trust me when I tell you that things are about to get real Western around here! You are a far cry from a cowboy. You are going to want to drop that rope."

Melody counts off loud and clear: "One... Two... Ludo." She is raising her right hand to unleash my 'get 'em' command. My hair bristles with excitement. I crouch down and snarl, showing off all my teeth. I am now in a position to launch my attack as soon as Melody releases me. *Just remember, pal, it's not my fault you forgot to wear a padded suit today. I know you are trying to be a tough guy, but this is probably going to hurt!* I am excited by the man's lack of a puffy suit. I have never gotten to latch onto an arm that is not hiding deep inside thick padding. I am certain my grip will be even better without all that stuffing in my way. I am finally going to show Melody my full capabilities. *Unleash me, Melody. I am ready!*

179

Suddenly, Mr. Sinister's scent changes; fear is seeping out of his every pore. He drops the rope and sheepishly says, "Geez, woman! I was just playing. I was coming to give you the rope myself, but—here, just take your crazy dog and go!"

I look over at Melody. She had brought her hand down to her side, and gives me a boring command instead. "Come here, boy!" I prance over to my Melody with my head held high. I am proud of myself for scaring a fowl-smelling odor from Mr. Sinister's backside. As I get closer to Melody, I can smell relief pouring off her. I watch her closely, still awaiting my favorite command. Melody never speaks it though. Dread starts to settle upon me. I am sure I will be deep in then doghouse when we get home! I turn and give Mr. Sinister one last growl, and a goodbye bark to Miss Not-Worth-It Golden Girl. Then, I trot alongside Melody as she leads me back home.

"Ludo, what am I going to do with you? I almost lost you, boy. Do you realize this could have been really bad if I didn't find you?" She sighs. I nudge her hand to reassure her. Melody is right. Today could have ended terribly if I had been taken by Mr. Sinister. How could I have let myself be so blind? Somehow, that Lab had driven me to insanity. I decide that all Labs are evil and vow to stay clear of them from here on out.

Chapter 24: Clipped

The following week passes with more awkward-ness than normal. Melody always seems to be in deep thought. She and Grandpa are up to something; they whisper often, but stop as soon as I mosey into the room. They are definitely talking about me. Is this their way of getting back at me for venturing out of the yard last week and almost getting myself doggy-napped?

Friday morning arrives, and the strangeness of our week continues to show itself. "Please, Melody, forgive me already. I can't take this anymore," I whimper as I rub my body along Melody's leg like a cat. I know Melody can't hear the words I am saying, so I make the most out of my gestures to get my point across. I waltz over to the front door after rubbing on Melody a few moments longer and pick up my leash. It is time for our morning workout and training session. Hopefully, after a good run, Melody will finally be able to put last weekend behind us. *Should I let her and Grandpa win the endless kennel war for a day? That might make them feel better.* I have been quite the stinker lately. Maybe I need make my gestures a little grander for greater for-giveness.

Melody walks towards front door where I sit

waiting for her. I watch patiently as she puts on her shoes. *Wait, Melody, what are you doing? Those are the wrong ones! You need your tennis shoes, not your flip-flops! Are you feeling okay?* Melody then says something that shocks me: "Sorry, not today, Lu. We are going for a car ride, though, to visit your friend, Dr. Jerry." *What? Wait a darn second, did you say Dr. Jerry?*

I bark my dismay as Melody's words settle in my mind. Then, I bark more as I run away from her. No way am I going to let her clip that leash onto me and lead me outside for a car ride to Dr. Jerry's. "The last time I saw him, he drugged me after you got captured by aliens in the cornfield. I will go to the vet, but you had better let someone else take me. I will never relive that nightmare. We have just gotten things back to normal and are starting to build the Ultimate legacy. No way am I going to that vet ever again!" Bark, bark.

I create a ruckus running throughout the house, so much so that Grandpa and Grandma come out of their bedroom. They are both dressed in their work clothes. Grandpa says, "What is all the commotion going on out here? Is everyone okay? Is someone at the door?"

"No," Melody replies. "It is Ludo. I told him we are going to the V-E-T to see Dr. Jerry. Now he is freaking out. You don't think he remembers our last trip there, do you?" *Melody, dogs can read, so we can also spell. You may as well just say 'vet' and save yourself the time. Also, yes! I am scarred for my life from our last attempted trip to Dr. Jerry's vet clinic.*

Grandpa laughs as he walks over and pets me to calm me down. "Melody, you are giving your dog too much credit. Ludo here doesn't have a clue. Dogs are not that smart." *Hey, we are, too! It's not my fault you can't understand us, Grandpa.* "Nonetheless, your mom and I were just in the bedroom talking and we think it would be better if I went with you. The last time you attempted to make that drive, you didn't make it, so we are a little apprehensive. Come on, you two, let's go. We don't want to be late for our big date with Dr. Jerry." Grandpa winks at me. Something about that wink rubs me the wrong way, and I don't find it very comforting.

I want to go on record here and say that I am agreeing to go with them to see Dr. Jerry for only two reasons today. Number one, and most importantly, because Grandpa is driving. No way will I let Melody and me make that drive alone again. Number two, this is a prime opportunity for me to get back into Melody's good graces by complying after my stunt last week.

Even though I am in agreement, I can't let my wolf and dog brothers everywhere down. I have to play hard to get and pretend I am scared of going to the vet. I dart around the house, and then the yard, until Melody baits me into Grandpa's Toyota Forerunner with my favorite Frisbee. Once we are all in the car, I calm down. I will save the rest of my theatrics for the clinic parking lot.

The whole idea of going to the vet with just Melody makes me anxious. I try to calm myself by thinking of all the ways that today's trip differs from our last one. *The day of our accident.* Today is different: Melody and I aren't rushed, and Grandpa is accompanying us and is driving. *Alpha Pa has it all under control.* Melody and Grandpa are sitting up front and I am sitting in the back seat with my head poking over the middle console between them. *Yes, today is nothing like before.*

Melody reaches back to rub me behind my ears as Grandpa drives. "I hate to do this to you, boy, but I will not lose you to some Lab—or any other gal in heat!" *What is Melody talking about? What does the Lab-loving incident have to do with the vet?* Come to think of it, I had my yearly shots recently, if my memory serves me. I am almost certain that Grandma took me about a month ago, in fact, I can vividly remember the day now. It was a nice sunny morning and Melody and I were about to get in the car, when she chickened out and nearly had a panic attack. Melody ended up staying home and Grandma took me to the vet by herself. Melody said she was not ready to make that drive yet, probably part of her PTSD. Confusion swirls through my brain. *What is prompting this visit to the vet? I thought I only had to go once a year?*

Six country songs on the radio later, the three of us arrive at the vet. We all unload from Grandpa's SUV and go inside. I don't put up much of a fight. I can tell that my Melody needs a solid win today. Once inside, I watch as Melody stands at the front counter and fills out some paperwork. Grandpa and I wait patiently by one of the exam rooms. I am now even more befuddled than before. Normal procedure for visits with Dr. Jerry is paper-signing and green paper transactions after my office visit, not before. An uneasy feeling creeps its way in. I look at Grandpa for reassurance. He must sense that I need some, but he says the oddest thing next. "Don't worry, big guy. Grandma made me do something similar after Kasandra was born. It's not as bad as it sounds. Plus, you will get lots of sympathy pampering, I promise! Oh, and for the record, I tried to talk Melody out of this, but she wouldn't hear it. It's your fault. You terrified her the other day when you ran off. You didn't give her any other choice." *Phew!* At least some of what Grandpa said is a relief. I mean, I didn't really think Melody would give me up for adoption. All the odd whispered conversations lately had made me second-guess my surety. Deep down, I know Melody could never give me up. We are soulmates! My nerves settle more with Grandpa's words, but something about this day still smells fishy. *And I doubt it is because Grandpa and I are standing by the cat food.*

Melody finishes playing with the papers at the reception desk and walks over to take the leash from Grandpa. "Come on, boy. They said they are ready for us." I follow Melody into the first exam room. Dr. Jerry is already standing inside waiting, and greets us as we enter. I don't catch his entire greeting because Dr. Jerry's previous customer had failed to sniff out a treat on the floor near his feet. *Not me, though.* I key in on it as soon as we turn the corner and gobble it up quickly before I greet him back.

Dr. Jerry and Melody continue to talk for a few more minutes. As they chat, one of his assistants comes in and gives me a shot on my right haunch. It pinches a little, but that is the worst of it. I sigh and yawn. I am bored, so I lie down by Melody's feet. I need to make a little noise and look sad so I will get more post-vet sympathy. I am only following the dog code, after all. "Okay, Melody, I got my shot. Time to go back home. I was a good boy. Now, let's put last week behind us. I promise to never wander off without you again." I grumble as I lie next to her feet, admiring her red toenail polish. It makes me think of my Frisbee. It's such a pretty color that, race care red.

Wait a second, since when do I care about colors so much. Am I stoned? I hear Grandpa's voice out in the reception area. He was standing over in the corner of the waiting room on his phone. Grandpa realizes I am watching him and gives me another sympathy-filled look. *Jeepers, maybe I should go with him to the vet from now on. He seems overly concerned and may spoil me more than Melody. It's okay, Grandpa. No need to be sad over there.* I want to go rub against Grandpa's legs to reassure him but for some reason I can't convince my legs to carry me over to him. I consider this to be one of my more pleasant visits to Dr. Jerry's. That being said, this exact moment is the last thing I remember. Everything goes black after that last sorrowful look from Grandpa.

I am now replaying everything over again in my mind, trying to figure out where things went awry. Melody and Dr. Jerry were talking, Grandpa looked at me with sympathy-filled eyes, and then, *poof!* It's all gone. It seems my memory was wiped after I got that special shot from his assistant. *This place and the drugs they use are something else. Someone should report Dr. Jerry. What he is doing can't be right.*

I remember our conversation on the way to the vet in Grandpa's SUV. I remember Melody doing paperwork at the desk after we arrived, and then we entered the exam room. *Could it have been something in that exam room? Gas leak, maybe?* Five minutes after I entered exam room number three and received my greeting from Dr. Jerry, things got hazy. I had scarfed that lost treat down. *Is that the reason I can't remember? Maybe it was a bad treat? Maybe Dr. Jerry's assistant is to blame for all this?* There are too many variables for me to work out. If I had to bet on the reason for my memory loss, though, I would bet Dr. Jerry, the voodoo doctor, was behind it in some manner. His assistant could be a witch. She had injected me with a syringe filled with who knows what. *That's it—it must have been the assistant!* My memories stop right after she stabbed me with that needle. I hate having a blank page in my storybook for the day. Dogs are creatures of the present, but somehow, I have lost almost an entire day and there is no way to get it back. I really am never coming back to see Dr. Jerry again.

All this thinking is making me dizzy. I seem to be stuck in a place between consciousness and unconsciousness. I can hear things going on around me, but I'm not truly aware of them. I try to respond and draw attention to myself, but none of my body parts will cooperate or move. "Melody, help me! Where are you? I have been drugged!" I finally manage to whimper and kick my legs in an effort to run away from wherever I am. My paws only find air and make no contact with solid ground. *Why is it so dark? Where have all the lights gone?* It was early morning when we arrived at the vet clinic, and now I can see nothing. *Am I blind?*

After who knows how long, I regain consciousness. I still feel very woozy and am unsure of how much time had passed. I can see now, so I immediately search for Melody. Thankfully, it doesn't take me long to find her as I frantically scan the room. Melody is sitting on a stool next to where I lie on a table. We are in a part of the clinic I have never seen before. It is a large, mostly white and stainless-steel room with obnoxiously bright lights. The room smells highly of antiseptic. The scent reminds me of when Melody came back after her long visit at the used car repair shop. I will never forget that smell. She smelled like that for a long time while her leg was wrapped in the colored toilet paper. I sniff harder at the air around me and realize that most of that scent now seems to radiate off me. My anxiety starts to grow.

Melody speaks. Her voice comforts me and squashes my monster back to a manageable size. "Welcome back, big guy. How are you feeling?" She kisses the top of my head and strokes behind my ears. I can hear her talking to the doctor and I try to listen, but for some reason I can't stay awake. I doze off again though this time I am a little more aware of the things going on around me. I still don't seem to have enough energy to respond though. I know I didn't walk out of the clinic on my own because I recall Grandpa carrying me out and placing me in his

Toyota. *Whiteness continues to bleed onto the next page of my storybook.*

Finally, I wake up. I mean, really wake up. It is now much later in the evening. Melody, Grandpa, and I are back at our castle, and I am lying on the couch. I am still disoriented, but relieved to be out of the clinic. I am going to protest more the next time the vet is mentioned. *I had better get a lot of sympathy for this one!* Melody is sitting next to me, with Grandma next to her. Both are staring at me as if they had been waiting all this time for me to come to. Due to my not fun, impromptu vet visit, I fully intend to milk the crap out of the spoiling that should be headed my way now that I am awake. I whimper and crawl my way closer to the girls.

The girls sit looking at me with curious faces. They were sharing a bowl of popcorn and watching a love story on the television before I woke up and crawled over to them. *A chick flick, I suppose.* I generally hang out with Grandpa in the garage when the girls watch this type of thing. *Is popcorn a food group of its own?* Melody and Grandma eat it several times a week. Thank goodness other people live in this house with us. If they didn't, those two would probably eat that for dinner every night. I do not understand their obsession with popcorn. The substance reminds me of cardboard, but with a much better flavor. Grandma butters it up quite a bit, so I usually indulge with them, as I love the creamy yellow goodness of real butter with a heavy dash of sea salt. If it weren't for the topping, the popcorn itself wouldn't be worth the chew time. I let out a whine to show that I am slightly disappointed as this is definitely not my first choice for an after-vet spoiling snack. If given the choice, I would have picked a nice, juicy T-bone. Melody works part time at a steakhouse while she goes to college. Every now and then, she brings me home a large, delectable T-bone and grills it to a seared, rare perfection for me.

I inch closer to Melody and Grandma on the couch. I want to join them in the sharing of the popcorn. I notice a strange twinge of pain between my back legs as I move though. *That's odd. I must investigate this after my snack.* The movie ends at the same time as our bowl of popcorn. Melody rises from the couch and says, "Okay, Ludo, let's get you outside. I'm sure you have business to tend to. Plus, we need to make sure everything still works. Then, we will get some real food." *What do you mean, still works?* I jump down off the couch to follow Melody towards the door and notice that pinch between my back legs again. *Seems slightly worse now that I am standing.* I turn and gaze back at my rear side. I don't see anything out of the ordinary. I will give it a good lick later; that always seems to heal all.

Once Melody and I are outside, I saunter over to my favorite bush to lift my leg and relieve myself. *What in tarnation is going on back there?* I look back as I lift my leg, and another sharp twinge of pain stabs at my nether regions. Something is missing! *A something I find very important and happen to be very fond of!* My boys, as I like to call them, are gone, vanished, *poof*—disappeared! I urinate quickly, then curl my head around to my backside for a better look. *You boys had better be hiding back there amongst all my fur! Come out, come out, wherever you are!* I poke at my rear side with my nose even though it hurts. *Where could they be? They aren't small.*

My highly important search is interrupted as Melody scolds me. "Leave it alone, Lu. I promise you will feel better in a few days!" *Um, no, I will only feel better when I find what is missing.* What have Dr. Jerry and his witch sidekick done to me? I am never going back to that clinic. I am about to really start making a stink about my current state of affairs when Grandpa comes out on the porch and calls to me with that same sympathetic look he had given me at the clinic.

No, he couldn't have known. Grandpa would never let anyone take my jewels. Boys stick together and back one another up! Grandpa is lowering down a heaping plate full of delicious leftovers from dinner as he whistles for me to come join him. The food is heaped on the plate like a large mountain peak. He has truly piled it as high as possible. The plate looks like a volcano of goodness just waiting to erupt in my mouth. I forget about my missing boy parts for a second and waddle painfully over to him as fast as my backside will allow. *Now, this is what I am talking about. Forget about cardboard popcorn!* Grandpa pats me on my head as I arrive at the plate. "Here you go, boy. I can sympathize with you. You, at least, have earned a proper meal tonight. No dog of mine is getting just dog food after a loss like you had today. I will mourn with you. For what it's worth, Grandma had me snipped years ago."

Ah, so it may be possible that Grandpa had

191

known what was going to happen at Dr. Jerry's. This explains why he kept giving me sad looks. I am not sure how this makes me feel. Perhaps it is Grandma I should be mad at. I mean, if she orchestrated Grandpa's snipping years ago, she may be responsible for mine, too. One thing I am sure of is that I will get to the bottom of this matter some other time. The smell of pork chops, mashed potatoes, and green beans with bacon is overwhelming my ability to process any more in-depth thoughts for the time being. I now have a one-track mind, a dog on a clean plate mission. I forget about my missing parts and finish shuffling the rest the way up to where Grandpa stands on the porch with my dinner. I will go back to solving this mystery once my belly is full. The large contribution of food is skewing my judgement about whether or not I need to reprimand Grandpa for not having my back at the clinic. *Surely, he could not have known?* Grandma must have some sort of trickery super power. There is no way Grandpa would have voluntarily gone to the doctor for an operation such as this.

I gobble up my food. As I do, Melody adds a circle-shaped cookie to my plate. I eat that first as it looks the least desirable. I save the pork chop for last. It will make an excellent dessert! The amount of food in front of me is enough to feed Melody and all my aunts. My first thought is that I should not be so gluttonous, but then I remember my tragic loss and think, 'heck, I am going to eat it all!' *I earned it.* For some unknown reason I get tired again before I finish giving my plate its final rinsing lick. I am like a dishwasher, always sure to complete the spot-free-rinse part. *After all, I am only helping whoever really washes the dishes later on. I am a true service dog. I aim to please and make people's lives better!* Something deep in the back of my mind sparks a vague memory from the time Stranger Lady took me to the vet. I think these oddly shaped cookies were involved then, too. *I must pay more attention to what I put in my mouth.* Again, this is a matter I will sort out later. For now, I have no choice but to lie down and nap as fatigue quickly overtakes me.

The next few days carry on like this. As soon as I forget about the last weird cookie and vow not to eat one again, someone gives me another. I always swallow it before remembering why I wasn't going to eat those darn cookies anymore. This is hard for me, though, because there is something addicting about them. They also seem to cause me to forget a lot. I can never remember not to eat them until the damage is already done. *Cookie down the hatch!* It is as if I have become the dang Cookie Monster from *Sesame Street.* I lose my mind when someone says "Hey, Lu, you want a cookie?" These cookies are the only consistent thing I can put my paw on. The sympathy food they feed me keeps changing, but those little cookies keep coming. *Always one in the morning and one in the evening.*

I remember that I am going to go on a mission to investigate something, but I can no longer remember what it was. *Darn cookies!* I know it has to do with a strange pain, but I don't feel pain anywhere. Is it someone else's pain? Perhaps it will come back to me later. For now, I will sleep on it, but when dinner comes this evening, *no more cookies!*

193

I must stop contributing to the stereotype that precedes dogs. People already think that dogs just sleep all day. We take naps, yes, but those are only to recharge our batteries. It takes a lot of energy to plan great daily homecomings for our humans. Plus, if we have to send any miracle vibes out into the universe, that really zaps our energy supply. If our humans earn a promotion at work, or a new corner office is obtained, or a new love connection, lottery win, or the beating of a disease such as cancer occurs, one can bet that their faithful dog was behind it. Feel free to award the four-legged superheroes working behind the scenes in your life with steak dinners, and maybe a cheese curd or two. Dogs love cheese! *And apparently strange cookies.*

Thankfully, as dinnertime arrives this evening, I don't have to remember to turn down one of those magically awful cookies. No one offers me any. *At last, my pack must have realized there is something strange about the cookies.* I finish my dinner and sit, reflecting on the last few days. Aside from the cookies, I had not realized that Grandpa and Melody seem to have given up on putting me in one of those dreadful kennels. I hope they will finally succumb to defeat on this matter.

To my dismay, this may have had something to do with the bizarre cookies. Due to these tasty treats, I have been sleeping away most of my days in a relaxed bliss, not a care in the world to give me any stress. I have zero anxiety, but I have also been oblivious to the things going on around me. I have failed to notice something major.

Chapter 25: Contained

Somehow, I have completely failed to notice all the work that Melody and Grandpa have been doing outside. I think I may have underestimated their ability to keep secrets from me. They have snuck nothing past me before, *I hope this doesn't become a new thing.* I thought we were a secret free household. Turns out Grandpa and Melody have been as sneaky and dirty as those darn cookies they have been giving my lately. *So much for thinking I had won the containment battle.* As part of my spoiling, Grandpa has been letting me nap on the couch when everyone goes to work. No one has been trying to box me up 'for my own good,' as they call it, and it has been nice. The cookies must have had more than a little something to do with that, because when I finally stop eating those laced little goodies, a new super kennel appears in my yard.

Sure, I normally get a little anxious when my humans leave for work, but that's all part of the separation anxiety the TV doctor diagnosed me with. My human pack-mates get irritated because my anxiety sometimes makes me a little destructive as I impatiently wait for them to come home. *I haven't ruined anything major yet, but I have made Grandma mad a few times.* My biggest offense has been with shoes. I'm telling you, it wasn't my fault.

195

Grandma's Coach shoes looked at me funny the other day. They practically begged me to eat them. I mean, come on—they were covered with the letter C. Everyone knows a big letter C stands for 'cat.' I would want to be destroyed, too, if I had to wear that letter all loud and proud. I was only helping the shoes; they no longer wanted to exist.

I will admit, I lack a little in the patience department, but no one is without faults. I do not see this as being overly critical. Melody and Grandpa got more serious about kenneling me after I killed Grandma's cat shoes. I know there has to be something to them always saying that "it's for my own good and safety." Melody is scared that I may eat something that could be fatal. I find it funny that Melody and Grandpa are the two who say "we are doing it for you" the most, and they were the ones who fed me the killer cookies.

Whenever I am put into a new containment box, I do what any smart dog would do: I escape. Then, I tear something up to pass the time as I wait for my humans! I have seen lots of dogs do similar things on the television. I believe this is just part of being a dog. I love all of Melody's faults, so she will just have to learn to love mine, too. *After all, all good relationships are give and take. We must learn to meet in the middle and embrace one another's faults. They call it acceptance. No one is perfect. However, dogs are pretty darn close!*

I am certain that with enough time, Melody and Grandpa will give up this kenneling war. I truly believe that there is not a kennel out there that I can't escape from. The only thing that has contained me so far, is our house with all the windows closed. Although, if push comes to shove, I know I can always break the glass in a window to escape if I truly need to. Yes, I am one hundred percent positive that there is no possible way to truly contain me. At least, I was until I went into a cookie coma for a week and Grandpa engineered what I call 'The Fortress.'

Grandpa may be more of a contender for the Alpha role than I give him credit for. My new fortress has sides that reach twelve feet high. It also has a black screen-like roof and large steel walls that frame in a generous ten by ten area. I have to admit that this is much better than those smaller boxes they have tried to keep me in, but I still want nothing to do with it. The walls of the new containment center are made of thick industrial steel woven together in diamond shapes. Grandpa also used a rocky cement compound to secure the perimeter. All these lovely new attributes put two of my main escape tactics out of play. *No digging under or climbing out.* I guess I will just have to chew through. Most wire is no match for me. I walk over to one of the walls and bite it; I need to test out my chewing through theory. *What is this stuff?* My teeth have finally met their match; the gauge of this wire is too large for them to contend with. If I try to chew my way out, I will do significant damage to my pearly whites and, more than likely, barely scratch the silver surface of the metal links. *Grandpa has been paying attention to those prison shows lately. It seems like he has taken notes, too.*

I am eyeing my new super box, and I don't like what I see. Escaping from this new kennel is looking less and less possible. However, I am not completely discouraged yet. The fact that nothing has contained me thus far still gives me hope. My father used to say, " If we are not challenged, we will not change." *Challenge accepted, Grandpa!* I notice a flaw in Grandpa's design, and I cling to this new knowledge of mine. This will be the one card I can hide with a poker face and play later to win my game against Grandpa. I will use this card to maintain my role as the smartest, strongest male of the house. *Why? Because I am an Ultimate Alpha in the making. I am the one true alpha here. Just you wait and see.* I can hardly wait to see the look of disbelief on Grandpa's and Melody's faces as I elude them once again.

I watched Melody and Grandpa work on the gate mechanism during the final assembly process. It is a simple latch that lifts with just a few fingers. *Ha, I will be out of there within five minutes. I will show you who the alpha is, Grandpa.* I am readying myself for the testing phase of my new containment center. Due to my newly hidden trump card, I am excited to play this game of ours. I love baffling the two with my brilliance. I have to hand it to Grandpa, he has been listening to all the complaints I have made about my other kennels. He has met all my previous grievances with this new super box. I can tell that Grandpa had put a lot of time and care into this; he used the highest quality materials I have ever seen. Not even a dinosaur could chew through this stuff. Grandpa really was thinking of me. It's nice to be loved. *Bit of a shame I will have to show him that all the time he spent out here was another wasted effort. Perhaps I could wait a little longer before escaping so Grandpa and Melody don't feel like complete failures.* I will let the two down easy. An alpha must always behave and act for the good of the pack. I need my actions to be received as constructive criticism instead of a 'nope, you two failed again!'

I visualize my soon-to-be escape in my head. I find that all my plans work best if I do a pre-visualizing exercise. I learned that from Marsha's book. Try it sometime. It works amazingly well. Anyway, as I envision my exit, I struggle to keep a devious grin from showing itself. I can't let Melody and Grandpa know I have a plan. My hair is bristling with excitement. *Prepare to be amazed, my humans. I am the David Copperfield of canines!*

Finally, Grandpa finishes tinkering with his new invention and orders me in with the famous "Kennel up, boy!" command. As Grandpa shuts the gate of my gigantic new kennel, Melody stands behind him, watching anxiously. Frivolity fills me. In a few short moments, my nose will fit perfectly under the kennel door's latch, just like a human's thumb! I will lift the latch with ease. *One does not need fingers when they have a glorious nose such as mine!* Once I free myself from these confines, I will gallop over to where Grandpa and Melody are spying on me from the shadows. Sorry, guys. Ready or not, I am about to be right behind you. *Now, hurry up. Latch that gate and walk away.* I can hardly wait to show them why their newest venture won't work, either. Hopefully, this will be the last time I have to escape, and they will realize the best option is for Melody to just take me with her everywhere she goes.

The door to my new compound finally closes. I

appease Grandpa by pretending to sniff around my kennel as he finishes closing the latch. Hopefully, my sniffing will get him and Melody to go hide more quickly. I want them to see my sniffing as relaxed and content. I am skillfully distracting them. Or at least, I think I am. I hear a subtle click when my back is turned. *What was that noise?* I whip quickly around to see Grandpa playing his final trump card. *Dang, he really thought of everything.* I didn't expect this at all. Shock creases my brow. The clicking noise I heard was a heavy-duty carabiner that he put through the latch to hold it firmly in place. I had not factored this into my equation at all. Without fingers, I am screwed!

Well, double dog dang. I am officially stuck! I sit, befuddled and practically gawking at the kennel. *Grandpa has done it!* My Admiration for him grows. Well, if I have to be kenneled while I wait for my Melody, this will have to do. This kennel is about as nice as they come, and it is outside. So, I can at least tell time using the daylight now. I didn't have that luxury previously when they tried to kennel me inside down in the basement. My new confines even come with my very own house. Inside the house there is a pad that heats or cools it depending on the weather outside and my needs. All Melody or Grandpa have to do is switch the settings and I will be toasty warm on a winter day or comfortable cool on a hot summer day. I think Grandpa may have missed his calling as an architect.

My new kennel is basically the Ritz. Melody made sure I have a fully stocked minibar (in the form of an abundancy of water) and a large assortment of bones and toys. My kennel lacks a food station, but that is okay with me. I am sure they decided not to build one because they know I never eat until someone is home with me. It's a rule of mine never to eat alone. Let's face it—I can't, even if I wanted to. My anxiety monster grows when my humans are gone. When he gets bigger, my appetite always gets smaller.

When my pack leaves, I can't help but stress. Then, my stomach fills with extra acid. That darn doctor told me what my problem was, but he neglected to inform me how to fix it. Maybe he did, but I fell asleep during that part. That Dr. P is a little dry in the humor department. Sometimes, naps just sneak up on me. I may have a touch of narcolepsy, but it doesn't seem as bothersome as my anxiety. If I truly need to stay alert, I don't have any trouble doing so. It is only when things become mindless and boring that I sometimes drift off to dreamland for a few moments. It seems that I am stuck with this anxiety problem, though, and unfortunately, I think it is getting worse. Maybe Grandpa and Melody are right, and this new fortress is best for my safety. I can't keep up with the cars when they leave for the day, and I don't want to come across any more Labs with witch-like love spells. I am sure they are truly putting me first, just as I always do in matters that concern them. *We are a family, and that is what families do.* We may not always understand the reasoning behind something at first—or even like it, for that matter—but we understand that our love for one another is always involved in the decision-making, and that helps to drive the choices we make. Hindsight is always twenty-twenty, so while I may not agree now, I am sure that with time, their reasoning will become clear and I will see why my new super box is necessary.

My test run in the new fortress lasts for four hours. Grandpa takes Melody for a ride on his new motorcycle down to a drive in called Sam's. It is the local ice cream and root beer shop. I know this because I see them leave and I can smell the remnants of sweet treats on them when they return. *Well, you don't have to rub it in, Grandpa. You won this battle. So what? I assure you, there will be others!* He could at least be more humble about it.

While Melody and Grandpa are gone having fun without me, I am delighted to find another great feature in my new outdoor room: a fairly large green patch in the back. A toilet, as I like to call it. I can pee as needed instead of holding it for hours in the house. Not going to the bathroom is easy for dogs. However, if we are given the ability to urinate at will, we appreciate the luxury and take full advantage. I am sure that is obvious though. I have seen none of my humans hold out from going to the bathroom for ten hours. Some days, Melody and Grandma pee about every twenty minutes. Their bladders must be the same size as a squirrel's nuts. *Dang tree rats, always speeding around and coaxing me into chasing them.* Perhaps my superior bladder control is yet another of my dog super powers.

I adjust quickly over the next few weeks to a new life of waiting out in my fortress for my Melody to get home from work. All right, I will just say it out loud: my new kennel has made my life easier and much more enjoyable. There is a song that plays in my head every day when Melody shuts and locks the gate to my compound. I believe they call it "Waiting on a Woman." I can't for the life of me think of who sings it, though. *Where is a car radio when you need it?* Irrespective of the singer's name, this new fortress allows me to de-stress a little so I can be fully prepared to cater to Melody's needs when she returns in the evenings.

If Melody has had a hard day, I am ready to snuggle or walk with her while she decompresses. We dogs are always happy to see our humans and are never mad when they are late. This is mainly because we are so thrilled that 'soon' is over and we can go back to our scheduled plans. All dogs love schedules; we spend a great deal of time training our humans to get on one that works best for us. Of course, we do this all while letting our human think it's their great idea. Did I mention that we are master manipulators? I assure you that when we do manipulate our humans, it is always out of love.

Chapter 26: Our new house

I feel as if I blinked and two blissful years have passed us by. Melody and I are just reaching the stretching part of our morning routine when I reflect on how quickly precious time has soared past us. I have a strange feeling that I will have to embrace yet another change soon as tension has seemed to mount in the castle lately.

Melody has been completely recovered for some time now. She has graduated from college and has already started a job at a private clinic. *So much for a little down time between transitions.* It appears that I have been embracing small changes all along, and mostly they have all been good. However, I can't say I am a fan of her new job. Melody always explains her terrible hours to Grandpa with phrases like "starting at the bottom and working my way up." *Pure poppycock, if you ask me. We are all created equal.*

I feel that veteran workers get lots of perks, just like veteran dogs. I know that older dogs get all the respect and leadership roles over time if they play their cards right. If veteran workers give all the undesirable shifts to the new people like Melody, no one will ever want to stay and work in their pack. Legacy companies, like legacies will only be born when everyone is treated equally and is working to obtain a common goal. Why they don't see this is beyond me. I have found humans to be slow learners. I suppose companies such as the one Melody is currently working for will have to lose the good employees or suffer high turnovers before they ultimately figure out the secret to longevity and legacy. There are plenty of ways to reward people that don't include treating others as lesser. *Everyone's time is equally valuable.* I find it sad that only a small percentage of people know this to be true. I must make sure that Melody grasps this concept and never acts in such a horrid manner.

Melody and I finally finish the stretching part of our routine. I am more than ready for my favorite part: resting and belly-rubbing. I am disappointed that the belly rub is not as joyous as the others. During my rub-down, Melody says, "I think it is time for us to move out of Grandpa's house. It's time we found a home of our own, bud. What do you think?"

Um, Melody, I think you are failing to see something. That's what I think! I let out a groan of disgust. "Surely, I have mentioned that I do not particularly care for change and take a while to transition. Have I not?" I stand and walk away from her, no longer willing to accept her belly rub. I can see it for what it is now: a bribe. I bark twice. "It took me months to learn to love my fortress while you were at school or work. Now I must adjust again?" This completely ruins my rub and my fantastic mood. So much for thinking I have life all figured out. *I knew a change was headed my way. Dang dog intuition. Why must I always be right?*

Melody rises from the grass where I had left her

and starts to pursue me. I pick up my pace as I head towards the house. I need my space. I will eat and think this over. Sure, life at what I'd thought was *our* house has changed a lot in the past two years. Apparently, I was mistaken on much of what I thought to be true of my life. I must have missed clues somewhere along the way.

My first mistake was thinking that I had a full pack already. *Wrong.* Aunt Kasandra moved out into an apartment with a friend about ten months ago, and Grandma left Grandpa in something humans call 'divorce.' Now, for what appears to be my second and biggest assumption, Melody is telling me that this is Grandpa's house, not ours. *There must be a full moon on the way. Melody, like other humans, always gets a little weird when those rise high in the sky.* Perhaps I should work on my detective skills a little more, they certainly aren't serving me at the moment.

Now I only see Grandma and Aunt Kassandra here and there, and not on a regular basis. I hate it. Aunt Bailey got married over a year ago, and I see her even less. All of my former pack members still seem to care when they come around or when we go visit them, and we are always happy to see one another. However, I can't handle the added stress of trying to keep all my loved ones safe when they keep spreading out and getting farther and farther away from me. I know I must hear Melody's idea out. I vowed long ago to do this with all changes.

Stop focusing on only the negatives. There is a method to Melody's madness. I must figure out what it is. Sometimes, change can be a good thing. The only problem with my current rationale is that my little monster, Lucifer, is shouting as loudly as he can. *If there is one thing I hate more than change, it's my dreaded little monster.* Just when I think Lucifer is finally gone, he finds a way back into my life through the fears, anxiety, and stress that arise within me. "When I reach the level of Ultimate Alpha, I will find a cure for everyone's Lucifers and get rid of them once and for all!" I growl at what Melody surely thinks is nothing as I send my 'not today' message back to Lucifer.

I have grown very fond of Grandpa over the years. I can't lose him as I have lost the others. My pack members are dropping like acorns in the fall. I can feel Lucifer actively growing bigger inside me. Lately, I have found myself sticking closer and closer to Melody in an effort to keep him at a more manageable size. My instincts have always told me that as long as I stay close to Melody, everything will be okay. I suppose that if we move to a house of our own, I will still be able to keep her safe. I guess I will just have to let the others go on some level. I will make Melody's safety and happiness along with building my Ultimate Alpha legacy my top, and now only priorities in life to get through this next adjustment.

In the meantime, all I can do is hope that my former human pack-mates are getting dogs of their own. Perhaps I should look for suitable handlers for them. Every human should have their own handler. Humans are terrible on their own. They mean well, but their green-eyed monsters often get the best of them, especially when green paper is involved. Dogs make this world go 'round.' If you want to live optimally and enjoy your time on earth, one needs a proper dog. Without one, you miss out on all the great things that life has to offer!

My anxiety continues to build as Melody starts house-hunting this evening. *Jeez, slow down, woman! You only told me this morning. Can't you give a guy a week or two to adjust to the idea?* I can tell that this will become part of our new nightly routine. I hate it already. Sometimes, I look with Melody and deliberately act disgusted with everything she says she likes. Melody shows the houses to me and points out all the good attributes with excitement in her voice. Then, I do my best to poop all over the glorious attributes she works so hard to point out. Sure, some sound nice, but I will not approve of anything I don't get to sniff out with my own nose. I feel that this should be obvious to her. She knows how I am!

Humans often overuse the phrase "a picture is worth a thousand words." I have a much better one: "A good whiff is worth a million!" I am not sure how Melody plans to get my blessing to move forward with this whole new house thing. Perhaps she wasn't entirely serious. Or if I am lucky, she might be starting to reconsider the idea.

I find myself getting extra annoyed lately as Melody always forgets to take me with for the viewings and inspections of the houses that excite her most. She sets up appointments with a new friend of hers that I have yet to meet. I only know she calls him Realtor. *What kind of name is that?* I hope she isn't losing her mind. I mean, I am the decision-maker in this relationship, so I ought to be there.

Another thing that really gets under my skin, is

the fact that Melody always remembers to take Grandpa along for the outings she plans with Realtor. This makes me incredibly jealous. I am becoming more agitated and upset with this whole new house idea of hers. *If this is to be our new house, shouldn't I be a part of the decision-making process?* I think we should just stay here. Grandpa's house is already broken in. The house and my kennel are nearly perfect! I try to use my mind tricks the best I can to persuade Melody to stop looking and stay here, but she seems more determined than ever. She appears to be developing some immunity to my puppy-dog eyes. I have noticed that it has lost some of its effectiveness over the years. *I can't say I appreciate her newfound tolerance to it.*

Three weeks pass agonizingly slow due to my super high annoyance with all of Melody's new 'I need to buy a house' activities. This crazy obsession and ludicrous behavior of hers has me almost wanting to adopt Grandpa as my soul-mate human and divorcing Melody. *Only an empty threat.* I would be lost without my Melody so I talk myself off the ledge of doggy-human divorce. However, I almost have to reconsider the idea again when Melody comes home today and shouts a dreadful sentence: "Ludo, come here. I have big news, I got us a house!"

Immediately a loud moan escapes me. "Correction: all you got me is more anxiety. What have you done? I haven't sniffed or marked a place yet!" The next two weeks drag on F-O-R-E-V-E-R as the kid says in one of my favorite movies *Sandlot*. Melody spends most of our time packing and rambling on excitedly about *our* new place. *I love how she says it's 'ours' when I still haven't seen or sniffed it!* She is

209

bubbling with excitement, and I am bubbling with irritation and diarrhea due to a nervous stomach. *I hate change.*

After another week of more absurd behavior and way too much enthusiasm pouring off Melody, I finally find a few things of my own to be excited about. The morning alone brings me some relief when Melody reveals over breakfast that she will finally take me to our new house for what they call the 'final walk-through.' At last, I get to view our supposed new house. *Now, the only thing I have to figure out is how to get Melody out of a house contract.*

After lots of thought on the way to our supposed new castle, I decide not to sabotage the whole house contract thing. The whole buying a house and moving out to live on our own idea clearly makes Melody very happy. I can't take that away from her, that alone has been part of my person mission all along. I must keep my pack moving forward towards positive things. Melody is my pack now, and this makes her happy. I get plenty of time to think all of this over as we are walking instead of driving to this house of ours. I think this small fact alone is a good sign. I decide to cling to it and let it help ease some of my mounting anxiety.

Fifteen minutes' pass as Melody and I stroll along familiar streets. We walk or run these same roads daily for our morning workouts. The surrounding neighbors all wave and smile. We get a lot of extra attention thanks to my cuteness. I am suddenly pulled from a daydream about my celebrity dog status with the neighbors as Melody says, "This is it

Ludo. What do you think?"

I look around and am slightly elated to learn that Melody has picked out a cozy white ranch-style house just over a mile down the road from Grandpa's. *Thank goodness I will be close to him.* I like that I know exactly how to get to Grandpa and my soon to be former castle on my own if there is ever an emergency. I hate to admit that I actually like something about this house so soon. I hide my gratitude about the houses proximity to Grandpa's from Melody.

First thing is first, if this house is to be ours then it needs to be marked as such, so before I start my walk-around and begin my full sniff interrogation I pee on the mailbox at the end of the driveway. Once I am done draining my bladder Melody pulls me toward the house's front door. Melody and I are almost to the big red door when a man I have never met before opens it. This startles me so I bark and growling immediately at the man and place myself between him and Melody. "Don't worry Melody I will protect you. Stay back, I don't want to have to bite you!"

Melody scolds me, "Ludo no, he is a good guy. This is my realtor and friend James."

With Melody's words, I cease barking. *Ahh, so Realtor wasn't his name after all.* James greets us and extends a hand out for me to sniff, "Calm down big fella, you must be Ludo. I have heard a lot about you. Hi Melody, you two come on in and have a look around. The documents from the inspection you had done are over on the kitchen counter."

I bypass James's hand as I push past him into

the house. I am leery of all people that instantly extend a hand out to dogs or humans. As I pass James, I pick up the smell of a blue heeler on his pant leg and decide he is probably a good guy. I quickly turn back and give his dangling hand a nudge with my nose to signal that we can be friends so long as he tries nothing funny with Melody. I thought it would be rude of me to leave his hand hanging in the air like someone who seeks a high-five after a job well done. Melody and James then being talking and I leave them to go explore my new house and yard. *I definitely don't love it, but it's not awful either.* I suppose I will just have to learn to adjust. What doesn't kill us strengthens us, or so I have heard.

Chapter 27: We're In

Shortly after Melody and I move into our new house, she and Grandpa fence in our large backyard. I like having all this room to run and play, and with the fence, uninvited outsiders can't join us without an invitation. Grandpa's house does not have a fence, and neighbors just come and go as they please. It isn't a bad thing, per se. Most people are friendly. I was essentially the celebrity dog of the neighborhood at Grandpa's house; everyone always greeted and petted me as they passed through so I never had a shortage of attention.

Only two things about Grandpa's open yard policy ever irritated me. Number one, people would come over to raid Grandpa's garden. Sure, Grandpa had given them permission to do so, but this meant I had competition for all the ripe produce. We all seem to like our veggies the same way. I especially love a fragrant, deep red tomato. The number two thing I struggled with was the neighborhood kids. Often, they would only stop over to tease me with a stick when I was out in my fortress. For this reason alone, I have learned to hate small humans and their mean teasing tactics. I would have loved the children if they had just opened the gate and thrown the stick so I could fetch it for them. For whatever reason, we never got along.

213

Yes, I like my new fenced-in yard. There are no kids around and no one can get close to Melody or me without permission. Now, I am only slightly upset with Melody and this whole new house concept. I try my best, but struggle significantly to give her my full support in this matter. Part of me is hoping that I will get lucky and Melody will just return it like she sometimes does with clothes. Sometimes she buys things on impulse, then later she decides she doesn't really like or need the item. Perhaps the house will be like one of her most recent shirt purchases. Or maybe we can still stay with Grandpa and just visit here often to play in the yard. We could just use this place as our own personal dog park. I like this idea as only the humans and dogs Melody and I choose could come in to play.

My private dog park daydream ends and dread floods over me like an overflowing creek after a long rainstorm. I will miss my fortress at Grandpa's. I had finally found serenity in there. He put a lot of time and love into my outside containment, and it offered me great comfort when he and Melody were gone. I will also miss the set schedule I had both Melody and Grandpa on. All of my hard work is ruined. Now, I will have to retrain Melody. *Crap, she took the longest in the first place!*

Melody is my favorite human, of course! She is my human soulmate, but she is just as stubborn as me, which is not exactly a good thing. I guess that is partly why we are such a good match. We are always pushing one another to go after our dreams and to dream bigger. Neither of us ever lets the other give up on anything until we have achieved whatever we are going after. Dreams plus work plus faith always equal success. This new house of ours is a prime, but unwanted, example. Melody dreamed of this house and worked very hard to get it on her own creating her success. I should be happier for her instead of worrying about how all this has affected me. *Sometimes, we must do things we hate for the ones we love.*

Thinking of the ones I love, Grandpa has grown to be a core pack member. I feel he needs to be with us full-time. If Grandpa will no longer be a full-time member, I will have to start thinking about recruiting some canine help for him. At least when Grandpa was around, I could take a day off now and then and let him be the Alpha. That was nice, especially on days I felt a little under the weather. Lord knows Melody is not ready for any sort of Alpha role or the responsibility and stress that accompanies it. *Some days, she still seems fragile.* I often worry that her path in life is more like a roller coaster with lots of ups and down. When she goes down, I have to make sure she can get back up. Without Grandpa around, this move may mark the end of my days off. *This is going to be a job for an Ultimate Alpha. Good thing I know just the dog for the job!*

Chapter 28: Adapting Slowly

Before Melody is even done moving boxes and furniture into the new house, let alone unpacking, she and Grandpa go to work building a new outdoor kennel for me in our backyard. *But I don't need a new one. I love my old one!* I, being resistant to change, rebel. The sides of my new kennel are only eight feet high, and the chain-link fencing used to make them is not as strong as my previous fortress. It looks like my old one, but doesn't even come close in comparison. I laugh silently to myself as Melody and Grandpa pat themselves on their backs when they think they have completed a masterpiece. I assume they think because I am now older and have adapted so well to my fortress a Grandpa's, that I will now be easier to contain. *Oh, how wrong you two are!*

Our first night in our new house is terrible. I can't sleep because there are too many new noises. I am not used to the sound of the furnace, or the ice maker on our new fridge. Each sound stabs at my eardrums and makes me shoot upright in bed. Grandpa isn't across the house anymore, so I am solely responsible for stopping any intruders who may wish to harm us. In our old house, I know where all the squeaky floorboards are. If someone were to come in the house, I would know exactly

216

where they are standing in every room without even being able to see them. The daunting task of having to re-learn these new floors as soon as possible only exhausts me more on my already sleepless night.

Finally, the sun rises lazily, and so does a tired Melody. I don't think she slept well, either. I noticed that she was awake as often as I was last night. I am relieved when we go out for our usual morning run though. We run to my favorite place, and what should still be our house: Grandpa's! Once we arrive, we let ourselves in. Melody makes coffee as she yells, "Get up, sleepyhead. Your new favorite alarm clocks are here!" I jump into bed with Grandpa with a two-part ulterior motive. My first reason for jumping into bed with him is to wake him up and steal a good belly rub. The second is to alert him to the fact he is on Melody duty for the next fifteen minutes so I can get a quick nap in. I immediately snuggle into the already warm spot on his mattress where he had been sleeping. Grandpa gets out of bed to go visit with Melody and drink some of that brown bean juice the two of them seem to be addicted to.

Melody calls my name as she finishes her cup of coffee, signaling that our visit with Grandpa is now over. "Time to go, bud. We have to get ready for work." *But it has only been twenty minutes.* I yawn and stretch before jumping down off of Grandpa's bed. I am not done sleeping yet. I drag my feet as I wander out and groan my opinion on this matter loudly. *Woman, why must you be so relentless?* Melody herds me outside like a good sheepdog.

Once I am forced outside onto the porch, I try one more trick. I slowly saunter out of Melody's sight

217

as she and Grandpa finish talking. I need a few more minutes of quality shut-eye. I hear Grandpa call his goodbye to us, and I assume that he is still standing in the same spot on the porch as he was when I disappeared a moment ago. Melody's voice calls out, "Come on boy, time to go. Where are you? Come now heel up. This is no time for games!" I have snuck away and hidden myself in my old fortress. I am already curled up in the comfy confines of my old doghouse, and I have no intention of coming to her call. I poke my head out of my doghouse when I hear her walk over, inviting her to either join me or shut the door and leave me here. Frowning, Melody walks over and clips my leash to my collar. "Come on, Ludo. We made you a new kennel. Let's go, now. I don't want to be late."

"I am only doing this for you," I groan as I pad along beside Melody on our quick journey home. I am disappointed that she did not receive my message. I have to get this communication thing down better, and hopefully soon. I would kill for the ability to speak human words. *Gestures don't always get the job done. According to Grandpa, women are supposed to be mind readers. Maybe that only applies to men, not dogs. What a shame.*

Once I am shut in my new kennel and Melody pulls out of the driveway, I put my newest escape plan into action. To be honest, it has been a while since I have gotten to play this game, and I look forward to it. I rip the fencing apart while Melody is at work. It takes a significant amount of time and energy, but I get it done nonetheless. Then, I jump over the much shorter four-and-a-half-foot fence that

218

frames our yard and keeps the neighbors out. I soar over it gracefully, like a competition horse over a hurdle. All it takes is one good leap after a nice galloping lap around the yard. Once I am freed from my new, subpar fortress, I head up to Grandpa's. I could have easily smelled my way there, but my journey is even easier since Melody had shown me the direct route on our morning run only a few hours before.

When I arrive, Grandpa is at work. I knew he would be at this hour, according to the schedule I had put him on when I lived here. I head out to the garden and pick out a nice big zucchini to snack on while I wait for Grandpa to return. Generally, I don't eat when my humans are gone, but breaking out of my new confinement had really worked up my appetite. After finishing my snack, I settle myself in the shade offered by the covered front porch. There is a nice wicker loveseat there that Grandpa and Melody often sit on to chat while I rest in the yard after playing a good game of Frisbee. Grandpa had recently put one of those nice plush pads on the loveseat for the summer, which makes it a far better option than my dog house, even though I love that as well. *This is the life. I could get used to snacks and porch naps on the daily!*

A few hours later, Grandpa pulls into the driveway, and I run up to greet him. He smiles and pats me on the head, laughing as he speaks. "You are going to be in big trouble when your mom finds out what you did!" *Trouble bubbles, I don't care about any trouble.* I just want to be here where Melody and I belong., I have puppy-dog eyes to get me out of any real trouble. I know Melody will understand even though she has built a tolerance to my power. She can never resist my sad eyes for long. Often, she quickly caves because she feels like she is being too hard on me. This is mean of me, I know, but if you had the special eye power, I am sure you would use it, too. I think about my power for a moment. Melody did buy our new house, so maybe it isn't as foolproof as I had thought. *Is Grandpa right? Will I be in a bit of trouble?*

I can deal with whatever trouble Melody throws my way later. I knew Grandpa needed me this morning when we left to run home. Lately, Grandpa has been lost in a dark place within himself. If I am correct in my assumption, it started when Grandma left. This is another reason Melody and I shouldn't stay at our new house. We need to be here. He needs us.

Melody and I should just bring our things back to his place. Grandpa needs me like Melody did when she was lost in her darkness after the accident. There are some things only dogs can help humans out of. There are all kinds of scientific studies on this matter. Don't believe me? Just Google 'therapy dogs' sometime, and thousands of medical journals will prove that we are a million times better than any pharmaceutical pill on the market. Those drugs only turn people into zombies and mask the symptoms and problems they are having.

Take agoraphobes, for example. Without dogs, these people can't leave their houses without being in a severely drugged state. Anxiety is the worst; I know because I, too, have it. I need Melody to help combat Lucifer. I can contain him when he is small like a black bird without his wings spread, but when my panic takes hold, he becomes a dragon-sized monster with massive wings! Lucifer has never succeeded in spreading his wings in giant form yet, but I can't imagine the consequences if this ever occurred. I can't stand my pack being so spread out. I feel that Grandpa's sadness will be enough of an excuse to validate my escape from our house this morning.

Grandpa and I go inside to watch television while we wait for Melody to get home. He calls Melody to let her know my whereabouts and promises to bring me up to our new house once she gets home from work. The two also make plans to work on reinforcing the new kennel after dinner. Grandpa tells her to pick up gyros on the way home. Some friends of theirs Chace and Macia own a small bar and restaurant called The River is Greek. Marcia is well known across the nation for her gyros—or, at least, she should be. They are excellent and nearly the size of my head! I love those spicy little lamb slices. I dislike the sound of the kennel reconstruction, but I like the sound of dinner. Instead of spending the rest of the afternoon worrying about what Grandpa will engineer to keep me in my new kennel, I choose to focus on the Greek deliciousness headed my way. The thoughts cause drool to pool in my mouth; a few long strings make their way to Grandpa's wood floor. *Sorry, Grandpa, but you brought up Meg's cooking.*

After dinner, Melody and Grandpa decide a slow transition will be best for Grandpa and me. As the week progresses, I only have to deal with short times in my new kennel, which is significantly better than long stints. This makes adjusting easier. Melody and Grandpa modify my new containment area and then test it while Melody is away from home for short periods, like trips to the grocery store. I, of course, escape in every way possible: I dig out, climb to the top and throw myself over, eat metal like it is kibble, and destroy gate latches like they are made of clay. What can I say? I am the true master of the escape game! *Jails should really consider hiring me for test runs.*

Melody runs me up to Grandpa's every morning before work to visit with him over coffee. Then, she puts me in my old kennel for the rest of the day. I am not very keen on her running back home by herself, but I want to stay in my fortress at Grandpa's. This is a compromise I can live with. At the day's end, Melody either picks me up after dinner with Grandpa, or Grandpa brings me down to her house and stays for dinner. This is a schedule I can live with, and my stress level lessens. I like this new arrangement much better because I get to see them both every day. I know Grandpa will eventually build a fortress of equal greatness at my new house, but I refuse to resign until that time comes. *Perhaps I will get lucky and Grandpa is thinking the same as me. Maybe he, too, likes this arrangement better.* I secretly hope that Grandpa will decide not to complete the task of building me a new, inescapable fortress though failing or quitting is not in his nature. That is why he, too, is an Alpha.

By the end of the third week, Grandpa has constructed a new, foolproof containment center for me. He made a pretty cool adjustment to my new kennel: I can go in and out of the garage. My new kennel has a shaded roof like my old one, so I can no longer climb out the top, and he reinforced the bottom with cement and wood. *There is no getting out! And I do not give up easily!*

I finally allow myself to accept this as my new home. At least Grandpa comes to visit often, and some days even picks me up to take me to work with him. I think it is time for me to read the classified section of the paper and have Melody and my aunts get Grandpa a dog of his own. His birthday is coming up, providing us with a great reason to get him a new doggy handler of his own. I can't stand the thought of Grandpa at the castle alone. He needs looking after still, and I have not yet figured out how to be in two places at once. I am unsure if dogs contain that level of magic. I read the paper while Grandpa and I take our lunch breaks at his work today. I am now determined to find him a new handler.

A few months later, I find the perfect breed and family lineage for Grandpa. I mastermind a plan with Melody and the aunts and direct them to get Grandpa a high-energy, bird-hunting machine: a German Shorthaired Pointer. *What can I say? I like German bloodlines!* Her name is Denali, and she is the perfect fit for Grandpa's current needs.

When outside, Denali reminds me of a big Super Ball. She goes bonkers, running over every inch of the yard and springing off anything that can be sprung from. She is like one of those extreme parkour athletes. Once in the house, though, she settles down quickly and just wants to snuggle. Grandpa loves his snuggling, and I am certain that one of his favorite things to do is take a nap. Denali will ensure that Grandpa has to get out of bed even on his worst down-in-the-dumps days. She is perfect for him! I know Denali will get Grandpa on her schedule in no time. He seems to thrive on a set schedule. I think this is part of why I love him so much. He is a lot like me. *Embrace the routine—it helps to ward off anxiety and stress!*

Time is passing, and I am finally adjusting to our new home. It isn't so bad, really. We go on a run or walk to Grandpa's every morning, where I get to wake him and Denali. For being such a little pup, she sure can snore! *She probably puts snoring hippos to shame. Assuming they snore.* Melody always gets the coffee started while I jump in bed and lick Grandpa's face like I am never going to see him again. Even though I know we will be back the next morning, it never gets old. Grandpa always laughs and pushes me away while he pretends to be upset by the complementary face-washing.

Rousing Denali is something I also enjoy. The two really are a perfect pair. Denali is a lot like Grandpa in that she is not very energetic in the morning. These two are more like night owls while Melody and I are morning larks. Denali always acts surprised at first when I assault them upon our arrival. Denali burrows down deep under the covers so I have to dig her out. I have outdone myself by matching her up with Grandpa. I believe the saying is "a match made in heaven." *Another perfect human-canine soulmate combo, complements of the Lu!*

Chapter 29: Dating Games

Melody, my former pack members, and I all seem to adjust. Life has been throwing changes at us all like candy thrown at a parade, but luckily, all the changes have been positive. *Life is what you make of it.* The past few months have passed us by with more ease and less stress than I had expected, which makes for a pleasant surprise. I am happy that all my former pack members are thriving as Melody and I make our regular rounds.

Grandpa and Denali are building a strong bond and learning how to best communicate with one another. Their relationship reminds me of the one that Melody and I share. The other day when Melody and I went over to Grandpa's house for dinner Denali was showing off just how well she has already trained Grandpa. Grandpa was sitting in his easy chair being lazy after dinner when Denali cracked the whip. I watched amused as she ran over to where Grandpa was sitting with a tennis ball in her mouth and plopped it in his lap. She then barked, "Come on Rick, just because Ludo over there calls you Grandpa doesn't mean you are one. Let's show Ludo and Melody our new game."

I always forget Grandpa's real name is Rick. Melody always calls him Dad and I call him Grandpa. Denali's bark worked like a charm and Grandpa reached over and patted her on her head while saying, "Good idea girl. Come on Melody let's take these dogs outside I have to show you a new game Denali and I came up with." Yes, it is safe to say Denali has her and Grandpa's communication on point and is off to a great start when it comes to training Grandpa.

Grandma is thrilled at her beautiful apartment and looks more content and at ease than I have seen her in years. My aunts Bailey and Kasandra have each got their own furry handlers. This allows me to take them off my list of people to worry about since I know that they are now being well looked after. As for Melody, I finally have her on a schedule I approve of. *It took longer than I wanted it to, but we are both in a better place now because of it.* I have really embraced that nothing changes unless we do. Without change, one cannot grow. I guess I am slowly learning to accept all these facts of life, though I can't say it is always easy to do.

One evening, Melody comes home later than usual. I am not upset or worried by this. I only know it is later than usual because my belly has growled from hunger. *Generally, that never happens.* Melody had promised me that morning she would be back 'soon,' and she has never broken a promise. Melody is a woman of her word, and I value that. Say what you mean and mean what you say. If only everyone would communicate in such a manner... I especially hate people and dogs who expect someone else to read their minds. Few in this world have that talent. If a dog or person does harness that power, I feel that it is being wasted if they are only using it to decipher what somebody wants for dinner. If the one being asked would just communicate what they want in the first place, it would save everyone a lot of time and agony.

So much talent gets wasted in this world. If only everyone could realize their potential and see their unique quirks for the gifts that they truly are. *Melody is especially bad at this.* I sit outside in my kennel, awaiting Melody's return, and list off all her wonderful gifts to stave off my worry due to her unusual tardiness. *She will be here soon.* I think I am only anticipating Melody's arrival more today because before she left for work, she gave me a treat. I remember her saying something as she did this, but I hadn't awarded her my full attention. Shameful of me, I know, but there was a squirrel in our yard that needed to chased. It was the pesky tree rat's fault.

I force myself to think back, which is challenging for a dog. I think Melody had said something along the lines of, "Here is a snack, Lu. I may be home later than usual. You don't have to wait to eat this. I promise we will still do dinner together, but I don't want you to go hungry." That was definitely the gist. I may not know her exact words, but I am close on the concept. Then, as I was kenneled this morning, she gave me the steak bone from last night's dinner to serve as my snack later in the day.

The bone still sits in the corner of my kennel, untouched. *It will stay that way until Melody returns.* Upon her arrival, I will devour it in a matter of minutes. *Come on, Melody. My delicious appetizer awaits.* Hopefully, it will be only a few more minutes. *Wait for it.* I am coaching my willpower while watching the evening sky take over. *Good lord, woman. What on earth are you up to this evening that doesn't involve me?* Melody and I are an inseparable pair, and I feel we should always eat together. Daily family meals are important and should never be skipped. They are the perfect time to communicate with one another.

Now that Melody is all healed up and settling back into a normal life, she recently started to date. I assume that this may be the cause of her tardiness some evenings, and I can't say it excites me. The whole dating thing is interesting though. Melody does not date often, so these are erratic events. She works long hours and usually gives the rest of her time to me, her close friends, and her family. I have never complained though I may start if I have to wait any longer to eat this steak bone.

I have not stressed out about Melody's dating too much yet, mainly because her dates are not often, and also because she is smart. I know Melody can see right through most of the men who come after her. She has high standards. I think she may even be referred to as high-maintenance. I know this because of her impeccable taste in canines.

As for dating, Melody only goes out with a potential date or talks to him on the phone once, maybe twice. Evidently, there isn't much to choose from in our area's male population. I find this a particularly good thing as it means more Melody time for me! *Time is so precious, something you can't get back once it passes you by. Grab hold of it and be present in the moment, don't allow distractions to cause you to miss a big moment.* This is where dogs differ from humans. Dogs think of the future; we don't have the time to dwell on past events. We also don't have the energy to waste being upset over something trivial. Dogs embrace each moment as it arises. I am training Melody to be better at this. *It's going horribly slow and is a slightly painful process.* It must be done, especially if I am to reach the role of Ultimate Alpha. *I love how that sounds!*

Melody is pretty good at seeing people for who they are and what they want. However, sometimes her perceptions have impeded her judgment, and she has misread situations. *By nature, she is extra cautious and paranoid. She gets it from Grandpa. Neither of them give trust away easily.* For the most part, Melody picks up on the person's intentions quickly and can tell if they are good or bad. When she misses something, I am usually there to steer her out of harm's way and protect her. That's why it is so important that we are always together. Melody and I have encountered more than a few weirdos at various parks over the years. *Another reason why everyone in this world should have their own dog*! Sometimes, I wonder if Melody has a canine nose. I haven't figured out which instinct she uses to read people with the most yet.

Nonetheless, I love our playtime together. Often when we play Melody recounts her most recent human observations from her not-so-grand and seemingly always failed dates. I expect one of these stories tonight. I look forward to Melody throwing my Frisbee in the backyard later with her musical laughter soaring through the air like my Frisbee. Her and I will laugh as she tells me the story of her most recent and often comically tragic date. Even when Melody hasn't been on a date, she tells me about the people she works with. I am always fascinated by all her stories. Sometimes, I get so enthralled that I miss catching the Frisbee. Some of Melody's greatest stories are about her coworkers' kids. They seem like a lot of stress and work. I am glad we have none of our own to worry about. Kids would surely send my anxiety through the roof. *I am not kid material.*

I decided a while ago that I need not worry about any of these men until one of them gets invited into our house. *The probability of that is low, and my happiness about that is high!* When the time comes, I will make my judgment and either accept or reject him from our pack, and will make it clear to Melody. If, for some reason, she can't get rid of the guy, I will take care of it with a simple glimpse of my fangs and a dash of a bad attitude. I do not foresee the last part as ever being necessary. Melody is a strong-willed woman. She typically has no problem telling people what she thinks. *You have learned well, my little grasshopper. I am so good at my job. Sometimes it scares me!*

Finally, the garage door opens and Melody pulls into the garage in our Jeep. *It's about time!* I celebrate Melody's homecoming by wolfing down the T-bone that had been giving me the stink eye for the last hour. After finishing my bone and licking the leftovers from my whiskers, I follow Melody inside to eat our real dinner. I sense a more hopeful than usual attitude coming from her. *This could be bad.* Melody and I eat our dinner together, and she talks highly of the guy who had the pleasure of her company this evening. Jealousy makes it hard for me to hear most of what she says.

Thankfully, whatever Melody is rambling on about does not seem to matter much. Three weeks pass by, and Melody always gets home on time. The worries I had about that guy getting a house invite dissipate quickly. As the weeks progress, I notice that Melody has been talking on the phone to a man named Peter more frequently. I find this only mildly concerning. Melody always seems happy while talking to him, so maybe this guy will not be as bad as some of those from her past. The only thing that irritates me is that these phone conversations are cutting into my playtime with her. This Peter is keeping my Melody from being present in the moments we are sharing while she is on the phone with him. I am getting my time, but it is subpar when compared to what I am accustomed to. *Strike one for you, Peter.*

On a Thursday evening, this Peter guy comes to the house to pick her up for an evening out. I am pleasantly surprised when Melody returns a few hours later without him in tow. When only Melody enters the house, my system fills with relief and I immediately sniff her for details of her evening with Peter.

Melody smells of beer and fried food. *Ha, no wonder this Peter character did not get invited into the house after their date.* He should have taken her some place nicer to eat. Melody and I are healthy eaters, and she rarely, if ever, drinks. I cannot imagine her having a good time at such a poor-smelling establishment. Aside from the poor dining choice, her mood seems happy, with a side of perplexity. *What should I make of this?*

Melody plops down on our big, brown leather couch after getting a glass of water from the kitchen and letting me out to use the restroom. As Melody rubs my ears, she says, "I don't know, Lu. He is nice, but there is something off that I can't quite place my finger on yet." Melody then throws my favorite ball, which I had placed in her lap when I had offered her my head for an ear rub. I run after the ball, and Melody gets off the couch and heads for the back porch. I follow with the ball in tow. *Woohoo! Playtime for me!*

Once we are outside, Melody sits on one of our patio chairs. Relaxation eases her face as she leans back and takes in the cooling evening air. I place the ball back in her lap to bring Melody back to the present moment. Peter has taken up enough of my time. Melody receives my wordless message and grins down at me as she grabs my ball. Then, she lobs it as far out into the yard as she can. I must admit, she really is not very impressive when it comes to throwing a ball. I can tell that she did not play a lot of sports with balls as a kid. I assume she was more of a swimming and running athlete back in her prime. I promptly retrieve my ball and bring it back to her for another go-round. *I love this game.*

"Maybe it is just me," Melody says with a sigh as I return with the ball for the eleventh time. Instead of putting the ball back in her lap, I nudge her hand with my nose and drop the ball at her feet. I can tell Melody needs some comforting.

My sweet girl, you have it all wrong. I climb my one hundred-pound butt up into her lap. We no longer fit well on the patio chairs together since I have grown into a beast of a dog, but Melody needs a hug and a dog kiss on her cheek. Worry and stress are trying to consume her and ruin our evening playtime together. There is nothing wrong with Melody. *If only she could see herself as I do.* Then, she would understand. I believe Melody is truly as close to perfect as I am, and I come from kings.

Melody is pretty amazing for a human, and I have no doubt that she would have made an excellent dog had she been born one. If others don't see that, then they do not deserve her time or kindness. I feel bad for humans. They often let their overthinking get the best of them. *Live in the present, my girl. This moment, the one right here and now, is the only one that matters.* Melody and I snuggle the rest of the night as I battle her overactive and illthinking brain.

Ever since Melody's date with Peter, I notice that my girl is more somber. I don't care for Melody in such a mood. Another week had passed us, and the look Melody seems constantly wear on her face reminds me of the same one she wore when she was recovering from our accident a few years ago. Melody seems to have reverted to thinking there is something wrong with her again. I know when she was healing up from our car accident she worried about all her new scars and how she looked for the longest time. *I thought she was past all that now?* Sometimes I feel like Melody lets others' thoughts and opinions matter too much to her. Then, and this is the worse part, she seems to allow these opinions of others to dictate her mood and feelings about herself. I struggle to understand her sometimes. Melody doesn't readily give away her trust to people, and yet when they say something about her she accepts it as true.

I only want Melody to be happy. If we need to add a male to our pack to accomplish that, then I will get on board and stop being selfish. *Though, I love hoarding all her time, and I am not much for sharing the things I love.* I decide that I need to be more open to this whole male pack-mate thing. That is part of being an Ultimate Alpha. I will search for a good male specimen myself since Melody seems to be striking out. If Melody thinks she needs a man to be complete, then I will find her one. Hopefully, I will find one sooner rather than later, as I can't handle Melody in this mood for much longer.

Chapter 30: Second Date

Saturday morning arrives. I am not looking forward to a weekend alone with somber Melody. Mid-morning comes and Melody gets a phone call. I eavesdrop on the conversation. This is standard behavior for me; we have no secrets from one another. Most of the time, Melody puts the phone on speaker, so I am included in the conversation, anyway. I gather some interesting information from this phone call of hers. Apparently, Peter is on the other end of the line. He has somehow earned a second date with Melody after what I feel is too long a period to go without talking to one another. *What has he been up to all this time?* To my surprise, as the conversation comes to a close, I find out that this second date will take place this evening. *So much for a night in with my girl.*

Melody hangs up the phone and immediately dashes about the house, like a taut rubber band on the verge of snapping. *Great, now this guy has her all anxious.* I am really starting to not care for this Peter fellow. Melody runs through the house like a madwoman and ransacks her closet. She stresses about what to wear as she gets ready, so I help her out by barking to confirm that the purple shirt she has on is a fine choice with her jeans and sandals. It appears to me that their date will again be at another casual place since no dresses or uncomfortable shoes are involved. This unfortunate fact will probably earn Peter a point or two in Melody's mind since she has never been one to enjoy having to gussy up for events.

Once Melody is ready to leave for her date, she gives me a treat and pats me on the head. "You can stay inside with the air-conditioning. It's hot out there today. I will only be gone for a few hours. Be a good boy. I will see you soon." She then leans down and kisses me between my large ears before heading outside to her Jeep. *What, the guy couldn't even come pick her up? She has to go meet him somewhere? Really? This Peter guy isn't acting the part of the great gentlemen she seems to think he is.*

Late evening falls, and Melody returns as promised from her date with Peter. As I hear her shut the door to her Jeep, I run to the front door to greet and interrogate her. As I wait by the door for Melody to open it, I hear another car pull into the driveway. *Who could that be?* I then hear the door of the newly arrived vehicle open and close. *Dang, it doesn't sound like Paige or Grandpa. What on earth is going on out there? Whose voice do I hear?*

Melody comes through the front door, and I immediately notice she smells like the same poor establishment she had visited a few weeks back. My hair bristles as I realize that I was not mistaken about hearing another voice in the driveway. Melody has barely made it through our front door when a man who I can only assume is Peter follows hot on her heels. *Back off, mister. You're a little too close for my comfort.* A short growl escapes me due to a state of shock that seems to have overtaken my current emotions and thoughts. *I can't believe this guy got an invite.* Melody calls over her shoulder to offer him a cocktail as they take their shoes off by the front door. Peter accepts her offer.

Now, it is my turn to judge him. *Will he be right for our pack?* I have serious doubts that Peter will make the cut since he already has two strikes against him. I gave him the second strike for waiting so long to call and ask Melody out again.

I like to turn my people-judgment sessions into a game of sorts. I particularly favor baseball. It seems to be my go-to in most situations. I start my judgment of Peter with a full sniff interrogation. I smell way too much cologne and aftershave. The man's stench assaults my nose, causing my eyes to burn and water. *Jeepers, Peter, are you trying to contend with the Avon ladies?*

I am not a fan of perfumes. One should not have to hide their scent. I feel that people and animals shouldn't want to, or need to, hide anything. Sharing makes everything better. Especially sharing one's true sent. Scent tells others so much about you. Just by smelling one another, we can learn each other's hygiene practices, hobbies, and favorite foods. If the world shared more, it would be a better place.

I fully admit to being a slight hypocrite on the sharing front as I know I like to monopolize Melody's time. This is not the point I am trying to make though. Besides, humans especially are far worse at sharing than dogs. Just look at how humans are when they eat. Grandpa, for example, swats me away from his plate and only gives me the crumbs at the end of his meal. That man will eat far beyond the point of being full just because it tastes good. *Gluttonous Grandpa.* There is one exception to the 'share everything' rule that some may argue falls into this category: bones. People think dogs are selfish when it comes to their bones, but it is one hundred percent acceptable to hide a bone for later consumption if it is not finished at the time it was found or given. Bones need not be shared since they have already been chewed upon. You wouldn't give your already chewed gum to someone. They wouldn't want it, anyway. Bones are essentially gum for dogs, so it is a different situation.

Melody always smells sweet, even after a workout. She reminds me of salted caramels after she and I go for a run and have a good sweat session. I enjoy the scent of her sweetness colliding with the salty sweat on her skin. The smell tantalizes me. I also love the taste of her cheeks after our runs. Melody bats me away every time I try to lick her face while we stretch. I can't help that she tastes good. *Everyone loves salted caramels.*

"Ludo—back, boy." Melody urges me away from Peter and throws me a dirty look as they enter the foyer. *I probably got the look for the growly greeting when Peter first entered the house.* Melody apologizes to Peter. *For what, I have no idea.* "Have a seat on the couch. I will grab us some beers," she says as she heads to the kitchen. I trot behind Melody so that I can note her feelings on this situation. I also want to grab a ball in case a distraction is needed. I find it best to always have a toy to distract people with. This tactic of mine allows me to regain control if things go awry.

You're Welcome

When Melody and I return to the living room, I notice right away that Peter has made himself at home. *Much too comfortable.* Peter looks as if he owns the place. He reclines on our sofa with his feet resting on our coffee table. Melody doesn't even put her feet on the table. She works hard for the nice things we have in the house. I refuse to allow Peter to slob himself all over our things. *The batter takes the plate. Will this be the third strike for Peter?* His future here looks short and bleak in my eyes.

To amend the slobby Peter situation, I pass quickly and harshly under his outstretched legs, knocking them off the table with my bulky shoulders. "Pluto," he scolds me. "Go on, boy. Go lie down!" His voice is a little higher than I prefer a man's voice to be. I would describe his voice as one with a slight edge of femininity. *Not good qualities for a future Ultimate Alpha. Peter settles into the ready stance over the plate.* I add Peter's voice to my list of mental cons as I continue my judgement. Perhaps I make him nervous? *Let's face it—he probably should be.* I am the king of this castle. If you want to get to my queen, you have to get through me first!

Melody gives Peter an odd look, then corrects him. "It is Ludo, not Pluto."

I give a low, playful growl, though I must admit that I intend it to have threatening undertones to Peter's ears. "That is right, Jerk-pants. My name is *Ludo*, not Pluto. I have a great name, one you will remember because I am the ruler within these walls. I am not named after the smallest, most insignificant planet in our solar system. If we are talking space, then you may as well call me the almighty

Sun. If you make me mad, or hurt Melody, I will burn you right out of this universe. Also, there is no way I will lie down. I only serve those who are worthy. You, my friend, are nowhere close." I sit by Melody's feet. I can sense nervous energy coming from her now.

Peter and Melody talk about life. Through their conversation, I gather that he travels a lot for work. Perhaps that is why he took so long to call back? Should I reconsider my second strike? *Nah, it is easy to pick up a phone for a few minutes. Melody does it all the time when she talks with Paige. It never takes them long to coordinate walking plans.* Strike two still stands! I can sense Melody getting even more uncomfortable as Peter moves closer to her on the couch. I think now is as good a time as any to deploy my ball distraction.

I bring my ball over to Peter and set it right in the middle of his lap. There is no way for him to ignore my presence now. *Let's see what you are made of.* Peter at first tries not to acknowledge the ball or me and just swats it away. As my ball rolls off his lap, I notice that he has his eyes set on Melody. He looks at her as if she is some prize—like she is a piece of meat, almost. *Um, dude. That is highly disturbing.* His eyes seem slightly crazy all of a sudden. I place the ball back in his lap, but with more force than before. I hit his hand with my nose to signal him to play ball. All I get is "Pluto, go lie down. Maybe you should put him outside?" in a commanding tone that is more instructing Melody what to do than asking.

Excuse me mister, Melody does not need to be

told what to do. She is a brilliant, self-governing adult who needs no instruction from you. My skin prickles in agitation. I need to maintain control and continue to help him fail himself right out of this situation, our house, and our lives for good. This man is trouble. I glance over at Melody and see a look of complete annoyance spreading rapidly over her face. I am grateful that Melody is picking up on all of Peter's terrible characteristics. I have no doubt that when Peter receives his third strike in my imaginary ball game, Melody will understand my judgment and send him on his way.

"It's *Ludo*, and he is fine. He wants you to throw the ball. He did not get his evening playtime in since the two of us went out to dinner. I realize that was a choice I made, but Ludo is not doing anything wrong by merely wanting you to throw a ball. Is it really that big of an inconvenience for you?" Melody asks through gritted teeth. *Um, earth to Peter. Your actions are totally pissing her off. And I love it!*

Melody reaches over and grabs the ball from Peter's lap, frustrated. At first, Peter seems excited by her up-close-and-personal actions, but then disappointment paints his face when she turns away from him and tosses my ball up into the air. *Sucker!* I catch it and bring it back to her. I am ecstatic that Peter is making my job so easy. I have already decided that I dislike him and he is not fit for our pack. I just need to make sure Melody understands my judgement. If Peter really understood Melody at all, he would know the two of us are a package deal. *Lu, the greatest pitcher of all time, takes the mound and hurls an out-of-this-world fastball towards the plate. Peter bears down on the bat and braces for contact.*

241

Melody and I have been through so much together. In fact, if I could figure out how to arrange it, we would be physically connected at all times. *Like Siamese twins.* I read about these twins in a gossip— or, as I like to call them—garbage magazine. I think it would be great to always be connected to the one you love most. *Nothing can separate those twins. I consider them to be some of the luckiest in life!* I never mind when Melody leashes me to walk or run because this is as close to Siamese twins as I can get with her. I love always knowing where she is, and it is even easier when she is at the end of our tattered and overused leather leash. Melody only leashes me in busy places with lots of people or traffic. I like it though; my leash makes it easier for me to lead her away from trouble. It gives me more control. *I love control!*

Even on hot nights when Melody and I sleep in the bed and can't snuggle due to heat, I still extend a paw to touch her. This allows me to know if she gets up for any reason in the middle of the night. Melody has a similar tactic of her own: she reaches out to hold the tip of my tail. *She needs our closeness just as much as I do.* We ease one another's anxiety. We are each other's therapy pets. No one can ever separate us. We are a two-for-one special. Sorry, Peter. Where she goes, I go, and vice versa. *No getting this girl without this old dog in tow!*

Peter started this ball game with his arrogance and bad attitude. Now, he has me determined to end it. I take the ball back to Peter after Melody tosses it one more time. I need to show him who is boss and get him to swing for the third strike. *Man, he is easy*

to bait! Hey, batter-batter! Hey, batter-batter! Peter
is struggling to hide his irritation; I put on my most
adorable puppy-dog eyes as I give Peter the ball. I
can feel myself recapturing Melody's heart as we
lock eyes for a second. *That's right, sucker. This girl
is all mine!*

It is a good thing that people think all dogs are
cute and innocent. *Disclosure: There is a serious manipulation taking place when a dog locks eyes with a
human.* People are unaware that our oh-so-cute
puppy-dog eyes are one of the greatest mind-
controlling tactics we are capable of. In fact, the
puppy-dog eye's power may be the greatest mind
control method that exists today, period! Grandpa
and I watched a documentary on the history channel
once that showed similar tactics being used to train
soldiers in our armed forces. It was brilliant. Nothing can keep someone or something safer than a loy-
ally trained, muscled to the gills, highly educated,
armed soldier. All those soldiers need is a 'why'.
Once a soldier has a why that means so much to
them, nothing can get in their way or stop them from
completing their missions! All anyone needs to complete any goal in life is a why. *Why's are the foundation of all successes.*

Getting back to the demise of Peter and Melody's relationship—the game between him and me
continues. Melody smiles over at me and looks at
Peter, waiting to judge his next move. I have placed
the ball in his lap; it rests there like a grenade, just
waiting to blow up what little chance he has at sal-
vaging a relationship with Melody. *If you don't pull
the pin, I will. It's over, buddy.* Peter is now getting
uncomfortable. He lobs an angry look at me. I am

sure he thinks he is on to me and my little game. He then smirks at me. Peter has just received the invitation to my challenge, and he clearly thinks he is going to win this battle. *Kind of cute and a little sad, really.* Peter then turns and smiles at Melody as he heaves the ball hard into the next room.

Peter says in an annoyed, high-pitched tone, "Well, if he missed his playtime, I don't see why you don't put Pluto out in the backyard to play."

If humans could hear dogs laugh, he would have heard belly thunder coming from me. All he and Melody hear is a loud snort I can't contain. "It is your funeral, Peter. Just keep digging your hole. You will be in China before you know it." I snort numerous times as I retrieve my ball from the next room.

Melody stands up, more vexed than earlier. "Well, why don't we all go outside, then. Also, it is *Ludo*, for the last time!" Her voice is now sterner than the other times she had corrected him. *Ha, this guy is a true moron.*

I bark excitedly and run towards our back patio door. *"That's right, Jerk-pants, Melody is coming outside with me. I am Alpha number one, not number none like you!"*

Peter follows Melody and me out onto the porch. I lead the way with a massive, uncontainable grin spreading across my face. The two sit down on the patio chairs with more space between them than on the couch. *How did that work out for you, Peter? You still want to play my game?* I taunt him, cockier than I had been before. I know his final strike is only moments away. Melody takes the ball from my mouth and throws it into the yard. I catch it with the grace of a trapeze acrobat floating through the air. I then stick my landing with the ease of a gymnast. *The crowd cheers, and the judges all lift tens!*

The tension grows thick between Melody and Peter. *Hey, batter-batter. Swing!* Finally, after more than enough time has passed in silence, Melody says, "Well, it is getting late and I have to work tomorrow, so you should probably get going."

Strike three! He is out of here. The crowd goes wild! The great Lu has pitched a perfect no-hitter! I love a good ball game, and if I am being honest, Mark Buehrle is a way better pitcher than me. He and the White Sox are my favorites! Plus, there is something about Mark's beard that I envy. *A dog can dream, can't he? If I had hands and could pitch, I would also want a beard like that!*

Melody stands up, signifying to all that the game is over and Peter needs to vacate the park—I mean, our house. Melody whistles for me to join her, and I run quickly over to assume my post by her side. We all head back into the house. *Come, Peter. I will show you the door!* "How about next Saturday night?" Peter blurts nervously as he follows us inside.

I watch the skin on Peter's forehead and around his eyes wrinkle up and can tell that he is racking his brain, trying to come up with a way to save this date from dying its fateful death. *Earth to Peter – the tombstone has already been picked out, and you dug the hole a while ago with all your 'Plutos.'* I should have known he isn't smart enough to just be a good boy, tuck his tail between his legs, and leave with what little dignity he has left. No, that would be much too easy. I can tell that this is not his style at all. He loves to have all the attention on him, and he is not a man who hears no often. Another reason he is not suitable for our pack at all. *I definitely made the right call this evening!*

As Melody and I walk him to the front door, I stay in between the two. I am enforcing my dominance and making it clear that I am there as a protective barrier. I can sense apprehension coming from Melody, so I rub against her leg as we walk and nudge her hand to give her reassurance. *Don't worry, my girl. I have your back.* "I will let you know about Saturday. I may have to pick up a call at work," Melody says sympathetically.

Melody works in the medical field, and being on call now and then is a part of our lives, but I know that she doesn't have an on-call night coming soon. She only has one every third month. I can see what Melody is doing, and it makes me smile. *Lucky you, Peter. She is letting you down easy. Now, take the hint and get lost.* What I really want is for Melody to say we have to wash our hair, or something more obvious, like women do in the movies. I guess it is always best to take the high road though. I am proud of her for that.

Peter replies with a look of disappointment. "Okay. I will call you later this week to confirm plans, then." *Gag me.* This guy is something else. I can't believe Peter is so arrogant that he can't see her kindly declining his invite. Peter then tries to lean in to kiss Melody goodnight. I could sense he was up to something just before this took place.

Since I am between them, I bump Peter hard in the knees, disguising my sadistic move to make it appear like I am just some dumb dog. To them, it looks as if I am just passing by to grab my toy alligator, which is resting by the front door. *Planted there earlier, of course, by yours truly!* Peter bumps his head hard against Melody's and lets out an agitated groan. He then tries a second time. Melody is now aware of Peter's intentions and turns her face, offering him only a cheek.

Melody smiles her award-winning smile and opens the door for him, saying, "Good night, Peter. Thanks for a great evening."

"Yeah, goodnight, jerk pants, and don't come back!" I bark at Peter as he walks away. I think it is funny how some people live up to the meaning of their names. Peter means rock or stone, which makes perfect sense to me. He is one dense, block-headed dude. What a D-bag. I think that is what I have heard Aunt Kasandra and Bailey call guys before. *Though I can't say I know what a D-bag actually is.* From the context I have heard it used, I am positive they would have used it just now, though!

Chapter 31: Darkness Comes

Weeks ease past us, and Melody has not dated anyone else since Peter left. We seem to be back to our normal routine. Secretly, I am rejoicing about this. I know that one day we will need to work on recruiting and growing our pack, but I want it to be just the two of us for as long as possible. *Perhaps I am selfish.* Just the pair of us is all I need. Grandpa is around a lot, so I still count him as a full pack member.

I consider my pack to be a pack of three. It doesn't matter that we are not all living under the same roof like other conventional packs out there. *Who cares, anyway?* The people who feel the need to judge others so harshly on their status only do so because they are weak and insecure. I find that it is always better to stand out and be unique. *Go against the grain, track new ground.*

One can choose to be a leader, or one can choose to be a follower. I choose to lead. That is how I am bringing my dream of the Ultimate Alpha to life. I must help Melody understand this concept. Sometimes, I worry that she feels bad because she isn't doing the same things in life as others her age. The truth is that she really has no interest in most of those things. Melody is making a bigger difference in this world in her own way by not acting like others or striving to be like them. I must teach her to embrace her own, and everyone else's, differences. It is these small differences that make this world amazing. *The world needs to cherish this, not chastised one another for it.*

I reflect more on our unconventional pack situation and decide that since I go to Grandma's new house at least once a week; I have a pack of three and a half full-time members. *Well, look at that. I don't need to worry about adding another member right now!* I don't know what the rules are exactly; heck, some rules, as they say, are made to be broken. There are so many types of rules and standards now days it is hard to keep up with them all. Some I don't really see as rules at all, some are merely challenges that entice one to push the limits. It is when one pushes past the limits of what is conventionally acceptable that they become more of an individual and define who they are and who they want to be.

I am not saying let's break all the rules and be rebels. Of course, there are some rules that should never be broken, but that should be common sense. Those are the right-from-wrong rules. You know, basic human decency. There are ethical and moral standards that should govern us all. These are the no-brainer laws of life; don't steal, don't cheat, always help the next guy or gal in line, you get the idea. I decide I will color outside the lines of the conventional rules of how to count my pack members. *I can count my pack members however I want.* It's my pack. That being said, I can't find a good reason to work on growing my pack just yet, especially when everything in life seems so perfect right now. Melody is learning and transitioning so much at the moment. She is finally taking time for her own personal growth and putting the thoughts and opinions of others out of her mind. So far, I am loving the outcome! I want us to stay just the Melody and Ludo Show for a while longer. *Maybe even forever!*

Weeks roll into months, and our always sunny and seventy-degree environment is growing darker and colder. Melody is no longer thriving and growing; she is succumbing to the pressures that others place on her. Her light is dimming again. She is becoming more unhappy and restless than usual. Melody has recently developed a new horrible habit: self-shaming in front of the mirror. *I hate it!*

Mirrors are evil. That is why dogs bark at and bite them. We can sense the corrupt consciousness lurking behind the glass. Everything has two shadows: a maleficent one and a charitable one. If only the world could rid itself of the villainous shadows. Reflections should only be looked at in water. When we look at ourselves upon a water's surface, the ripples help us fight away the mistaken beliefs. I must destroy these terrible mirrors and rid the world of them. *If only I had hands!*

Melody is slowly slipping back into darker territory. Some days, we miss our morning walk because she is too tired. *I think they call this depression. I have seen it in Grandpa, too.* Melody seems to be reverting back into the same state she had been in when she was confined to the chair with wheels. I notice that she has not been taking care of her body as much as she used to; it seems to me that she is starting to give up on life again. I need to figure out what is going on with her. I did not give her the gift of a miracle for nothing. I refuse to sit back and let her waste away along with my legacy.

I bump my observational detective skills up a notch so I can discover the problem and amend it ASAP. After all, German Shepherds are known worldwide for our amazing detective skills. *Cops don't like working without us. I bet even detectives long to be us at times. To be honest, if cops had our noses, crimes would be solved much faster.*

My detective skills sense that Melody has an issue with her self-worth. It seems to be tied to finding a male pack-mate although I don't have the foggiest idea why. I think television shows and magazines target women and try to make them feel helpless without a man. Wrong—women can be Alphas, too, and I am sure Melody is one. I have to get her to realize this. *Come on, my girl. Open your eyes already!*

Chapter 32: Fire Burns

One evening, Melody comes home a little later than usual. Normally, this would have concerned me slightly, but she wears a smile on her face. I am curious to find out the reason behind the upward curve that had been lost to her lips as of late. I sniff her immediately for clues. To my dismay, I can smell other dogs and a man.

My brow furrows. I am unhappy due to her lateness, and I don't care for the scent of the dog breed she had spent her time with this evening. Worry finds me instantly. The smell of the man and his dogs is not something Melody should place any of her trust in. *Am I overreacting out of jealousy?*

One thing I have always been certain of is the information I get from my trusty sniffer. My nose has never been wrong. As twilight falls fast upon us this evening, an ominous darkness creeps in. I sense another of life's storms brewing. What I wouldn't give for a human tongue to warn Melody of the treachery headed in our direction. She needs to take cover.

Over the next few months, Melody comes home late more often. At first, she is happy, but as the weeks pass by, all the looks of satisfaction vanish. Melody's brow creases due to the constant frustration that threatens to permanently paint itself on her face. I need to find a way to warn her. Melody is playing with fire and, more than likely will get burnt. Fire damage is irreversible. *Come on, Melody. You are stronger than this.* I need to get her to crouch down below the smoke so she can find her way out. *Why can't you see the danger?*

Melody continues in life as a zombie from *The Walking Dead*. It pains me to watch her blindly walk through the smoke from the fire in which she plays. I hate feeling helpless, too. Some of life's lessons must be learned the hard way. I smell Melody upon her late arrivals and learn more each time. The size of the dark threats that Melody's bright future faces grow larger each time she visits with her new friends.

The man she is spending time with has a male and a female dog of the same breed. While there are no bad dog breeds, there are bad owners. I can tell that these dogs are the products of such a case. *If we will add dogs to our pack, I will be the one picking them out.* There is no way I will ever allow these untrustworthy meatheads and their owner into our house, and most certainly not our lives!

I decided long ago that I will allow Melody to have some say on the humans we add to our pack. This is fair since she is one. *Let's face it: Melody is the one who must interact with them more than me, anyway.* I, however, will never, ever, let her pick out the dogs! I have standards. I don't think they are high, but rule number one is no meatheads, and number two is no unintelligent dogs! The breed I am sniffing acts on impulse and is not known for thinking things through. The fact that they have been raised poorly only worsens the bad behaviors and habits they have learned in life thus far. *None of this will stand in our house!* I am already tasked with the job of training Melody. I can't add two meatheads and a sinister male to my list. *Life is short and time is precious.* Melody and I are destined for greatness; we don't need anything or anyone holding us back! I must get this message to Melody even if it kills me!

The evenings when Melody comes straight home from work are the best. They give me a chance to breathe. There seems to be a crappy fifty-fifty split lately between coming straight home and coming home after stopping over at Mystery Man's house. At least when Melody comes straight home, I get my evening walk in with lots of playtime and extra snuggles on the couch. I think she feels guilty and is struggling with a lot of internal feelings. I feel that Melody should feel a little guilty, especially since she is putting someone else not just before me, but also herself. I don't put anyone else before her. Nonetheless, I will take whatever time I can get with her. I need as much time as she will allow to find a way to guide her out of the massive relationship firestorm she has landed in. Melody is still far from being her one-hundred-percent, bright, shiny self again, but seeing her struggle with guilt right now gives me hope. There are days I can see her light cutting through the darkness that has settled into our lives. *Grab onto and harness that light, Melody. I will lead you out!*

Unfortunately, Melody sticks fast to her weird zombie-like auto-pilot mode. She is settling in life and can't see it. My heart breaks for her. There are lessons and paths in life we must walk alone and learn the hard way. I see now that this is one of those times for Melody. All I can do is be here for her and help her pick up the pieces after this fire burns out. *Will there be any of my Melody left after it runs its course?* Only time will tell. My internal monster grows bigger himself. He is feeding voraciously on the stress and anxiety from the current murky state of our lives.

Presently, the best moments in our lives are when we are out mowing the lawn together. *Sad, I know.* We play Frisbee the entire time, and my joyful acrobatic catches always bring a smile to Melody's lips and a warmth and the sparkle I love so much back into her eyes. I have noticed that lately her eyes have lost their luster for life and seem to get increasingly darker with each passing day. I notice that when we are out doing yard maintenance, Melody's mood lifts significantly. *That's it. This is the key!*

Since meeting this Mystery Man, Melody has given up on all the self-maintenance she used to practice religiously. This man is putting pressure and time constraints I don't approve of on Melody. He keeps making Melody choose between herself, and me, or him and his needs. Melody's biggest problem right now is the poor choices she keeps making. She is choosing Mystery Man over herself and ignoring herself and me to appease him! She has elected to give herself a backseat in her own life! *Wake up, my girl. We are not back-seaters. We are drivers, innovators, and creators of happiness!* This world needs us at our best. *I need you at your best!*

255

Melody is a lot like me. We are always happiest when we are outside and active. She and I are not lazy. I am struggling to figure out why she is slipping into the unsatisfied, lackadaisical life she always detested seeing others in. Before this man entered her life, Melody would often scoff when she saw others living sub-optimally. When we saw them, Melody would explain that she didn't understand why people would choose to live an unmotivated and unrewarding life. *How do I alert her to the fact she is doing the same thing now?*

Melody has always seen other people's potentials. *It is one of her gifts.* Melody always tries to help these people see the error of their ways and lift them up with positivity when they allow her to do so. She learned long ago that you can't help someone who is unwilling to help themselves first. *Another of life's brutal lessons.* I am worried that Melody may have burnt herself out trying to help Mystery Man and now it has somehow sucked the positivity right out of her. Lately, Melody just passes by these people who need her help. She is applying the same dismal existence to her own life and can no longer help others. *Don't settle, Melody. Settling is the worst thing you can do!*

In the past, Melody has always understood that the people she meets in life that have fallen on hard times have to change their current circumstances. Ultimately, each life of ours is the byproduct of all the choices we have made along our life's journey. Melody has always at least tried to reach these people as she has crossed paths with them and help them understand that they, and only they can make things better for themselves. She has offered them a kindness by showing them the richness that lies within them. She hoped that once these people see the gold inside themselves, they will want to grab hold of it and therefore make a change. This is a big part of the vision I have for my Ultimate Alpha legacy. I thought I had already achieved this part by teaching Melody to give this gift to others. Once these people have the gift, they will pass it on as well to the next person they meet that is struggling with something. *Like ripples on the water's surface, the happiness spreads! Joy gains immortality.*

Recently, Melody has lost sight of the luminosity within herself. I can only attribute this to her spending time with Mystery Man. Unfortunately for me, this setback of ours is detrimental for my quest for my legacy, it has forced me to return to 'GO'. In the process, I was not allowed to collect my two hundred dollars. Melody and I are starting back over in a nearly bankrupt state. *I loved the game Monopoly until now. I hope she learns this lesson of hers soon so we can move forward again.*

Another year passes Melody and I by in this subpar manner. It seems like Melody is barely getting by at this point. I consider this depressive slump far worse than when she was in her wheelchair after the accident. I miss that chair. Right now, I would give my nuts, *if I still had them*, to go back in time and start over. I must have missed teaching her something vital. We need a do-over, but life does not give do-overs. Life lacks a rewind button. The only way forward is to admit to and own the mistakes we have made. Only then can we gain the strength to try again and find success. The darkness surrounding us is the blackest it has ever been. I don't like how Melody seems to look at pill bottles and knives lately. She gazes at these items longer than what I feel is appropriate. When Melody looks at them, her eyes are vacant and she appears lost. This frightens the hair right off my body and chills my blood to an icy temperature. I am shedding like never in the dead of winter!

The only thing I can attribute all Melody's changes to is her inability to tune out the opinions of others, and the arrival of this mystery man in her life. My evening time with Melody is being more affected by this unknown man, and my distaste for him is growing stronger. If Melody is not with him physically, then she spends part of the evening talking to him on the phone. It is because of this that I fault him most for the bereaved state of my girl. This man is playing mind games with her that are ultimately destroying her. *I hate manipulators!* He must have figured out the puppy-dog eye power and is using it to exploit Melody. Sure, I use it here and there for my personal gain, but only for an occasional extra treat. I have never harmed Melody or threatened her state of mind.

Mystery Man's intrusion on my time and quality of life with Melody has gone far enough. I too have the power of choice, and I choose not to stand for this any longer. It seems as if Melody and his relationship is only on and off again. *It is whatever is convenient for him.* Melody and I have lived almost another entire year with a sad, dismal existence, and it is all thanks to this unknown infiltrator. I draw my line in the metaphorical sand. I need to meet this man and either accept him or get rid of him. I can hardly believe two years have passed us by and I have still never met him! I am leaning strongly towards getting rid of him as being the only option at this point. Something in my heart tells me that this man needs saving also so I should be careful with my judging, but I fear I can't save them both. *Melody is my priority.*

Melody's work life is also going stale and not helping our situation, either. Unbeknown to her, the private clinic she works at has become a ticking time bomb, and it is on the verge of exploding. The stress in her life has become a volcano of molten lava that will erupt at any moment. Between Mystery Man—who, in my opinion, doesn't deserve the title of a man—and Melody's work, our life is falling apart! The sparkle in Melody's eyes is fading fast; I have no doubt it will soon be gone entirely. I vowed never to let this happen again, so it is time to intervene and keep my promise. If Mount Melody explodes, she will not survive. I cannot stand by and let her be burnt alive by her own lava. I can see no other way out of our situation, I have to give Melody one more miracle.

Melody means more than anything in the world. If I lose her, my life will not be worth living. One thing I have learned over the years is that life is always worth living. Once I get Melody back from this depressive state, I will make sure she never gets lost again. I got cocky and arrogant over the years. I took things for granted. It is time for Melody and me to eat some humble pie. We will not make the same mistakes again. Melody and I will have to up our daily training after this miracle, but we will survive and thrive again! *Perhaps I could get Melody a shock collar. Then, if she seems to be reverting to nonsense thinking, I can zap her back to reality.*

First things first: Melody needs a new job. That is number one. My number two task will deal with this mystery douche bag. It is far past time for him to be exterminated. Melody is always irritated and stressed out when returning from her current job or his house. I will not stand for this any longer. *It ends now!* Emotions storm through me, fueling my powers. *Nothing is stronger in life than a passion-filled 'why'!* I have had enough of my always positive Melody becoming increasingly negative lately! Melody needs to see life as it is and should be: fun, positive, and beautiful. When Melody leaves for work today, I unleash an epic and explosive two-part miracle out into the universe.

Kaboom!

Chapter 33: Don't Count Your Chickens

Monday morning arrives and when Melody gets to work this morning, she is greeted by some FBI agents and an unpleasant surprise. Fear not–my little gem of a girl has done nothing wrong. However, the lovely agents inform her that her work licenses will be in jeopardy if she does not immediately quit. The doctors she has been working for, unbeknown to her, have been up to some fraudulent billing. It is far pastime it catches up with them. *Task number one, check. Stressful job: gone.*

Having a now jobless master does not stress me out in the slightest. Melody is very intelligent and good at her job. She and I need a vacation. By its end, Melody will have multiple job offers. Melody returns home from work in the early afternoon. She didn't have much of a choice since the agents forced her to quit immediately. Melody walks through our front door, wearing a mask of stress on her face and carrying a large bottle of wine in one of her hands. The wine is opened almost immediately as it comes into our house. One thing is clear: I am not belabored by her now jobless state, but Melody is.

Melody greets me as usual with a quick massage-like rub down on my neck and shoulders, and tops it off with a kiss on my head. Then, she prepares my dinner. This is a few hours earlier than normal, but I don't mind. Melody is home with me where she belongs, and where I can continue to fix this mess, we are in. This is the only thing that matters in our lives at the moment.

As I eat my early supper, I am surprised to find that I am not fatigued or tired at all from my miracle work this morning. Perhaps the universe has thrown me a bone and do this one for Melody without charging its usual price. *Thanks for the two-for-one, universe!* This is the only thing that makes sense. After all, the doctors Melody had been working for are corrupt. The FBI and karma would catch up with them, eventually. Melody speaks, interrupting my thoughts: "Sorry, Lu, we can't walk tonight. I have to find a new job or we will be homeless in no time!" Melody settles in next to me on the floor with her glass of wine and tells me all about the crazy events of her day. I give her my listening ears and my most concerned 'it will all be okay' face. She rises and pours a second glass of wine, then fires up her laptop. *Let the job-hunting begin!* I rest my head on her feet to show her my full support.

I cannot keep the smile off my face. I know that rainbow-filled days are headed our way as soon as the rainstorm that is putting out the fires that threaten our lives clears. The original miracle I had summoned up this morning has two parts, and I am sure that the last half of my miracle will not be another universe freebie. The only way I will get a two-for-none special out of the universe is if this mystery guy is a bad man like the doctors. I have serious doubts that this is actually the case, though, especially since he is bright enough to own dogs and not cats. I will need to be strong for the second part of this miracle. Getting Melody out of her lousy job was the easy part. I have no idea what exactly to do when I come face to face with Mystery Man.

This man has strung her along for years now, and somehow, he still eludes me. *I am sure he has some sort of power.* I thought dogs and small children were the only ones capable of the innocent eye-catching power of manipulation. Somehow, Mystery Man must have hung onto it as he grew up. *This makes him very dangerous in my book.* Visions of baring my teeth with a lioness growl while he pees his pants and runs away dance in my head as Melody e-mails off countless résumés.

Mystery Man calls Melody as she is job searching this evening. As I listen to his and Melody's quick phone interaction, my hatred for him grows even thicker. Not only did he interrupt my much-needed nap, but apparently Ghost Man had not answered his phone earlier when Melody called him on her way home to vent about her stressful day.

Isn't that part of being one's partner in life? Aren't they supposed to be there for one another in times of crisis and stress? I am, and always will be, there for Melody with everything! I refuse to let any lesser male who is not willing to do the same into our lives. It is time for Mystery Man to be gone. Melody needs someone who will be there for her. When we get a new male pack member, he will be someone who makes Melody a better person, and me a better dog! He will be a man who adds value to our lives, not one who devalues them, as Mystery Man does.

He is a pessimistic parasite. *All parasites can, and will be, exterminated!* The battle is about to commence.

The next part of my miracle is deploying. It will boost Melody's self-esteem and get rid of Mystery Man for good. *At least, I hope this is how it will unfold.* I need the headlines of history to read: 'The Great Battle of Ludo vs Mystery Man Ends in an Epic Defeat. Mystery Man Vacates the Premises With His Metaphorical Tail Between His Legs!' Melody is so beaten down. I need my happy-go-lucky girl back. I don't exactly know how the next part of my miracle will unfold, but I know I am ready for anything!

Melody and Mystery Man argue more than they talk on the phone. Finally, the conversation ends with Melody hanging up without a goodbye. She then throws the phone into the living room, saying, "What a jerk! What am I doing with my life?" *Could it be that I have worked my two miracles in one day? Am I getting that good?* This is not quite how I had planned it, but I will happily take credit for it. *Is the battle over before it has begun?*

Another two weeks pass Melody and I by. They are wonderful. I have my Melody back full-time. She is stressed from not working, but has gone to several job interviews. I know that Melody will get more than a few offers soon, so I am just enjoying our time together while it lasts. I know that it will end shortly and I will have to train her on yet another new schedule.

My hope that the battle between Mystery Man and me is over are unfortunately squashed. Mystery Man continues to call often, and Melody always answers. I am filled with even more disappointment when Melody gives in and goes to visit him. *I must figure out what power he has over her. What am I up against?* I have one thing working in my favor now: when Melody goes to visit Mystery Man; she returns heavily annoyed. I must work extra hard to cheer her up upon arrival. Even though I am tired of this, I see it as something that will only aid my cause during our upcoming battle.

It is time to get rid of Mystery Man for good. I realize that the only way this is possible is through a face-to-face meeting. I have to show Melody his true colors. The next time Mystery Man calls, I get Melody to demand that if things are to continue between the two; he needs to start coming over and making more of an effort. Her exact words are: "Why should I always have to drive to your house? You haven't worked in months. I have a life, and I like being at home where I can relax with my dog. I should not have to cater to you. If you want me to be a part of your life, then you have to be a part of mine!"

I hope that things are over between them after that conversation. Ghost Man has not come to our house once in the past two years, and I seriously doubt he plans to start now. *Take that ultimatum and shove it, you cowardly excuse of a male.* I prance proudly through the house as Melody hangs up the phone.

The next week comes, breathing more fresh and invigorating air into our lives. Melody receives two job offers. She chooses the most local job since our house has not sold yet. *I didn't even know our house was for sale.* I had been so caught up in getting rid of

Mystery Man that I must have missed that conversation. Also, I had failed to notice the 'Dickerson Niemen' sign in the yard. It isn't until Melody states her reasons for choosing the local job I catch wind of this.

Melody and I go out into the backyard to frolic and celebrate her new job. A joyous play session is underway when suddenly, we are interrupted. I wouldn't have believed it myself if I wasn't standing right next to Melody to witness the next set of events. Melody had just finished telling me how good of a boy I was for making an excellent Frisbee catch when an ominous presence arrives outside the gate to our yard.

Prepare yourselves, people. You are about to witness the arrival of—drum roll, please.... Mystery Man! This occurrence shocks a fart right out of me. I wish it would have been louder to really represent my opinion on this matter. At the least, I hope that it smells rotten. I want it to reflect the situation that stands facing us. Unfortunately, it does not. Melody and I eat too clean for that. *That's right, folks. My farts smell like roses!*

Mystery Man has come over to our house uninvited and unannounced to congratulate Melody on her new job! I also assume he came over because she gave him an ultimatum when they spoke last week. To my knowledge, the two have not spoken since. *Dang, Mystery Man is more of a contender in this battle than I thought!* I feel his congratulatory hello to Melody lacks sincerity as he arrives and lets himself in through our gate without an invitation.

I find his actions to be peculiar. I can smell cigarette smoke clinging to his clothes, which is unacceptable. Arrogance pours off of him for reasons unknown. Mystery Man is a jobless, unmotivated, and self-absorbed man. *What is there for him to be arrogant about?* I would kill for Melody to have an ounce of the confidence that this man walks with though.

The battle is about to ensue. My only option now is to win. Never will there be a smoker in my pack! My instincts alert me to Mystery Man's ultramanipulative and negative personality. He has such a dark presence about him that I have a hard time not growling the second he sets foot in our backyard. *Be smart, Lu. You must defeat him with kindness and chivalry.* Calmness and determination settles over me. The time is now!

Mystery Man relaxes and really let out his evil personality. He makes himself comfortable on one of our patio chairs. Every time Melody says something positive about her new job, he counters it with a negative fact. *Hey, jerk pants, why can't you let her be happy?* I am struggling to maintain higher ground. I do not understand people who feel the need to voice their crappy opinions whenever someone else says something positive or talks about something that makes them feel good. I spit at Mystery Man's words in disgust, but disguise it with a sneeze. Melody is getting annoyed. I plan to use this to my advantage.

My temper grows hotter by the second. I really want to rip one of his pompous hands off when he tries to sound educated and superior as he talks down to Melody. *I thought you came to celebrate with us. What a waste of a human.* Mystery Man is making Peter look like a suitable choice, and I didn't think that was possible. *Life's full of surprises!*

I am grateful that Melody and I stay outside when Mystery Man arrives. Melody never likes to be close to people when she is uncomfortable. I recall her making the same move when poor Peter was over. I almost wish Peter was back now. He was far easier to defeat. Mystery Man keys in on Melody's annoyance and tries to butter her up by not being as much of a butthead. Melody isn't falling victim to his game though. *That's my girl!*

The past two weeks have allowed Melody to gain some of her dwindling strength back. She stands on the back porch, looking out into our yard. I think she is considering what to do. Since Melody is not giving Mystery Man the time of day, he walks over to her and puts his arms around her waist. I have to fight a tremendous urge to bite him in the meaty part of his butt cheek. I especially struggle not to attack when she moves away from him and asks him not to touch her.

Mystery Man says, "Calm down. I am just kidding around. I am not working right now, you know that. I am just jealous you got another job so fast." He reaches for her again, and she backs farther away. Mystery Man pursues her one more time, and I decide I have seen enough.

I bite down hard on the hammy part of Mystery Man's thigh. I had not intended to resort to violence, but he left me with no choice. "No!" Melody says. I growl up at him.

I make sure not to break Mystery Man's skin. I

only want to send him a message. *More of a warning, really.* Mystery Man needs to leave Melody alone! I place myself directly between the two. Mystery Man yelps like a schoolgirl and swings quickly. He hits me so hard on the top of my head that my teeth make an awful sound as they clank together. All I can see is stars. When Mystery Man does this, I let out warning bark. This is a battle I will die fighting if things go much further south. I am not sure Mystery Man is prepared for what he is up against. "Consider yourself warned, D-bag. It is about to get real western up in here!"

Melody reads a series of Joe Pickett novels by C. J. Box. It is our all-time favorite series! Anyway, whenever situations in the books are about to get hairy or a battle is about to ensue, Joe Pickett always says, "Things are about to get real western!" I have a much better understanding of the statement's meaning right now! *Where is Nate Romanowski when you need him though?*

I fight to get the stars in my vision sorted out. I need to figure out my next move. Melody moves as fast as a bolt of lightning and thrusts herself between Ghost Man and myself, yelling, "Knock it off, both of you!" Her voice is filled with fierce determination. I sit and obey immediately. I have never seen her like this!

If Mystery Man was smart, he would have done the same thing. Instead, he raises a tight fist in Melody's face as he snarls, "That dog needs to be taught a lesson!"

I shrink further behind Melody, half seeking protection and half staying close in case she commands an attack. I know that today will not be like any of my previous practice sessions when her or Grandpa wear the big puffy coat. Adrenaline courses through my veins more intensely than ever before. This is real life, not pretend. I have never wanted to hurt anyone for real, and I don't want to start now. I know what happens to dogs if they break a human's skin. I want none of the possible fates that follow those situations, but I am not about to let my Melody get hurt, either. *It's do-or-die time.*

Melody's eyes turn from ocean blue to red. Like me, Melody has been overtaken by a protective rage. I saw a mother Grizzly bear do this on a documentary once when a pack of wolves came after her cubs. Melody is the spitting image of that mama bear right now. I prepare myself for a fight with Mystery Man. I am ready to go down the road of no return. I give a final warning growl and raise all my hair to look as big as possible. Melody always calls this look of mine 'porcupining.' In the past, I am always scolded whenever I do this. Today, though, she doesn't say a word.

Melody grabs my collar and pushes me farther behind her. I have never seen her assume such a threatening, vehement stance, nor did I know that she was even capable of it. *She makes my porcupining look like a fluffy, cuddly bunny.* Pure anger and hatred pours out of Melody. I think even the mother grizzly bear would have abandoned her cubs and run in the other direction if it faced Melody in this state. *Heck, I am about to run to Grandpa's and seek shelter.*

Melody is a nuclear weapon on the verge of exploding. "Touch me or one hair on that dog's head again and I will end you right here, right now!" I step towards Mystery Man, growling for effect, but Melody places a firm grip on my collar and pulls me behind her once again. In reality, I am just as shocked as Mystery Man is. I have no intention of doing anything but what I am told so as not to make Melody any angrier. *Running seems like the best option for both Mystery Man and me at this point!* If I disobey Melody's command while she is in this state, I risk losing part of our bond, or a body part. I decide that I will act only if Mystery Man strikes Melody as he had me. At that point, I will have no choice but to end him here and now as Melody promised! *No way will I let Melody go down the road of no return.* I will be the one to go for his throat if needed.

Mystery Man receives Melody's message loud and clear. Gratitude fills me when he turns and retreats, leaving the yard in a fury. I bark at him to make sure he continues towards the driveway and out of our lives for good. *Ludo for the win! Mystery Man is out of here! The crowd goes wild, chanting, 'Ludo, Ludo...'*

If there was a crowd watching the events that just took place, they would have chanted Melody's name. I am so proud of her for realizing her worth! Mystery Man turns as I bark our final goodbye and yells, "Screw you, and your stupid, crazy dog. Enjoy living your life like a crazy old lonely cat woman!"

How can Melody be an old lonely cat woman? Melody isn't old, she will never own a cat so long as I am around, and I will see to it she is never lonely. The only stupid one around is Mystery Man, and I

271

think it is finally safe to say we will not have to worry about him anymore. Melody kneels next to me and hugs me around the neck after Mystery Man leaves. She is crying as she says, "You are always looking out for me. I don't see it sometimes and I am sorry. Thanks, Lu."

I know, Melody. That's what I am here for. Don't worry, your eyes are open more than ever now! I am so proud of us. Our battle against Mystery Man could not have gone any better. I am also elated that neither of us had to go down the fatal road of no return! I know now that Melody would kill for me, and I for her. Our bond is now stronger than it has ever been before.

Chapter 34: The New Job

Monday arrives, and Melody and I are determined to start the week off right. We run up to Grandpa's performing our normal alarm clock routine. It is a pleasant spring morning; the smell of dew-covered cherry blossoms hangs in the air. There's only one thing that I don't like about spring: it leads to summer. Call me crazy, but I like winter. I love the way the cold air bites at my wet nose and how the snow and ice crunch under my paws as I walk on top. Winter and fall are my favorite seasons. If there was a way to reduce the seasons down to three and get rid of summer, I would be all for it.

Summer is just too darn warm for me and my plush fur coat. Between the heat and the humidity, I look like a cross between a melting snowman and a molting rabbit. Summers are awful. I'm grateful that Melody took the time to find me a good groomer who shaves my heavy coat off when summer rolls in. I look like a giant squirrel when shaved, and some neighborhood dog's laugh at me as we run by, but my comfort is worth a few laughs! I am trying to teach Melody not to place so much value in others' opinions when it comes to appearances. I figure me walking around like a giant squirrel is the Ultimate Alpha way to lead by example.

273

After visiting with Grandpa and Denali for a quick pep talk and a cup of coffee, Grandpa wishes Melody good luck on her first day at her new job. Melody and I head back home to ready her for work. I am not sure which of us is more excited for this new step in our life. I know good things are coming our way now she has rid herself of Mystery Man and her other stressful job. Sometimes, we must fall down so we can get back up and stand taller than before. The last few days have not been pretty, but the sun now shines brighter upon us because we have survived the storm!

Melody is more jubilant than she has been in months. I think the loss of Mystery Man was much needed. After he left the other day, it worried me at first; I thought she might be sad or try to win him back. Melody pleasantly surprised me when she instead seemed happier and more relieved than ever. I watch as Melody straightens her hair in our bathroom this morning. Positive vibes bounce back and forth between us as she moves on to do her makeup.

Melody never wears much makeup. She only ever puts on a little mascara and some coconut lipgloss. I often try to lick the gloss from her lips when her face is close enough. It tastes so good! Melody must have read my mind because she extends a coconut-flavored finger out after applying gloss to her lips. I gleefully lick her finger clean. Next, Melody heads to her closet to pick out some clothes.

Due to the chill in the air and the ominous spring clouds, Melody decides that it would be best to leave me in the house while she is at work today. Upon leaving, Melody says, "I will be back early today. The first day is only orientation. Hold the fort down. I will see you soon, big guy!" It is nice to have my spritely Melody back. She bends down and smooches the top of my head like she always does before leaving for work. I quickly tilt my head up and extend my tongue, getting myself another tongue full of her coconut lip gloss! She falls for this trick every time. "Gross, Lu! Really?" She wipes at her mouth with the back of her arm, then smiles at me. I got my baby back, baby back, baby back! Great, now I am thinking of ribs... But all I can taste is coconut.

As promised, Melody returns home a few hours later, stress-free and all smiles. She quickly packs a 'we are going on an adventure' bag and commands me to grab my leash by the front door. We then head out to our Jeep. Woo-hoo, adventure time! "Where are we going?" I bark.

Even though I can't speak human words, Melody often knows what I am saying. She answers my question as we both load into the Jeep. "Ready to go see Grandma? I thought we could celebrate today with dinner and a stroll."

"Yes! Yes! Grandma! It has been too long since we last saw her!" I bark excitedly to speed Melody up. Sometimes, she is so much like Grandpa she drives me crazy. After a short car ride, Melody and I unload our things at Grandma's apartment. I am excited to see that she is doing very well! The mood in her apartment is cheery, and I greedily coax extra snuggles and cuddles from her.

Grandma has ordered delicious takeout from the Italian joint in town, and it arrives at her apartment a short time after we do. Melody prepares my dinner in the dog dish that Grandma keeps in the cupboard next to her other dishes. We should come here more often. Grandma always treats me like a king! While we all eat, Melody gives Grandma and me the abbreviated version of her first day of work at the hospital. The dark clouds that had loomed over Melody's head have finally floated away. Ludo the Great has done it again! Insert chanting crowd here: Ludo, Ludo, Ludo!

As Melody recounts her day, I notice that she keeps circling the conversation back to a guy who sat next to her at orientation. Melody describes him as the dreamiest, most intriguing male she has ever met. What? A new guy? We just got rid of the last one, and it took us over two years to erase him! I am about to get anxious and annoyed all over again when thankfully; she eases my thoughts by saying she will keep her guard up this time. I am also excited to hear Melody thinks nothing will come of her meeting this man since he had recently gotten divorced and was likely doing the same. Melody uses a word I don't quite understand: "I would probably just be a rebound, anyway." I decide that her words are music to my ears! I have a feeling that there is more to Melody wanting to keep her guard up than just the possibility of being a rebound. I don't want that for her at all, and to be honest I don't know how it would be possible anyway. She isn't a basketball.

You're Welcome

Melody is moving forward in life, but she is bearing few new emotional scars now. Perfect. At least this means she learned a few things from our last experience. I hope she doesn't feel like she needs to go man-shopping on my account. I think we are just fine the way we are now: alone! If I have learned anything over the past year, it is that Melody officially sucks at picking men. I don't know if she is blinded by their good looks, or maybe they are just smooth in the talking department, but either way, I gave her way too much credit a while back when I said she was good at picking up on people's intentions. I should have said other women's intentions. There is something about men that Melody seems to be blind to. I am currently helping her work on her self-esteem, which seems to be a large part of her problem. I think men prey on nice women like Melody. It is almost as if they seek the women who struggle with self-confidence issues. After our encounter with Mystery Man, I have decided that I, too, will pick out the male human pack-mate when it is time to grow our tribe!

I believe these are called 'arranged marriages.' These types of relationships are more popular in other countries, according to the History channel. I see arranged marriages as an acceptable and practice for our current circumstances. I hope that Melody will be open to the idea when I finally bring it up. I am waiting until I have the right man lined up. No way can we survive another two years like the last few were with Mystery Man, that was miserable!

Chapter 35: Meet Kenner

Spring has already sprung, and summer is now burning its way into our lives. I hope that the past few weeks of nice weather are the cause of Melody's increasingly happy mood. *Yes, probably the weather.* I find it weird that humans love summer so much. I am sure it's partly because they lack permanent fur coats. I find it most gratifying that humans have adopted the custom of wearing clothes over the years. Humans have hairless bodies that are often skinny, and they look awkward walking around in their inefficient vertical manner. I have seen my fair share of naked humans over the years, as I slept on the cold, tiled bathroom floor when Melody and I lived at Grandpa's house. I didn't care for the views that often came with being in the bathroom, but it was the coldest room in Grandpa's house. Naked humans are almost as odd-looking as the hairless cat or the Chinese Crested dog. Those are the only two kinds of animals that can get away with wearing sweaters and jackets and not look like fools while doing so.

Melody has made new friends at work. She has also started going out with her old friends more often. She is finally embracing life again. Melody's eyes glitter more brightly than I have ever seen them before. Finally, Melody appears to have pulled herself free of the giant black hole in her life that had been trying so hard to suck her in. *Have I finally prevailed in my quest to get through to her? Does she see now what I have always seen?*

Melody wakes each morning with the energy and vibrancy of a lark. She has started dreaming bigger again and has stopped living small. I am so proud of her for drawing her line in the sand and not falling victim to a life of settling. Two paths were placed before Melody and me. As her loyal and trusted sidekick, I would have happily followed her down either one, but I am beyond ecstatic she chose the path of opportunity, not the safe and easy road of the mundane. Together, Melody and I can weather any storm that comes our way. We can climb any mountain we choose! *Melody will be an Ultimate Alpha after all! I am good at this being-an-awesome-dog thing. Ultimate legacy, here I come!*

I am enjoying more walks and twice the play time with Melody due to her new job. Her previous job never afforded us such luxuries. I attribute the extra quality time I am receiving to the fact that Melody's new place of work is thirty miles closer than her prior one. *Less commute time equals more me time!* Why I didn't orchestrate a new job for Melody years ago is beyond me. *Perhaps I was settling, too.* Oh well. Hindsight, as they say, is twenty-twenty. Dogs do not live in the past where regret lies. *Onward we march!*

Along with our warm weather trend, I key in on another contributor to Melody's increasing happiness: she has been returning from work smelling of the same human male. *Please be a patient. Please, oh please be a patient!* I desperately hope that the scent I'm picking up on is not a potential male pack-mate for our family! The last relationship Melody had with a human male was calamitous. I fear ever having to battle another ghostly shell of a man. That being said, I am not sure one could classify what Melody had with Mystery Man as an actual relationship. The man was a ghost, and was only around sporadically over the past few years. *Personally, I don't think it counts.* I note that every time Melody smells of this new man when she returns home; she is also in a chipper mood. Aside from hoping that this guy is a patient, I can only hope that Melody's choosing skills have gotten better. Hopefully, Melody has learned from our prior situation, as well as the lessons I have been trying to teach her over the past six years. Time passes so quickly and it is so precious. I am truly blessed to be spending all my time with my human soul-mate.

Humans miss out on so much of this wonderful world. They look at everything through half-open, jaded eyes and closed minds. I feel bad for them. Their senses are so poor, especially their sense of smell. For example, they think dead fish smell horrific when, in reality, they are missing the fish's true depths and undertones. The smell of a dead fish is out-of-this-world magical and beyond mouthwatering. If they could truly smell the real thing and see the beautiful circle of life it represents, they would want to roll in fish guts as well!

Two more weeks pass, and the phone rings. This new man is now calling my Melody. I have decided that even if it is a patient, this guy is interested in her and Melody is interested in him. I wish humans would just sniff butts and get it over with. Instead, they play silly cat-and-mouse games and waste heaps of time. Just the other day, Melody asked me how long she should wait before calling this new guy back. Of course, I said forever! Melody, however, ignored me and called him back right away. *I swear, sometimes she only hears what she wants to!*

To my disappointment, Melody and this new man talk on the phone frequently and for what I feel is an overly extended length of time. I fear the phone may try to attach itself to Melody's face. This reminds me of Stranger Lady from all those years ago. Often, Melody will set her phone down and switch it to the speaker setting so she doesn't have to hold it any longer. I can only imagine how cramped her hands and neck must be after some of their long conversations. Most the time, Melody and this man talk about the most random and seemingly unimportant things. *Humans...* I try to listen and learn as much as I can about this new man when Melody puts the phone on speaker, but usually after a few minutes pass, I become uninterested and end up wandering off to play with my favorite orange gator. Sometimes, Melody and this man even talk me to sleep. *Madness!*

I guess I can't really complain, as I really do like the phone's speaker setting. It makes me feel like I am being included in the conversation, and I can keep tabs on Melody's mood and what is being said when it fluctuates. I have to admit; I find this man's deep timbre fascinating and calming. His voice isn't feminine like Peter's was, and it is not whiney and arrogant like Ghost Man's. *So that is a plus, I think.* Also, this new man seems to make her happy. I mean, thrilled. I have not witnessed Melody ever being upset or moody after she talks with him. Their conversations always end with Melody wearing big, goofy grins.

I have decided that this potential pack-mate can have two check marks in the pros column. Because he and Melody talk so frequently, I figure I may as well judge him now. This way, I can intervene sooner if needed. I realize that part of my newfound leniency could be because we are coming off a major losing streak in the man department. I am just as rejuvenated as Melody lately, and I, too, feel like it is time for a win! *So, you get a point. You get a point. And you, New Man whom I have yet to meet–you get two points!* I love Oprah. She is always so happy-go-lucky!

Friday night of a speedy work week arrives and I notice a nervousness has settled over Melody. At first, I do not understand what has my girl so anxious as she walks through the front door, but I quickly figure it out. Melody smells more strongly of this new man than ever before. The scent isn't coming directly from her though. I peer past Melody's legs and find the reason why. The origin of the smell stands right behind Melody on our front step. New Man enters our house cautiously behind her. *Is this man the one who talks with Melody on the phone? Or are there two different men?* I don't know why I hadn't thought of this possibility sooner. My initial thoughts are instantly confirmed, as New Man speaks in the same deep timbre I have become so familiar with. He gives me a confident greeting:

"Hello, big guy. You must be Ludo. I have heard a lot about you!"

All good things, no doubt! Surprisingly, I find myself very excited to meet this man. I am not sure if it is because he has become a constant voice in my life, or if it is because I can now further my judgment of him. Regardless, I am happy that this man will not be a mystery for two years like the last one. I just got happy Melody back and am not going to let another dumb male ruin it! Plus, Melody and I are not getting any younger, so it is time to start looking a little more seriously for a human male to add to our pack. I am already six human years old and working on seven, which means that I am just over forty-four in dog years. Melody is fast approaching twenty-five. *No spring chickens here!*

I begin my in-the-flesh interrogation after my excitement from his arrival wears off. I am happy that he walks in with confidence but seems humble, not arrogant. I deeply inhale his scent as he approaches me: he smells very woodsy. *Perhaps he spends a lot of time outside.* I pick up on a wide mix of trees, fresh air, and cut grass. *Were you out mowing before you came over?* Melody and I love to mow the lawn. If I am lucky, he does too! I find these small facts to be positive attributes; he likes the outdoors and does not bathe himself in aftershave. I award him two more points in the pros section as Melody introduces him. "Kenner, meet Ludo, the world's best dog. In my opinion, anyway."

Nice to meet you, I think. Oh, and Melody's opinion is the only one that matters! I am a sucker for names, and I love the name Kenner. It means 'brave guard' or 'chief.' I see this as a sign of independence. This man follows no one. He, like me, is the firstborn of his family. I can tell this is true by how he carries himself. Melody is in the process of learning to be more like that. She is no longer clinging to others' thoughts and opinions. Because of this, she is really finding and embracing herself. It is wonderful! *Get back to judging. Celebrate your accomplishments after Kenner leaves for the night.* Six, almost seven years, and I still do not have the focus of a true Jedi.

When Kenner first came into the house, he semi-ignored me until Melody made the introduction. Ignoring a dog is not a bad thing. Honestly, it is a practice I wish all humans would take up. I wag my tail inviting him to further greet me. Kenner kneels to my level. I sense he respects me, so I will respect him. *Another point for Kenner!*

Over the years, I have found people's unwillingness to ignore dogs upon first meeting them to be a real problem. Everyone wants to shove their hands in a dog's face. Part of it is due to bad teaching from other humans. "Oh, just offer the nice doggy your hand first." So I can't blame them entirely. We all do what we believe or are taught is the correct behavior in any given situation.

I must caution everyone that hands may not be returned if one goes about meeting and greeting canines in such a manner. A person should always wait for an invitation or approval from said canine. This is an okay of sorts. *We are, after all, royalty. You can't just walk up to us without some sort of permission granted.* Dogs need a few minutes to adjust. We don't deal with change well. This should be obvious as humans shake hands with this same principle. First, humans talk for a minute or two, then they lead with a hand once the feeling is mutual. It is only then that the handshaking—or, in my case, butt-sniffing-can begin. *Why this is not common sense is beyond me.*

Okay, okay, get off your soapbox now and continue with your judgment. After Kenner gets down on my level, he proceeds to give me the best ear rub I have ever had. I give him extra points on the scoreboard for all of his astounding actions. First, he ignores me, then he kneels to my royal self, and now the ear rub. *Ohhh my goodness, the EAR RUB!*

An embarrassing and almost orgasmic-sounding groan escapes my throat as I wag my tail and tilt my head to allow Kenner deeper access to my ear canals. A light sadness finds me as Kenner tells Melody that he misses his dogs. I can tell that Kenner is a dog-lover, but sympathy fills me as I think of his dogs without him. Surely, Kenner would not have left them without extenuating circumstances. Maybe his dogs left him after falling victim to a Labrador love spell and an evil dognapper. *It could happen to any one of us if we aren't careful. Evil, loveable Labs!*

I make a mental note to investigate this part of Kenner's story further. I give him another two checks in the pros column while trying to maintain my composure from my ear massage. I have to admit, part of me almost wants to hand him the keys to our house already. *Just give him a third check mark and hold on to the keys a little longer.* The rub is so enjoyable that my thinking is being clouded! That's it, I am making it a firm rule that points can no longer be awarded during ear rubs. These rubs of Kenner's could be a form of mind control or manipulation. *I must maintain my guard!* I regroup my thoughts as my ear rub comes to an unfortunate end. As I do so, I realize that I have not yet found a con. *How can this be?* I rack my brain to come up with a negative quality as I study the previous moments. I can't find one yet!

Over the next few months, Melody and I get to know Kenner. I find that I am falling just as hard for him as Melody is. If she goes to his house, I go with, and when Kenner comes to visit, he always gives me treats, respect, attention, and the best dang ear rubs on the planet. *Can this guy really be perfect?* It is seeming so. Kenner is six feet tall and has sandy blonde hair with a reddish hue and intense blue eyes that remind me of the waves of an ocean glittering in the sunlight. He has a solid, muscular build, and from what I have seen so far is also athletic. I imagine I would look similar to Kenner if I were a human. Perhaps I would be a little taller due to my higher level alpha status, and more than likely my hair would be white and I would have a lot more of it, as I refuse to look like one of those hairless cats. Irrespective of what my human form may or may not look like, I find myself growing very fond of all Kenner's characteristics. He is a man who looks like he can keep up with Melody and me. Melody seems to like all his attributes, too, because her heart always beats a little faster whenever he is around. I think it is cute how Kenner can make Melody's hands sweaty just by walking through our front door. I have found one thing odd, though: when Kenner is near Melody, her scent changes to a weird, sweet-salty scent of anticipation. *Is that good or bad?*

Weeks turn into months and pass us by. Melody, Kenner, and I spend lots of harmonious time together and continue to grow closer. I adjust to the idea of adding to our pack. *Why not Kenner?* Melody likes him, and, to my astonishment, I too. Everyone around him grows fond of him quickly. *He is an extrovert, though, and they generally have that ability.* I don't want all of Kenner's likableness to taint my judgement of him, so I add something to his con list today. My plan is to even up the score so I can see all of him more clearly. I need to counteract all the positive check marks I have awarded him thus far with some red X's. I worry that in light of her past relationships, Melody and I may have gotten ahead of ourselves and are being overly hopeful since Kenner is such a breath of fresh air.

After sitting in deep thought for a while I find a reason to award Kenner with his first X. Lately, I have heard Melody make strange and sometimes alarming noises. These events of hers only seems to happen when Kenner is around. He is the only constant I can come up with that could be the cause of Melody's strange cries. Melody and Kenner play so well together that when I am out in the yard, so I often allow myself the luxury of getting sidetracked and playing with my gator. *Always good to embrace a little me time after all.* Anyhow, before I know it, these bizarre noises start to pollute the quiet air, so I run to investigate. The only problem is that when I try to rescue Melody, I find myself staring into the glass of our closed backdoor instead. My reflection mocks me and says, "Now what are you going to do, tough guy?" Melody and I have always had an open-door policy around here. *At least, we did until Kenner started coming around.*

I can't decide if these odd sounds are Melody experiencing pleasure or pain. Unfortunately, I have not been able to fully investigate these noises or the situation that the two are engaged in that causes Melody to cry out. I feel as if the universe is keeping me from this discovery as it seems to keep Melody and I separated whenever these noisy events of Melody and Kenner's occur. Once the noises end, I bark to gain Melody or Kenner's attention. One of them always comes to the back door to let me in within a few minutes of my sound off. When they let me back inside the two seem hunky-dory and act is if nothing had just happened. One thing I have noticed for sure, is that when these odd events occur Melody and Kenner reek of joyous, salty pheromones, and she seems to have a new glow about her.

I find these situations annoying as I get to sit perplexed for the next few hours while the two of them can't seem to stop smiling at one another. It is almost as if the two are playing some joke on me. *I don't know if I like the possibility of Melody being in cahoots with Kenner against me on this matter.* I can't see Melody ever playing a joke on me at my expense either, she knows I hate surprises and change.

The fact that everything seems hunky-dory when I enter the house after these occurrences has me lost. I admit I am struggling with the question of whether or not Melody making these noises is actually a true con for Kenner. I am not yet certain if I need to be concerned when these things happen, or even if I need to know what is actually taking place when they do. Perhaps part of me has a weird fascination with putting something on that side of the scoreboard. I promise to investigate this matter further. If it turns out to not truly be a con, I can always revoke it. My only other option would be not going outside to go the bathroom when Kenner is around so I can keep my eyes on him better. I have noticed a small connection with my bathroom breaks and these events. *But I can't hold it all day!*

Chapter 36: Long-Distance

July is scorching, but aside from the miserable temperature, life is going grandly. I conclude that Kenner may be just the male pack-mate that Melody and I need to complete our family. Perhaps the heat has completely exhausted me, or maybe I am suffering from a fried brain, but I am ready to award Kenner with the keys to our castle and let him into our lives permanently. I plan to make my final judgment of Kenner known to Melody and give her my blessing to move their relationship forward tonight. Kenner understands and embraces the fact that Melody and I are a package deal. Even on nights when Melody goes to his house for dinner, Kenner always invites me along. *Kenner has earned a place in our pack!*

Melody returns home from work and I run out of our bedroom, where I had been sleeping and cooling myself on one the register that cools the tile floor in Melody's bathroom, to greet her. I am excited to give her the good news regarding Kenner and our pack. I know that Melody has been waiting for me to be comfortable with Kenner and the whole relationship thing for quite some time now. I run towards Melody with my tongue hanging lazily out of my mouth, sporting a goofy grin and an erratically spinning tail. I am so excited that my tail is flying around like a small bush plane propeller. But as I reach Melody, I sense that she is upset, so I put my plan on the back burner for the time being. *What's wrong, Mel?*

Melody has a red face and watery eyes. She wears the smell of the ocean on her, and I can see dried salt crystals on her cheeks from crying. Defeated, she pats my head as she enters and passes me in the house, then she throws her exhausted self upon the couch. I can tell that Melody is mentally worn out, so I jump up to console her. I need to figure out what has saddened her so deeply. She looks as if she lost her best friend, but I know that is not possible because I am here with her. *Maybe it's the heat? It makes me want to cry, too!*

Melody strokes my furry head as I lay it on her chest. *I love that I can calm her so quickly.* Then, like in all the other broken moments we have shared over the years, Melody unloads all of her troubles on my listening ears. I never in a million years would have expected the next sentence that comes out of her mouth. "Well, Lu, it looks like Kenner has a new job and will be moving away soon. So much for that one, huh? Too bad, I really cared for him. I thought what we had was it. It seemed so perfect. Too perfect, I guess."

What? Kenner is moving away? He has broken Melody's heart and destroyed the trust that I—no, wait, WE—had built with him! This is absurd. I am furious! I will be sure to bite him if I ever see him again. I think I can find the way to his house with my nose. I should go there and rip him apart. I am so disappointed in my judgment skills. Kenner is no better than the other two men. I consider going down the path of no return if he ever dares to show his face at our house again, but that will probably only hurt Melody more.

Anger fills me as depression and sadness tug at my heart. I had fallen for Kenner just as Melody had. I had given Kenner a small piece of my heart. I admit that the other ninety-eight percent is reserved for Melody, but this two percent is more than I have ever given anyone. Another thought hits me, a more selfish one: *No more ear rubs!* If I am lucky, Kenner taught Melody the secret to dazzling ear rubs over the past few months. Only time will tell, though, as Melody is in no mood to give me one at the moment.

Melody pushes herself from the couch and I know exactly what she will do next. She will call Paige, for some advice and a good vent session. I long for the ability to speak in actual words to Melody as others do. All I can lend her are my comforting gestures, and that saddens me on days like today. Melody crams the phone between her ear and shoulder so she can use both hands to open a bottle of wine while talking. "I guess we will try the long-distance thing and see what happens," Melody says with little excitement. "Yeah, it sucks. I really liked him. I fell for him. Hard! Long-distance rarely works out. But you never know until you try, right? Illinois and Iowa aren't that far apart I think he is worth it."

I had thought Kenner was worth it too. *Keyword being 'was.' He has broken my heart and upset my Melody.* I bark at her, "Are you sure we should forgive him so easily? You hate long drives. You hate driving in general!" Melody still battles some lasting PTSD issues from our car accident. We mostly have good days, but now and then, I can tell that it is a real struggle for her to be in a car. Her therapist has helped her a lot over the years, but what helps her the most is me sitting next to her. "I have gotten you through worse things, Melody. This is nothing. If you want to try this distance thing, I will get you through the drives." I groan and lay my head in her lap. Melody is now sitting on one of the bar stools next to the kitchen table. She reaches down and puts her hand on my head. Even though Melody is talking to Paige on the phone, I know that she received my message.

I decide that we need to approach this long-distance relationship with great caution. I immediately reopen my judgment case against Kenner and hastily fill the scoreboard with red Xs to even out all the green check marks. This option is better than going down the path of no return. I will just make him start back at ground zero. Now, Kenner will have to work twice as hard to earn the keys to our castle, let alone our hearts.

Summer falls away, and fall flies past us as fast as the leaves on some of our windy day walks. People say the older we get, the faster time goes, and that is no joke. The more I think about it, the more I think it sucks! *Twenty- four hours should be the same every day, according to science and basic math—and yet, somehow, it's not!* Winter screams by as well, though with little snow. We have made it all the way around the calendar and are back in the month of May. Melody and I celebrated my seventh human year of life back in April. I am now the ripe old age of fifty human years; I have long since surpassed Melody and Kenner.

I passed them with my genius years ago, but no one likes a bragger. The intelligence level of dogs is grossly underestimated. By the time a dog reaches the age of three in human years, there are few, if any, humans left on the planet who are smarter than they are. I read somewhere that dogs have the intelligence level of an advanced four-year-old. Wrong. They need to update the literature to say at least a forty-year-old if they want to be accurate. *Although, I have met some not-so-bright forty-year-old humans, so that may not be accurate, either.*

Anyway, Kenner has finally relocated for his job and is now residing in Iowa four hours north of where Melody and I live. The two decided that he and Melody will travel back and forth on weekends and see where the relationship will take them. Melody and Kenner share a deep connection that is apparent to everyone around them. They often remind me of that cliché soulmate in feel-good Hallmark movies. This isn't a bad thing, considering how I love to see Melody so happy. I, too, share a deep connection with Kenner, even though I am currently trying very hard not to like him and to be the reasonable one between Melody and me. *Nonetheless, it's there, and it's only growing stronger with each passing day.*

Melody is so much happier when Kenner is with us. She becomes even brighter, shinier, and more full of life than I would have ever thought possible. Yes, at first this made me horribly jealous, but over time I realized that it wasn't just Melody who he had that effect on. Kenner brings out the same cheery side in me, too. I have to keep reminding myself that either Melody or I need to keep our guard up at all times. Kenner has made Melody cry once, and I will not allow anything like that to happen again. I rarely give out second chances, but for some reason, I know that I have to allow Kenner this one do-over. *You'd better take advantage of this, or get ready to kiss us goodbye!* Melody is thinking with her heart and not her brain when it comes to Kenner. Therefore, I make sure to do most of the thinking for us. I will not allow him to break her heart again under any circumstances.

Besides Melody's crying, I cannot say I have found a reason to truly dislike or distrust Kenner. *He was upfront with us about the job relocation as soon as he knew about it. Kenner has never hidden anything from us, to my knowledge.* As much as I hate it, Kenner seems to be a straight shooter. I value that immensely.

On a very happy note, our new weekend schedule translates into lots of good things for me. I always get to go with Melody since she isn't capable of driving more than an hour without me in tow to keep her calm. This means more time with her, so I give Kenner a check mark.

To lessen the drive time on the weekends that it is our turn to go north, Kenner and Melody found a place for me to stay near her work. This helps to reduce Melody's anxiety, as well as shorten her drive time, because now she doesn't have to backtrack to our house to get me. Melody found that if we leave right after her shift at the hospital, it takes forty-five minutes off our drive to Kenner's house. The place that Melody and Kenner found for me to stay at while she works is called doggy daycare. *I call it Heaven!* I feel that the development of such establishments is one of the best inventions on this planet.

I admit that I was very skeptical and not very excited at first, but seriously, if you own a dog, do them a favor and get them to doggy daycare! Your dog will thank you and love you even more than you thought possible! Dogs give everything to their humans; doggy daycare is an excellent way for humans to give back! I swear, every time I set paw inside the daycare, the Fred Astaire song "Cheek to Cheek" plays either on the speakers or in my head. Pure bliss!

Heaven—I mean, daycare—is freaking fabulous. I am really struggling to find words that do it justice. Since Kenner is the reason we discovered the daycare, I give him another check-mark. *Congratulations, Kenner. You are back on the board!* He continues to amaze me. I put him down at ground zero after he broke Melody's heart, and he is already climbing his way back to the top. Sometimes, I want to pretend to be Kenner. *I think it is called a man crush?* Now, now, don't twist my words or get excited by the term 'crush.' I really admire the amount of gumption and grit that Kenner has!

Anyway, getting back to the daycare. Melody drops me off on Friday mornings with a lady named Kathy. Kathy owns this glorious organization, and she loves German Shepherds. She loves all dogs, but I happen to be her favorite breed. *Another smart woman in my life with excellent taste in dogs!* When I am at the daycare, I play all day. I am often so exhausted from my daycare adventures that when Melody picks me up to head to Kenner's house, I have to sleep for the first few hours of our trip. Daycare makes my anxiety level a big fat zero, so I can't amp up Melody's anxiety with mine. *Double bonus!*

I was right the first time I scented Kenner nearly a year ago: he loves the outdoors. Going to Kenner's new place is also like going to daycare since he always keeps us busy. *Seriously, the man rarely sits still.* There is always an adventure to be had somewhere. Lazy time on the couch with a movie is only reserved for when one of them is feeling under the weather or it is raining. Kenner is always getting us to try new things, and all of them have been amazing thus far! Last time we went to visit him, we went hiking through tall grass fields. As we were walking, brightly-colored birds made loud *kurkurk* noises as they flew only a few feet ahead of us. It was amazing! However, I got a strange feeling that Kenner hadn't gotten quite the reaction out of me he was hoping for when the birds had exploded out of the grass. *I was grateful and excited. What more does he want?*

Kenner lives in a large, white farmhouse. There is corn as far as I can see in all directions, but a few miles down the road there are bluffs, creeks, caves, and rivers all waiting for us to play in and explore. Summers, as I am sure I previously stated, are my least favorite season, and it doesn't take Kenner long to realize it. *The man knows me well. He is clearly after my heart.* I get overly hot quickly in my permanent fur coat, and I can't help but wonder if my age is starting to affect my internal thermostat. I read an article at Grandma's house the last time we were there that said our hormones go haywire as we get older. Regardless of the true cause, Kenner has my back on this matter. During the hot months, he always makes sure I have access to water during our daily adventures. Kenner and Melody always schedule in a break time so I can cool off and rest up. If it weren't for these various water sources, I could never keep up with them.

Melody, Kenner, and I have all survived a full year of the once-dreaded long-distance relationship. To be honest, I am enjoying it. I get Melody to myself all week and then play hard all weekend long with Kenner. Needless to say, their relationship has transitioned way better than I had expected it to. The three of us learn more about one another as time continues to blissfully pass us by. One of the things we learn about Kenner is that fall is his favorite season, too!

Kenner has different reasons than I do for liking fall so much. With fall comes the hunting season for him. Grandpa and Melody hunt deer in the fall, so I have some knowledge on the subject. Kenner hunts deer as well, but one thing he partakes in that Melody and Grandpa don't is bird hunting. Kenner is addicted to the sport, and understandably so, as the little creatures make amazing delicacies when grilled. I now have some learning to do, as I lack knowledge on this feathered sport. *Perhaps this is why Kenner looked slightly disappointed in me when we walked through the grass-covered, pheasant-filled fields in the spring?*

I listen diligently as Kenner talks about the upcoming season. I am mainly looking for clues and hints on what our next greatest adventure will be. I feel that I can better prepare myself since I now understand Kenner's expectations. Dogs love to please their humans. *Wait, did I just call Kenner my human?*

Kenner is a divorced man like Grandpa. I guess his ex-wife got custody of their dogs full-time. *Makes sense. I would stay with Melody if these two ever split.* Perhaps that is the standard protocol for these situations. *Women do need protection.* Anyway, this left Kenner without a hunting partner. I have learned so far that when a human hunts fowl, they need a dog to be their partner. *Good news, Kenner: I am ready for the job!* I am excited to learn something new and have a passion I can share with Kenner. The more I learn, though, the more I find that I have more than a few concerns. I am worried about leaving Melody alone on the farm, and I really do not have a clue how to be a duck hunter. I am secretly relieved when Kenner and Melody talk things over one night and decide that I can't offer much assistance in the duck-hunting department. There are two key factors in their decision. Number one, I don't have even the slightest interest in birds. *Unless you count eating them after they are obtained.* Which brings me to the number two factor: I am not a fan of the loud gunfire it takes to knock these feathered meals out of the sky.

Melody and Kenner sit on top of the picnic table in his yard while I play with an antler. I stopped paying any real attention to what they were saying once I heard I was off the hook for duck hunting. *Phew!* I know that they are devising some sort of plan to get Kenner through the upcoming season.

So long as it does not involve me, I don't care what transpires. I soon lose interest in chewing my antler as well and drift into a peaceful nap as the gentle sun warms my slightly achy hips and back. *Dang, excessive adventuring.* I can tell that this is going to be a love-hate part of my life soon. I will always love going on adventures with my two favorite humans, but I will hate how my body feels afterward.

Before I know it, a decision has been made by Melody and Kenner, and Melody is waking me so we can pack our things into the Jeep. *Time to go back home for the week.* I am slightly surprised by how much I am looking forward to a lazy, mundane week with Melody. Hopefully, since we are leaving later than normal, we can skip our morning run up to Grandpa's house. I can't seem to get enough rest today, and my hips are killing me.

Note to self: never again stop paying attention to a conversation that involves one of my humans needing a hunting partner, especially when said hunting partner is a dog! The work week flies by, and Melody and I find ourselves back up at Kenner's place as the weekend arrives. *I thought it was his turn to come to see us.* This is not a big deal to me at first. However, I find myself quickly thrown for a loop as the weekend progresses.

Saturday morning comes, and with it, another big red X for Kenner. The day starts out on a highly positive note when he and Melody drop me off at a new doggy daycare by Kenner's house. I love exploring new places and meeting other dogs. Plus, if I get tired, I can lie down and nap in the shade. I relish my time at daycare because there are so many distractions there that I don't worry about Melody at all when we are apart. One of the things I love about daycare is its 'no humans allowed' rule! Don't get me wrong, I love being with Melody and Kenner, but when those two aren't around, I don't have to keep tabs on them. I know that Kenner will keep Melody safe when I am not with her, so daycare is basically a paid holiday for me.

When Kenner and Melody drop me off, they tell me that they will only be gone for half the day. They promise to pick me up by late afternoon. *Heck, don't rush on my account. Take the whole day. I will be just fine here.* It isn't until they come to pick me up from daycare that my day turns sour.

Melody and Kenner are not alone in the truck. *A giant red X just found its way to Kenner's con column.* Kenner has gotten himself a dog with no input from me! *The audacity of this situation is absurd! What has he done? What was he thinking?* I know he is not my primary human, but I have become very fond of him. Until today, that is! I thought that Kenner and I had something serious going, something special. *Hello, I was doing a trust fall. You are supposed to catch me, not step out of the way!*

Chapter 37: Winston

First impressions are everything. Kenner's new dog, our supposed new pack mate, is not off to a good start. Since I always try to stay positive and optimistic, I will start with what I do like about him. First, I like that he is a German Wirehaired Pointer, and second, that his name is Winston. Unfortunately, this is where my list ends.

Kenner had to choose his new dog's name because he was never properly given one. How sad is that? A dog who was never given a name! Winston is already one year old, and he seems to be a few kibbles shy of a bag of dog food, *if you know what I mean.* He speaks mostly German, with a smattering of English. He has either never been taught English, or he is a very slow learner.

Luckily for Winston, my mother and father made my siblings and me learn our native language. When our parents were teaching us both languages, Father always said to be sure to respect our German heritage and where we came from. *Perhaps this is why life chose to bring Winston and me together.* I am able to understand ninety percent of what Winston is trying to say, so teaching him English won't be that hard.

As it turns out, teaching Winston English and servings as his translator is slightly more challenging than I had anticipated. *I guess that is what I get for assuming again.* Winston speaks with a thick German accent, I know the language but that accent of his really muddles some of his words. I find Winston especially hard to understand when he gets excited, then the sentences he speaks are all broken. There is one other thing that aggravates me about Winston: he has absolutely no manners. *Zero!* When Melody or Kenner call Winston's name, he doesn't even turn his head or acknowledge them. *No respect!*

At first, I was worried that Winston may have hearing problems. This theory of mine was disproved when a bird flapped its wings a half mile away which caused Winston to instinctively stand proudly at attention and point in its direction. I suppose that comes from the pointer in him. Regardless, he seems to have very selective hearing. *I like to call it 'butt-headedness.'* Kenner seems to have it at times, too. I have connected Kenner's selective hearing with football on the television. I don't shame him for this at all though, there is something about that delightful game where large humans fight over a ball that very much intrigues me. I have to admit that when football is on, I sometimes don't hear Melody calling my name either. As for Winston, I have not yet figured out the cause of his selective hearing. *I have news, pal: no one is better than anyone else around here. Snobs will not be tolerated!* So far, my introduction to this ill-mannered male is off to a bad start.

My disappointment with Kenner furthers over dinner as he talks about an upcoming hunting trip he will be leaving for on Monday. This news means that Winston is going home with us at the end of this weekend. Not only did Kenner bring home a

one-year-old moron, but now he is making Winston
our full-time responsibility. I agree with Kenner
when he says that Winston is clearly not ready to
accompany him on a hunting trip. He should have
waited a few more weeks before picking him up,
then.

I have no choice but to make the best out of this
situation. Since it appears that I will not get any say
in this matter, I decide to give Kenner another X. I
start a separate judgement tally for Winston and
give him two Xs. The only silver lining I can see at
this point is that my new living arrangement will
not be permanent. At least there is a metaphoric
light at the end of the seemingly dark tunnel that
Melody and I have involuntarily entered. I am not
sure if Kenner knows the severity of what he may
have just done by bringing Winston into our lives
without first consulting me. Now, if Winston does
not prove to be worthy of Melody's and my pack
while Kenner is gone, I will be forced to rid our pack
of them both. *We must lie in the beds we make, Kenner.*

After dinner, I try to be a good dog and get to
know Winston. After all, we are equals and I fear
that I am being a pompous butthead by judging him
so quickly. Outside, I show him the property lines
around his new yard so he will know where it ends.
He needs to know this vital information so he can
mark his territory later. If he is to be Kenner's dog
then this will be his place. Our peaceful stroll is
suddenly interrupted by those familiar yet strange
noises coming from inside the house.

"*Horst du das*? What is making *das schreck-*

lichen Larm?" Winston says with alarm on his face as we make our way back towards the house.

Winston wants to know if I heard the noise and what is causing it. I answer him slowly using both German and English in hopes he will deduct which words are what so he can learn English faster. "Yeah, I heard it. It won't be the last time you hear it either. It happens at least once a weekend whenever Melody and Kenner are together. You will get used to it, I finally am. I have no idea what to make of it either so don't ask." I nonchalantly say to Winston. "There is no reason for alarm as the two of them will be oddly happy once we finally get let back in the house."

I tell Winston that this has been an ongoing thing that started not too long after Kenner started coming over to Melody's house. I also tell him I that I am about to give up on trying to find out what causes them to makes these noises as my investigation on this matter thus far has been fruitless. I continue as Winston listens intently to everything I am staying. "It's weird the sounds that the two make over and over again when these events occur remind me of the same noises Melody or Kenner make when they stub their toes. Oh, and this is the strangest part of all, when I finally am let back inside the house everyone's feet are in perfect, unharmed condition. I really have no idea what causes them to unleash these moans and screams. I only know Melody and Kenner are always inexplicably happier after they occur."

I have a feeling Winston senses my slight annoyance with him and he wants to get into my good graces so he says, "I *denke*, I *kann* help *sie*. I am a good *detektiv*. I *kann* always *finden, der Vogel* that makes the noise. I *kann* help *sie* with this problem."

I am pleased with not only what Winston has just told me but also with the fact that he is using some of the English words I have just taught him. Winston informed me that he is a good detective and that he can always find the bird that is making the noise so he thinks he can help me solve this noisy conundrum of mine. As it turns out, Winston's name should probably be Watson. *As the alpha of our pack, I, of course, have already obtained the starring role of Sherlock!* Winston claims to be very good at solving mysteries and finding the source of unseen noises. I wonder if they teach these skills better in Germany. Why they had not taught Winston both languages fully while he was there is beyond me. From what I have seen so far, Winston is proving to be very resourceful and a speedy learner. *I just need to get a better grasp on his accent and it will be smooth sailing for both of us from here.*

Winston and I start our investigation. We follow the noises with our ears, constantly turning and adjusting like small satellites until we reach the point at which the sounds are most prevalent. I can now hear Melody and Kenner more clearly than ever before. *Is Melody being beaten? What is going on in there?* I quickly inform Winston that we are standing outside of Kenner's bedroom. Winston says, "Okay, das bedroom *fenster* appears to be offen and only blocked by material."

Translation: The bedroom window is open and only blocked by a screen. Winston and I devise a plan. We will jump on top of the air-conditioning unit, then nudge the screen that blocks the open window, forcing it to give way. This way, we will gain entrance to the house without Melody or Kenner's aid. Once we are inside, I will finally be able to figure out the cause of the muffled squeals. "*Geheimnis* solved once and for all!" *Geheimnis, aka mystery.* Clearly, I was being a jerk for judging Winston so harshly before getting to know him. *The dog is brilliant.* I am also finding that I enjoy his broken English. Something about it soothes me, maybe I don't detest his accent so much after all.

I climb on top of the air-conditioning unit first. Winston waits his turn below me. As I make my climb, Winston gives me a boost. The nearly ninety-degree angle is hard on my hips and back; I had played excessively at daycare today while awaiting their return and don't have much strength left in my reserves for the day. I didn't even ask Winston for help. He just kindly boosts me when he sees me struggling. *What a guy!* Winston just says, "*Sie brauchen steigern meine, freund?*" *Translation: you need a boost, friend?* Then, he boosted me before I even had a chance to say yes!

I decide that I will reevaluate my feelings about Winston after we have solved our mystery. I am still irritated with Kenner for not consulting me on a new pack-mate, which seems to have put me more on edge and makes me quicker to judge than usual. I think this reason alone is why the next part of our mystery-solving mission isn't executed as cleanly as the first part. I have just adjusted to standing on the slippery top of the air conditioner when I hear my Melody let out a much louder cry. I instantly panic and give the window's screen more than a little nudge. It sounds like Melody is in trouble. I have no choice but to abandon all reasonable thought and take immediate action.

I unleash a powerful growl and spring at the screen with all my might, leaping through the bedroom window with my teeth bared and gleaming in the light. I want to look as threatening as possible. Though, I have to admit; I land like a five-hundred-pound man doing a belly flop into a pool. I splatter onto the wooden floor like one of the many bugs I have seen career into a windshield. *Karma.* I struggle to cover a slightly pained whimper with a roaring growl from deep within my belly. *The police in the movies make busting down doors look so easy.* My forced entry was done with zero grace, and more than likely did not appear threatening, so I make sure I at least sound like I am in charge of the situation.

I gather my wits and get my legs back underneath me as I continue to growl. When I look up, all I see is Kenner's bare behind streaking out of the room. Thunderous laughter reverberates from Melody's chest where she lies on Kenner's bed. I immediately jump up onto the bed to check Melody and assess the situation further. Melody appears fine. *Heck, she is better than fine.* Melody has a very relaxed and content look on her face. Through hysterical laughter, Melody says, "Silly Lu, everything is okay. No one is being hurt. Calm down, buddy!" She hugs me and soothes my anxiety.

Moments later, Winston comes in through the window. His entrance is smooth and graceful. He walks over to join Melody and I, wagging his stubby tail. I quickly warn Winston as he approaches us, "Watch out for Kenner. I fear he may have lost his mind. He just ran down the hallway in his birthday suite screaming like a scared hairless cat."

As I finish cautioning Winston, a now clothed Kenner appears, slowly peeking his head around the corner. "Is everything okay in here? You alright, Lu?" Kenner approaches me nervously and proceeds to give me a spectacular ear rub as a form of peace offering. I let out a partially satisfied groan, then turn my head away from him. I need to refuse the ear rub he is trying to manipulate me with. I want Kenner to be fully aware of my currently angered state.

I am being dumb. This is what some would call 'cutting off my nose to spite my face.' I desperately want, and should have accepted, Kenner's ear rub. However, I jump down from the bed, unwilling to accept any loving attention from Kenner. He needs to know who is in control around here. He also needs to know that I don't approve of him trying to put the same moves on Melody as I did with the loveable lab a few years back. Maybe I just jealous because Kenner still has his Mojo sack, either way I decide I am going to make a stand. *I can't believe I am turning down one of his amazing ear rubs.* Melody tries frequently but is nowhere near a contender in that department. *I must stay strong.* I have to make my message clear.

Winston tries to reason with me by saying, "Ludo, *paarung* is only *naturlich.*"

I reply dryly, "I know mating is only natural,

and you would say that. You and Kenner both have your mojo sacks intact. Just because it may be normal doesn't mean I have to like it and I can't interrupt them so they do it less often.

Winston walks over to Kenner to accept my ear rub. As he is receiving it he says to me, "Ludo, don't be bitter, that is how you miss out."

I suppose he is right, it's not Kenner's fault I lost my mojo. I decide to put this whole event behind me and accept a not as amazing ear rub from Melody.

Chapter 38: Housebreaking

At the end of the weekend, Melody and I head back home with Winston in tow. The next two weeks are going to be interesting. Winston has no clue about living with humans. He and I talk on our jeep ride back to my house. As we chat, Winston informs me that he had spent the first year of his life tied to a doghouse after being flown here from Germany as a five-week-old puppy. The only time poor Winston had interacted with humans over the past year was once a day when a sixteen-year old boy would come to feed him. *Sad!* First, five weeks is much too young to leave home, and second, the humans who had him sound terrible. Winston does not stand much of a chance with the upbringing he has had thus far.

Winston's story reminds me of those gut-wrenching animal commercials with the Celine Dion music. I always thought they were just to get people to open their pockets wider and give some green leafy paper they all love so much to the organization. *I had no idea that this kind of cruelty really exists!* I feel bad for Winston. He had missed out on so much by being torn away from his family so young. Not to mention that he had zero choice as to who he went to live with. Deep sympathy finds me, and I decide that I will give Winston a chance to become a part of our pack. *After all, Winston did solve the mystery I have been working on for over a year in only a matter of minutes.*

I tell Winston that I will teach him the basic skills of life. But first things first: Winston needs to learn better English since that is the only language Kenner and Melody speak. With my skills and Winston's eagerness, I have no doubt that we can accomplish this, as well as some other very necessary skills he will need to be successful in life. The two of us will work hard every day for the next few weeks while Melody is at work and Kenner is away. Winston wags his stub excitedly. He is elated by the time and attention that Melody and Kenner have given him already. I am still a little upset by the new situation and the dog who had been thrust into my life without my input, but I will make the best of it. *An Ultimate Alpha always shows kindness and compassion to all living things.*

Winston needs my help, and it seems that he has only been given very unfair circumstances so far. To be honest, I am impressed that Winston has made it this far in life and somehow found his way to us. *Our relationship must be a necessary step in both our lives.* My mother and father made it very clear when we were pups to always help others in need. It is a good practice in general as one never knows when they will need a favor returned. Winston and I have nothing to lose by befriending one another. *We can only gain!*

Boy, do I have my work cut out for me! Winston has so much to learn. I thought Pointers were supposed to be smart. *Remember, it is not his fault since he was tied to a doghouse during one of his best learning years.* Either way, Winston has a lot of catching up to do. When we first arrive home, I bring Winston inside to show him around. He immediately walks over to our couch and lifts his leg. The obscenity of it almost kills me! Winston is going to pee in our living room, on our snuggling couch. *Preposterous!* I run over and bite the back of his head to warn him off the couch. At the same time, Melody chases after Winston, yelling, "No, no!" This gives me flashbacks to my younger days. I remember getting the same treatment at Grandpa's house when I first came home. *This must be the required welcoming practice for all dogs when they first step foot into their new castles.* The only difference is that this time, Melody is yelling, "Winston, no!" and running after him, waving her hands frantically in the air. The whole scene causes a small, smug grin to take over my face.

Melody captures a puzzled Winston. Once she has a firm grip on his collar, she guides him to the back door to show him our backyard. I can tell by the mystified look he wears that Winton does not understand what is going on. I remove the smugness from my face and walk out in front of Winston so I can show him what he should be doing right now. I pee in the grass. *Some are better visual learners, others like to read, and some learn better by listening.* Winston and I have not discussed his preferred method of learning, so it is probably a good thing that Melody and I start with the show-and-tell method of training.

I tell Winston what I am doing as I do it. "This, my friend, is the only place we pee. Now, you go." I

313

allow Winston to urinate where I had just gone. Standard procedure would have been for me to get the final pee on top since this is my yard, but today I decide that this is acceptable. Melody and I will have to change a few things and give Winston special training due to his circumstances. I will lose no credibility in the alpha world by sharing my territory with a fellow dog in need. I once saw little kids on a television show peeing on Cheerios in a toilet so they had something to aim at. Winston is a kid of sorts, and he needs all the help we can give him. *This is a dog's way to Cheerio train: urinating first gave Winston something to aim at.*

While we all meander about outside, Winston explains that he was just trying to establish his territory. I inform him that inside and as far as he can see outside are all mine. There is no need for him to establish anything here at my house because I am not going to give it up anytime soon. I inform Winston that I am happy to share and teach him what he needs to know, but at our house, he is only a guest for the time being. Winston can save his territory-marking business for Kenner's house. Since Winston will be the full-time hound on Kenner's grounds once he returns from his hunting trip, it is only fair I allow him to call that his territory.

For the time being and for training purposes only, I tell Winston that he can pretend to mark his territory in various parts of our yard. I give him a few bushes and trees to call his own. "Every time you need to go to the bathroom, you can do it here, or over there." I point out scrawny bushes and immature trees in the yard as I walk him around the perimeter. "And Winston? This is the most important part, so pay attention. You can only use the restroom outside. Never go inside the house unless you are sick and having some sort of emergency." I explain to Winston that when dogs and humans live together, dogs mark their territory inside the house with the scent from our oily fur coats and by dropping a few hairs here and there to make our presence known. "Inside the house, you can rub on the carpet, rugs, and couches, which will leave your fur and oil behind. Besides, the only people or dogs that get let in the house are the ones we invite through the door. If you don't want them inside, then deny them entry. We do not under any circumstances pee in the house! Got it?"

"Got it, boss," Winston replies.

Boss? I like the sound of that! Winston is leaps behind where he should be as a one-year-old. I will need to remind myself of that and adjust to this lower learning curve over the next few weeks. Winston knows nothing about how to train a human, or even how to play the sit-and-stay game, so I work with him on these things constantly over the next two weeks. I even enlist the great trainer, Grandma, to help me. She is ten times better than that Cesar character on Animal Planet. I must say, I do really like Cesar, though. He, too, is an excellent dog whisper. Grandma helped me a lot when Melody was in the hospital after our accident. I know that I need all the help I can get when it comes to training Winston. *Why not employ the master?*

Grandma comes over daily to help Melody and me train Winston. I, of course, do most of the training by giving presentations and explaining to Winston the rules of the games we are playing in both German and English. After a week and a half, Winston gets the hang of it. I find this promising. It at least confirms that Winston is in no way dim. He is only a victim of circumstance. I am proud of him and how he is now taking responsibility to rise above his poor, insufficient upbringing

During our training, Winston tells me that his dog parents weren't able to teach him much before he left their house. He said, "I guess *das* American family that wanted me had lots of *geld* and they paid extra to get me shipped to their house early. I was a *geburtstag* gift for the families oldest son who turned sixteen. I don't think he ever really wanted me though. He gave me a name he barely ever spoke, and tethered me to a dog house outside with a chain because he didn't like me getting into his things. *Das* boy only came to feed and water me, and not even daily. For the longest time I thought something was wrong with me. Finally, I realized something was wrong with the kid instead and I was fine. The kid's mom and dad felt bad for me and placed an ad on a website and that is how Kenner found me."

After Winston' story, I am even more amazed by the speed with which Winston is picking up the English language. He barely got any training from his parents, he received none from his human, and he didn't have any other dogs to socialize with until he met me. For the most part, Winston now understands everything that is said around him, and he can communicate what he wants to in English. Winston does not always say the correct word and sometimes says things in the wrong context, but I understand him well enough. This at least means he is well on his way to speaking perfect English, well perfect with an accent anyhow.

I ask Winston more questions about his parents and Germany. I am intrigued by the way things work in this world and how we have come to be standing next to one another now. Winston says that he really doesn't remember much, but there is one thing his parents made sure to teach him and his siblings that he will never forget. I have to admit that I am a little disappointed when Winston tells me that the one thing he will never forget is what waterfowl and upland birds smell like. *Really? That's it? That is the one big tip your parents gave you in life?* Winston continues sharing and says they also taught him to play a game called 'Fetch the Bird.' They told him that if he wanted a good life with humans, he had to do everything in his power to capture these flying animals and bring them to the humans. *Ah, so this is why Kenner wanted him!* Kenner's motives have now been revealed to me.

I am intrigued by this so-called bird-hunting game Winston speaks of, which leads us to a very interesting conversation. "I have never encountered a mean duck or pheasant. I do not feel they are out to hurt our people. Why must you capture them for the humans?" I inquire.

Winston responds, "I do not think they are out to get our humans. I must admit, I am a little fuzzy on the details as it has been so long since I learned this lesson and my time was brief. I got very few lessons from my parents before being thrown into a crate and shipped to my American family. I think we are supposed to get the birds because the humans like to eat them. Perhaps we can figure this conundrum out together. The last mystery we solved was so much fun! I can teach you what I know of the hunting game when we return to Kenner's place. I do not see any birds around your place to practice with. Plus, the fence will get in our way. I suppose I have seen a few butterflies, but I must warn you that butterflies are not ideal to practice with. The last time I caught one of those glittery, flying insects, it tasted appalling and it took me forever to get the taste out of my mouth."

I tell Winston to be careful playing this game with the birds, as I may have played it once before. "A few years back, Melody and I encountered a goose with some babies in the park we run through on our way to Grandpa's house. We were jogging along on our usual route when a giant, hissing mother goose came out of nowhere. She was lunging and flapping her wings at us. She went after my Melody and tried to hurt her. I have sworn to protect Melody to the death, so I had to take action. Mother Goose started biting and snapping at Melody like a seventeen-foot crocodile!" Winston's stubby tail quivers in anticipation as I continue the story of me versus Mother Goose.

"I knew the goose was out for blood and meant to bring harm to my Melody, so I did what any good dog would do: I moved in to protect her. I only meant to warn Mother Goose away from us, so I got between the two of them and growled. She snapped at me with blinding rage and drew blood from my nose as she connected with my snout. The pain made my eyes water, but I quickly reacted and snapped back in her direction! This is where things get ugly, I must warn you. This story is not for the weak. Should I continue?" I ask Winston.

Winston jumps up and down, spinning in excited circles. "Yes, don't stop. I must know the ending. Are there more evil geese at the park? Will we see some tomorrow? I can't wait to have a goose adventure of my own!"

Ha, he wants to have a deuce adventure. That sounds poopy. I can't help but laugh a little because whenever Winston says the word goose excitedly his accent makes it sound like he is saying deuce. I wave my paw at him to settle him down. "Okay, but if you can't stomach the rest, let me know and I will stop. Apparently, I had snapped too hard at the mother goose. I know this because she went instantly limp in my mouth and her wings stopped flapping. Instead of getting a thank you and a hero's praise from Melody, I got scolded instead! I was trying to save her, but Melody didn't see it that way. It was all the goose's fault. She started the fight in the first place! Melody said that I killed the mother goose and that it made her very sad. Anyway, I wanted to tell you this story so you know to be careful when you capture these birds. I think the humans may want them taken alive, not dead—"

Winston interrupts me. "Maybe that is why we are to capture these evil, feathered beasts. Perhaps they are plotting against our people after all!" Winston sits there, looking at me with astonishment. The two of us are still pretty perplexed by the whole bird-hunting concept. We put our training on hold for the rest of the day and try to figure out the intentions of the mysterious, evil long-necked birds that flock to parks.

As our day comes to an end, Winston and I conclude that we will indeed need to investigate these birds and why Winston is to obtain them. I say, "I think my mother and father would have warned me about birds if they really were some evil force to be reckoned with. You may be on to something, though, back when you said that you think our humans may want to eat them. That is exactly what we did with the Mother Goose. She was our dinner that night, and let me tell you, she was delicious. Grandpa grilled her into a delicacy! I know what you are thinking right now, so just stop! We did not eat the goslings. Melody and I gathered up all the babies and took them to a wildlife rehab place. Melody explained what had happened once we got there, and a lady named Kay scolded me once more for my wrongdoing. It was a never-ending day of shaming. Neither Melody nor Kay realized that the day's events were traumatic for me, too. Unfortunately, sometimes humans only think about themselves. Watch out for them too, Winston. In general, Melody and Kenner are usually pretty good in this department, but everyone drops the ball now and then. Kay, the bird rehab lady, said she was upset that Melody and I had not been more careful, but she understood that I had to take action because Melody and I were under attack!"

Winston yawns. I am losing him now. I finish my story quickly. "Melody and I would have made terrible parents to the tiny goslings. Birds aren't smart like us. They can't survive without their mother. That is why they travel in huge flocks everywhere. Melody said something about the babies not being able to grow older without an imprint from their mother, whatever that means. Kay then gave us a special permit for the mother goose. That is why we got to eat her for dinner. No sense in letting her go to waste. That would have been the real tragedy of the day."

Chapter 39: Kenner's Home

In the short time that Kenner has been gone, Winston and I have grown amazingly close. I am now very fond of the little fella and his accent. But I am saddened slightly by the thought of Winston going to live with Kenner full-time once he returns. I really enjoy having him around, and I admire how relaxed he is all the time. I am always on Melody-protection patrol, but Winston does not seem to have a care in the world. Sure, he seems happier when Melody is around, just as I do, but he also seems happy without her, so long as we are together. *Perhaps this is because Melody is not Winston's human. Maybe Kenner will have a different effect on him.*

Winston loves that we have turned him into an inside dog, and he welcomes any attention he can get from Melody. He often makes me laugh because when Melody stops petting him, he finds a way to pet himself by rubbing his head on Melody's feet like he is tracing a large letter V. Winton really enjoys Grandpa and Grandma time, too. *He calls them fresh feet!* Winston always rubs his little noggin between anyone's feet that dare to rest upon the ottoman by our oversized chair.

The thing I think I like most about Winston is that he never stresses when Melody leaves for work. *Perhaps I could, and should, learn a few things from him.* I don't seem to have the drive to learn the bird-hunting game. I will leave that one all to him. *My prior angry mother goose situation still haunts me.* I do, however, want to become a master of his cool-as-a-cucumber and ultra-relaxed ways. He reminds me of one of those super chill people who work at those yoga retreat spas in the mountains. *Maybe I am watching too much women's TV during the day.*

Anyhow, I feel that the few weeks during which Melody and I have shared our house with Winston have gone by much too quickly. I don't want this new trio we have formed to be broken apart. Perhaps Winston should just stay with us full-time. Sadness tries to creep its way into my heart today when Kenner calls to say that he has crossed the U.S. border and is headed to his house. *Kenner will want Winston back. I don't want to give him back.* I know that I am being a total hypocrite because I made such a stink and didn't even want Winston in the first place, but time has a way of changing things.

Winston and I are now lying out in the backyard with two antler chews. I look over at him and see he is chilling out like some California surfer dude without a care in the world. I, on the other hand, am buried deep within my internal struggles as I try to devise a plan to keep Winston here with Melody and me. I find it funny that I been having so much fun with Winston that I can't even remember why Kenner had left in the first place. Melody is walking laps in the yard around us as she talks with Kenner on the phone. She is a lot like Grandpa: if they sit still, they fall asleep. I find it adorable.

Winston and I have both been listening in on

Melody's side of the conversation. Melody doesn't have the speaker option turned on, so the following is what Winston and I have deduced from her side of the conversation. Number one, Kenner had gone to Canada to hunt geese with a longtime friend of his. Number two, geese are evil, and many of the Canadian farmers refer to them as flying, feathered devils! Some farmers even offered to pay them to hunt the geese on their land.

Winston says, "Kenner is telling Melody that the farmers told him the feathered devils decimate their crops and eat up their profits. Should I follow Melody so I can hear the whole conversation?"

I tell Winston not to worry about it. We will know soon enough. I find that I am jealous of Winston for being able to hear so much better than I can. I say, "Knowing Kenner, he probably turned down the money and said he was just grateful for the opportunity to help them out." *He is a standup guy like that.* This is all great information, though, as I finally get to let go of my guilt for protecting Melody from the menacing, snake-necked mother goose.

Geese must be related to that Medusa chick I read about in one of Melody's college books. Perhaps geese are the more current edition since they only need one hissing head to get their job done. I have never really cared for geese. For one, they poop on everything! *Hello, there are designated places for that!* Two, they never shut up. I thought my sisters never shut up before, but I was wrong on that matter. These birds have my sisters whipped with their constant honking chatter! The endless and deafening noise they make reminds me of fishing boats out in the bays on foggy days. The boats all blast their various horns in an unrhythmic manner, nothing but honk after honk to get smaller vessels out of their way as they troll. I know this because Kenner took Grandpa and me out trolling for salmon once on a foggy weekend, and for a week after that adventure, I heard air horns every time I tried to sleep or nap.

On a more positive—and not goose-bashing—note, Winston and I decide that Kenner will probably bring some of these evil delicacies home. Kenner always likes to savor his most recently sought game as he tells Melody about his successful adventures. Kenner brings everything he hunts home. Seriously, the man wastes nothing! He is like one of those homesteaders who live on the Alaskan Frontier. Once Kenner gets whatever he had hunted home, he cooks it and then shares it with all of us. I don't know much about hunting, but I do know how excited I get for Kenner's return after he has been on one.

These thoughts alone have me licking my lips with anticipation. My salivary glands flow like a waterfall as I recall the amazing flavors and smells of the grilled goose that Melody and I had experienced once before with Grandpa. Served her right. I let Winston in on my mouth-watering thoughts, and we share a laugh. We will get the last words on those mouthy avians once and for all! *Revenge is a dish best served grilled. One's goose should always be cooked to a nice medium!* Melody and Kenner continue to talk, and as they do, we can tell that they are devising a plan to meet back up during the upcoming weekend. It sounds like the three of us will commute north to Kenner's place. It is time for Winston to return to Kenner's farm and run the house there.

The thought of leaving Winston up there with Kenner at the end of a fun weekend puts me in a gloomy mood. Envy colors my nearly all-white body green as Winston continues connecting the rest of the dots of Melody and Kenner's conversation for me. *Dang, how is Winston able to hear Kenner's voice when Melody is not using the speaker option? I need to get my hearing checked.* As Winston talks, I finally remember Kenner telling us he was going to hunt geese in Canada before we all drove home a few weeks ago. Seems my long-term memory is becoming spottier. *I will have to watch my blood sugar levels a little more frequently, as that has been linked to forgetfulness. Surely, it is only that.* Nonetheless, I have named my increasingly frequent memory loss 'Sometimers.' I have found a small silver lining to this aging cloud that has loomed over my head lately: bones and treats I hid and have long since forgotten about become an exciting new discovery. *I found another one earlier today!* I feel that a small disclosure is only fair as it has become evident to me that Winston's and my roles may be exchanged in the near future. Winston makes a much better Sherlock than I do. It appears that I am more of a Watson, though I am choosing to blame age instead of giving him full credit.

Apprehension is caving in on me. When Melody and I drive back to our place next weekend after visiting Kenner's farm, I will have twice as much missing to do during the week. *I have given away two more pieces of my heart.* I find this to be a preposterous thought since I have only been with Winston for a short time. How the little turd won me over already is beyond me. *It has to be his accent, and those ridiculous eyebrows, and the expressions he always makes.* Winston is so funny-looking, but it makes him extra cute. Everywhere we take him, people stop and comment. We get lots of extra attention because of this, so it is definitely not a bad thing.

I am almost completely in gloom-and-doom mode when I remember one of the best parts about going up to Kenner's place: daycare! This thought blows the dark clouds above my head away and suddenly fills me with excitement. I will get to watch Winston get his first taste of doggy daycare. This may be the event of the year, and it will put all of our training in the past few weeks to the test. I explain to Winston that daycare is where we temporarily stay on Fridays while Melody works. After work, we begin our four-hour trek up to Kenner's place. "Daycare helps tire us out for the long drive north. It is nice and makes the miles fly by." As I explain daycare to him, I notice that Winston has a very concerned look on his face. I quickly continue to ease his concerns. "Don't worry, Melody always comes back to pick us up at the end of the day. Remember, I will be with you the whole time, and Melody would never in a million years forget me or leave me behind." *Especially not for a road trip.* Melody is not capable of driving longer than an hour without me in tow. I serve as her therapy dog in vehicles to ward off her panic attacks. *You can be one, too, Winston!*

Winston starts to inquire why Melody cannot drive longer than an hour without me, but I avoid the question. I decide that not telling Winston about Melody's accident is probably the smartest thing to do since I don't want to make Winston any more worried than he already looks, and Melody doesn't need any more anxiety in the car. Her less-than-stellar driving record may put Winston over the edge of the concerned cliff. *It appears that I must serve as both of their therapy dogs this Friday.* I thought by giving Winston a job, I would lessen his anxiety, but his skin still seems to crawl with unease. He begs me to promise him we will not leave him behind at daycare.

I have Winston speaking almost perfect English now, with a small side of accent. Regardless, it fills me with pride. I listen to him grovel. "Ludo, I will follow all the rules and do as you say. You have my word. I will never try to pee on the couch—or anywhere in the house, for that matter—ever again! I have grown much too fond of you and Melody. I love my new luxurious, indoor, rope-less life. I absolutely cannot go back to being tied to a doghouse with no name!"

The thought that this would be a little scary for him due to his past had not occurred to me. *Could I, or should I, use this as leverage in the future? Nah, that would be taking advantage of the poor fella.* Winston is like a kid: he sometimes does things that irritate the crap out of me, but he is so darn cute I can't seem to stay mad at him. *If he ever figures this out, I am screwed.* I opt to reassure him that Melody and I will do nothing of the sort. "Relax, Winston. Just enjoy your time at daycare. That is why Melody takes us there. It is like a spa, but for dogs. Don't worry. You are, and always will be, a part of this pack now! I will not let anything happen to you. I will make sure you are never forgotten!"

I ease Winston's stress further by telling him about the cute females who are usually at daycare on Fridays. This piques his interest enough to reduce his anxiety—finally! I know this because Winston raises his furry left eyebrow, giving him a 'tell me more' look as I describe one of the poodle twins who I find the most intriguing. Of course, the twins are much too young for me at this point in my life. I am no cradle-snatcher. *No harm in looking though.* I always enjoy the show that the pretty poodles put on as they prance around. They wear their hair in a way that makes them look like ballet dancers with leg warmers on. A dog can not help but turn his or her head as the poodles' saunter past.

Winston wags his stubby little tail with interest. "Do you think I have a chance, Lu?"

I replied with a basic "Only time will tell." *I cannot promise love to anyone.* Love is something I have not fully figured out. *I don't know if I ever will.* From my research, I highly doubt I will ever have the power to make someone fall in love. *Therefore, I won't promise it.* I have found that love seems to find someone when they least expect it. If one tries to create it or goes looking for it like it is a treasure to be hunted, it only makes it that much more elusive. Melody's dating life was a prime example of that. Crashes in the Indie 500 had a much higher survival rate than her previous relationships. *At least, until she and Kenner collided one day.* I am not sold on Kenner yet though. I am keeping my judgment on him open until a clear decision can be made. *Kenner keeps throwing me curve balls, and I don't adjust easily.*

Love is uncontrollable. When I think of it, I remember the first day that my sweet Melody scooped me up in her arms. I had no intention of leaving my dog family that day, but I was indeed struck by one of Cupid's arrows. I have it bad, and will follow Melody into a fire if needed. *There is nothing I wouldn't do for her, and her for me.* Love comes in the form of unspoken and unbreakable bonds. Reminiscing on moments that Melody and I have shared over the years plasters a satisfied smile across my lips and warms my heart. Winston and I are in the middle of growing these same bonds. I also know Winston will grow them with Kenner once he overcomes his trust issues. This is a big, exciting step for a dog who once had no name. *I am blessed to be a part of one of life's most beautiful components.*

Chapter 40: Daycare

Ladies and gentlemen, the verdict has been delivered. *I will withhold the 'I told you so's for now.* Winston not only likes daycare—he *loves* it! However, the two of us got in trouble on more than a few occasions today. By mid-day, Kathy would only let one of us out in the yard with the others at a time. I thought at first this was because Kathy was lonely or needed a good therapy dog herself. *Let's face it: I am the best.* I am sure Winston and I are her two favorites even though she claims not to have any. *And why wouldn't we be? We were the best two gentlemen dogs there!*

However, when Melody picks us up from daycare today, Kathy gives her our daily report card, and a different version of how the day went is revealed. This is the first time ever—I will say it again: *EVER*—that I did not get an A! *I fully blame Winston.* In my defense, my record has always been more than stellar until Winston accompanied me. *I am a straight A guy. A is for alpha! This is unacceptable.*

I am appalled as Kathy greets Melody at our usual four in the afternoon pick-up time. There is no hello. Kathy instead leads off with, "Well, today was interesting. I am not sure if you are aware of this, but these two boys do really well together, but can't be together with others at the same time. Ludo kept trying to protect Winston from the other dogs when they would play with Winston. I don't know if it is jealousy, or if Ludo is just trying to keep him safe. Some dogs play rougher than others, you know."

"Of course I had to protect him!" I grumble at Melody. "Kenner would be furious with us if we returned Winston untrained and harmed!" Melody looks at me while I am groaning and pats my head. She is obviously not receiving my message. *Stop listening to this poppycock and pay attention to me!* I step on her foot to distract her from the lies that Kathy is telling her. *I thought we were friends. Doesn't Kathy know Kenner has excellent taste and high expectations?* Winston is to be Kenner's king's hand. The two are to play a game called 'hunting,' and Winston needs to be in tip-top shape for that.

Kathy must not watch the hunting channel or be privy to all this information. I suppose it's not all her fault. Winston is going to teach me the hunting game. I have started researching it while Melody is at work, just to get a better grasp on it. Winston and I both have been getting ready for Kenner's return. From what I have learned so far, we absolutely cannot bring Winston home damaged and sore. *I will chalk up our D grade to Kathy's lack of knowledge of our future with Kenner. I don't feel Winston should be at fault, either. Kathy can have all the blame.*

Kathy continues, "So, I started letting Ludo and Winston out separately. They seemed to do fine with this and we made it through most of the day. I would put them out in one-hour shifts and keep the odd man out at the front desk with me. Finally, that stopped working, and I ended up keeping them both up here with me. I could tell that Ludo was getting sore from all his playing, and he was starting to limp a little. I may start keeping him up at the front desk with me more often, if that is all right with you. He is great company, and everyone who comes in loves him! I am just worried that he won't be able to walk well tomorrow from playing so hard today." *That is true. My hips aren't what they used to be. These young pups are hard to keep up with.*

"And then there is Winston. I had to keep him up here with Ludo and me for the rest of the day not long after I pulled Ludo. I think Winston will be fine once he gets the hang of things here, but he kept trying to steal piggyback rides from unwilling parties today!" Kathy says, while winking at Melody.

Melody erupts into laughter. "Kathy, are you trying to say he was humping other dogs all day?"

Kathy giggles back. "Yes, excessively!"

Melody looks down at Winston and shakes her head. "What are we going to do with you two? Come on, let's go. We have a three-hour drive ahead of us, and Kenner is patiently waiting for our arrival." She thanks Kathy, and we head out to the Jeep to start our journey.

So, I was right—Winston liked the ladies I spoke of earlier. I want details. I have to live vicariously through this younger fella, after all! I admit, I am jealous of the fact that Winston not only has younger, more flexible, non-achy hips, but he also still has his mojo sack hanging down below his stubby tail. *Winston, that lucky son of a gun, was out there stealing piggyback rides from the poodles!*

Winston and I roar with laughter in the back of the Jeep as Melody drives. I pick on him and he picks on me. I remind Winston of the story I told him a week ago, about when I was four years old and fell asleep while visiting the vet. *When I awoke, poof! My mojo sack was missing!* I fear this has become a mystery that will never be solved. Ever since I told Winston this story, he has been sure to check on his little bag of marbles every morning when he wakes up. Winston yawning, along with the statement "Oh good, they are still there!" serves as my daily alarm.

Winston and I have heard stories about some tooth fairy that comes around and steals little kids' teeth. We can't help but wonder if there is a creepy little sack fairy wandering about this world. Perhaps no one tells this story because the first guy it happened to didn't want to admit that some fairy robbed him of his marbles while he was asleep! *Maybe the creepy sack fairy waits until we are a certain age to steal them. Maybe she waits until we sleep more deeply because our hearing is dissipating. Perhaps our sacks contain more mojo if they are aged like a good cheese or a fine wine.* The only thing I know for sure is that Sherlock Winston has assured me he will one day solve the case. But for the time being, we are exhausted from our play date at daycare and need to rest up so we can greet Kenner in a proper form.

Chapter 41: Northbound

Winston really loves car rides. He sticks his face as far out into the wind as he can get it. He looks hilarious with his beard and eyebrows blowing back in the strong breeze. His facial hair really cracks me up at times. I find it amusing that he sports the same beard style as Kenner. The two are practically twins! "This has been the greatest day, Lu," Winston calls back.

I smile, tired and sore. I find myself letting sad thoughts slip into my mind once again. We will be leaving Winston up north at the end of the weekend. I still have more to teach him, and I have not learned Winston's serenity methods yet. I have come to really enjoy his company; he helps me relax during the day when Melody is at work. *Well, I guess I am not sure if I am relaxing, or if he just distracts me and helps the time pass by more quickly, because we are always playing or talking. I need him!*

Melody pulls into Kenner's driveway, and I instantly sense another dog! *What in the heck is going on here?* Anger burns all the way to my core! Winston picks up on this and follows my lead. As we exit the Jeep, Kenner stands in the yard with a dog who looks similar to Winston. Kenner senses our unease and quickly introduces us to the Pudelpointer, who

335

stands by his feet. His name is Harley. Apparently, he was Kenner's dog before he and his now ex-wife got a divorce. I am grateful when Kenner explains to Melody and us that his ex-wife Jody has full doggy custody and that Harley will only be staying with him for this falls hunting season. Kenner doesn't feel Winston will be ready to hunt with him this year.

As much as I am relieved by the fact that Harley is only a temporary part of our lives I am still beyond irked. I had taken Winston in under my wing and accepted him. No way am I about to let another male dog into our pack. If we are going to add any more dogs to our pack, they will be females! *Perhaps one of the poodle from daycare Winston now fancies, but definitely not this pompous Pudelpointer!* Harley stands before Winston and me, a smug look painted on his face. He acts as if *he* is the king! Harley thinks he is above the king's hand! I can't believe his audacity! *News flash, Harley. You are not a king just because you are named after something that is referred to as 'King of the Road'!*

I play nice at first, mainly to humor Kenner and Melody, but so long as I am standing, Harley will never be the Alpha here. I explain to Winston that he is supposed to be Kenner's Alpha, not this Harley imposter! Immediately, Winston is on my side. His young, testosterone-filled mojo sack causes him to lose his mind briefly. A pecker fight ensues, and I have to back Winston. Winston and I tango with Harley for a mere minute. If I am being honest, it feels like an eternity with my achy backside. *Show no weakness!* Melody and Kenner quickly pull us all apart. Neither party is the clear winner; our scuffle only makes our situation worse. *No one likes a tie when leadership role is at stake.*

I remind Winston and myself that our new set of circumstances is only temporary. We all calm down long enough to make it through a tension-filled Friday evening. The three of us dogs decide to meet on common ground: none of us are happy about this current arrangement and none of us were properly informed! *What on earth was Kenner thinking?* On Saturday morning, Kenner takes Harley hunting for a while. This really chaps Winston's butt. He starts to pout and vent at me: "I may as well go back home with you and just become a full-time house dog!"

I do not know if I should be offended by this or take it as a compliment. I also do not know if I truly want to share my full-time house dog duties with anyone. *Or do I?* Funny how some things sound good until they are stated out loud. The whole 'be careful what you wish for' saying comes to mind. "Calm down, Winston. We will figure out a plan to get rid of the new guy. If we don't, you can come live with us and Kenner will be out of the pack. He can't just add males whenever he feels like it! I am sure this is just a misunderstanding of sorts." *Did the evil geese get to him up in Canada? What have they done to our Kenner?*

Melody stays home with us Saturday morning while Kenner and Harley are out hunting. She cooks in the house while Winston shows me what the hunting game is all about in the yard. We do not have any ducks or pheasants to learn with, so Winston improvises and teaches me with rabbits. *This is more fun than daycare! And I didn't think that was*

337

possible! The chase we go on is exhilarating. Adrenaline courses through my veins as we run as fast as possible after these little bunnies. Then, it gets even better when we catch one and get a delicious snack!

Our game ends abruptly when one of the rabbits lets out a high-pitched squeal and tells on us, making Melody come out into the yard. The bunny's scream is music to our ears. Apparently, it is more like nails on a chalkboard to Melody's, though. She yells at us, and she means it! Winston is smarter than me—or maybe it is ignorance. He has not seen the wrath of a mad Melody yet. He snatches the little ball of fur and bolts into the cornfield that surrounds Kenner's property.

"Lucky dog!" I call after him. Winston swallows the bunny whole before Melody can get to him. This hunting game is amazing, and Winston is superb at it! I have a lot to learn to be even half as good as him. At least he is willing to share his knowledge of this sport with me. He says he can teach me all his insider tricks. I can hardly wait to play again later when Melody is not looking. *Maybe I have a new addiction.*

Finally, Sunday afternoon arrives, and it is confirmed that Winston will spend the fall with us since Kenner has Harley to hunt with. Kenner feels that Winston will not be ready to hunt this season. *Poor Kenner. You are so sadly mistaken.* From where I stand, Winston is one of the best this world will ever know! It is planned that at the end of the hunting season, Kenner will take Harley back home. *I bid you farewell!* I cannot remember where Kenner said that was, nor do I really care so long as the smug little thin-haired guy leaves. He is not built for our winters. *Pfft. And to think he thought that he could be the King. One needs way more hair than that to survive around these parts.* The dog is clueless; his mojo sack is much too big for his body. The boys, as I used to call mine, have tarnished his way of thinking and given him some sort of false reality.

Once Harley returns to his home, Kenner will take Winston full-time. I take this as a blessing! Winston and I are really getting along. Maybe once all is said and done, I will want him in the pack with Melody and I full-time and will not give him back to Kenner. Either way, I give Kenner a check in the pros column for bringing Winston into our lives, and a red X in the cons column for bringing Harley. *Seems you are destined to be stuck at ground zero.* However, I still like Kenner a great deal, so I hope he figures it out soon so he too, will make the pack full-time. I like our traveling long-distance relationship, but I don't think this will work forever. *I am getting older. How will Melody ever make the journey without me?*

Chapter 42: Winter

The hunting season flies by quickly, just like the many migrating flocks of ducks in the sky. We still go to Kenner's on most weekends. Winston and I tolerate Harley, though I can't say any of us are overly thrilled when the weekends roll around. Finally, the season ends as winter roars in and establishes itself, and with that, Harley goes back home. This is the last time Winston and I ever see him, though Kenner still talks about him from time to time and shows pictures to Melody, so I know that he is still around somewhere. We wish him well from afar, but secretly hope he never comes back. Two male dogs are all a pack needs. *A lead and a successor.* From the sound of it, Harley is doing well and has a couple of kids who love on him daily. He is not a bad dog by any means. He was just not the right fit for Winston and I.

Along with Harley's departure comes a bittersweet moment for Winston and me. It elates us to see Harley go, but this means it is time for Winston to move in with Kenner. We will only see each other on the weekends now. We had a lot of fun while Melody was at work. I taught him how to be a great house dog, and he taught me how to relax. We discovered that I still have a much longer path ahead of me to acquire all of his relaxation skills, but Winston, on the other hand, has learned all there is to learn about properly running a house. He is ready to leave the nest, as they say. He, of course, understands that when I am in town, he will assume the role of the second in command. I stand as the alpha of the weekend. *We may not be brothers by blood, but we will always be brothers!*

The weekend after Harley leaves, we celebrate by going for a hike. Hiking this time of year means we are going shed antler hunting. Antlers are my favorite thing to chew on. *A delectable treat that's good for my teeth!* Once we are all worn out, Winston and I load into the back of Kenner's truck. We drive to a little hole-in-the-wall town so Melody and Kenner can get something to eat. It is warm for a winter day, about fifty degrees. The two stand outside the back of the truck, talking in a tone that seems almost argumentative.

Melody says, "I don't think we should leave the truck topper window open. I think Ludo will jump out and try to find me!"

Kenner disagrees. "Ludo will not jump through the screens in is not like they are all the way open anyhow. Come one don't worry, Winston is with him. They will be fine back there. It is warm out today, so I want to make sure they have fresh air. Besides, we will be only a block up the road, and we won't be long." Kenner reached for Melody's hand to pull her away from where she stood apprehensively alongside the back of the truck's open window staring at Ludo and gauging his next move.

Melody sighs hesitantly but concedes and gives into the pull of Kenner's hand holding hers. "I guess, but I am going on record and saying that I don't like it. This is a terrible idea. I know my dog, and I do not think he will do well with this!" The two start off towards the small dinner. Melody's anxiousness oozes from her pores. During their argument, she had told Kenner about my jump through the kitchen window years ago. Kenner assures her that this is a different situation.

Kenner says, "You will see. He is a different dog now. Plus, he has Winston!" Kenner does not know me as well as I had thought. One thing is for sure: Melody does!

She attempts one more time to bargain with him. "Can we at least get it to go?"

Kenner replies sternly. Being the leader he is, I expect nothing less. "No, you and Ludo need to learn to relax. You are both always so anxious. He feeds off of you, you know? I promise that you will both be fine." He grabs her hand and escorts her through the diner's doors.

Winston and I sit and watch as they disappear into the restaurant. Once they are out of earshot, my anxiety monster sinks his claws into my chest. I hyperventilate, then shake and whine. Winston tries to help me calm down. "They are fine, Lu. They went to eat. They'll be back with treats in a half hour. You heard Kenner. They are right there. You can see the door they went into. Look at the door. Focus on it—or on me, whichever makes it better."

I pace back and forth in the truck and continue to come unglued. "We have never been to this town, I do not know if she is safe. Who knows who or what is in that restaurant? So many security protocols are being breached at once!" I explain my racing thoughts to Winston at the speed of a NASCAR racecar headed towards the finish line. *I will find her, and I will save her!* I lose my ability to reason. My body is in a full-on tingle from head to tail. My heart pounds; I can hardly breathe. My muscles are twitching as I inch towards the only barrier between Melody and me.

Winston stands in front of the open window, trying to block my exit. "Now, Lu, just hear me out for one minute—"

"No!" I give him a low warning growl to get out of my way. He understands and quickly steps aside. Then, I burst through the screen of the truck toppers side window, leaving Winston behind.

He calls out after me, "What are you doing? Have you lost your mind? And you are going the wrong way!"

I have lost my mind. Sheer panic and fear have overtaken me. I have to find her. My vision is starry and my world is spinning. I think this may be what they call a full-blown panic attack! I have to run, but I do not know which way. I bolt this way and that, trying to scent her. I cannot smell Melody due to the restaurants around the area and the steadily blowing wind. She has vanished like an air-washed quail. I have lost the ability to isolate only Melody's scent and track her. Hysteria has taken over my body and mind.

Thankfully, Kenner had parked our truck in front of a house that contains a nosey old lady. She had watched them get out of the truck and argue briefly before heading up the road to the restaurant. Luckily for me, she continued to watch over us, and when I evacuated the truck, she called the restaurant immediately to inform them of my escape. Soon, I am found by a terrified Melody and a disappointed Kenner, who had run the streets calling my name. Once Melody makes sure I am all right, she scolds Kenner. "I told you this was a bad idea. I knew this would happen!"

Kenner, laid back as always, replies, "He is okay. Calm down, everything is fine. I don't know why he did that. I have taken both dogs places before and left them alone in the back with the windows open. Last time I did it, I stopped at Tom's, and when I came back to the truck, Ludo was sleeping like a baby. I think you two just stress each other out." *Wrong, my friend. It is the exact opposite. We calm each other.* That is why we thrive together and dive into a big, dark, anxiety-filled hole when we are apart. I am much worse than Melody. *Oh, Kenner, why can't you see this yet?*

Kenner seems perplexed by the situation as we return home. He admits that it scared him, and he thought I may have gotten hurt. He was grateful when they found me unharmed. *Turns out he was not as composed about the situation as he had let on.* He talks to Melody about her and I needing to work on our anxiety. "You two are missing out on some of the fun things in life because you are too busy stressing to enjoy yourselves." Melody doesn't reply she only sits silently next to Kenner as the truck drives us home.

Once we reach home and everyone settles down

and forgets about my recent escape scare things return to normal. Winston and I lie in the living room as Kenner and Melody prepare dinner together in the kitchen. Winston says, "Ludo I can help you work on some relaxation techniques. You can use them when your anxiety creeps in. Better yet, I could teach you, and then you could teach Melody. I think she needs just as much work in this area as you do. What do you think?"

I was about to tell Winston I was perfect and didn't need any more help because I am the Alpha One of our pack, but I don't. Instead I reply, "You're right Winston I think that is an excellent idea. Melody does need my help in this department." Neither Kenner nor Winston is wrong about us needing to work on this and an Ultimate Alpha takes responsibility and learns from his mistakes.

Chapter 43: Happy Birthday

Spring arrives, and I am turning sixty-four—eight in human years. I am more than halfway to one hundred now, and as we celebrate my great birthday weekend up at Kenner's, Father Time gives me a very unwelcome present: severe arthritis. It has slowly been establishing itself over the last few years, and I have always been able to fight it off until now. Finally, it has made itself at home in my lower back and hips. I hope today's bout is the worst it will ever get since I have to live with is daily now. I liked it better when it was just an occasional flare up. Too bad my birthday wish of being forever young didn't come true again this year.

Some German Shepherds get degenerative hips or dysplasia. I hope what I have is not either of those. Perhaps this arthritis of mine is the universe's way of coming to collect what I owe it from helping me with my two miracles years ago? If that is the case, then each painful hip is worth the look that is now always on Melody's face. Her positive spirit shines out of her every pore and blesses everything in her wake. She is always so blissful now, like a beautiful, sunny spring day after a harsh winter comes to an end. It's fitting that she has finally found peace in the spring—and on my birthday, of all days. *Wishes come true after all. Melody is lead-ing the life of an Ultimate Alpha and I taught her everything she knows!* I fight off the pain and stand proud enjoying every second of my birthday.

As the Sunday morning sun rises and my birth-day is officially over I cannot hide all the painful grimaces from my face as I step off my dog bed and stretch. I am sore after playing far too hard on Sat-urday. It was worth it though as it was one of the best birthdays I think I have ever had. Yesterday the whole family and I went hiking along the river bluffs. Winston and I chased Turkeys, we swam and fetched floating Frisbees in the water, and then we ate like kings as we shared a picnic next to a fresh spring waterfall that flowed almost magically from up high on the bluff.

Today would not be nearly as grand. I was grateful when Melody and Kenner noticed almost instantly as I woke that I was in pain. Instead of getting ready and leaving the house for another weekend day adventure we share a low-key family Sunday at home. I lie on the porch and listen most of the day while Melody and Kenner talk at the picnic table about where their relationship is headed. Win-ston is off hunting somewhere in the cornfield. My heart aches to chase Winston, and my hips and back ache worse keeping me on the porch. Even a turtle could outrun me today.

Eavesdropping on Melody and Kenner has a much more comfortable appeal. It is much easier, and people-watching is always entertaining. People are some of the worst communicators, but they serve as excellent sitcoms for us dogs! People just need to say what they mean and stop skirting around what they want or leave things open for interpretation. That only ends in disappointment. Dogs always do what they want and get their message across while doing so. We avoid nothing and leave nothing to be decoded. We also know when to cut our losses and walk away. *Say what you mean and mean what you say.* It is as simple as that and takes so much stress and guesswork away. Father used to tell us that my sometimes-hangry Uncle Thompson would say said, "If you can't eat it or hump it, then pee on it!" *Great words to live by in most situations.*

By the end of their conversation, they decide that Melody should look for a job up north. It is time for us to join Kenner and Winston full-time. This is a change I am actually excited for. I am blissful as we drive home tonight. Melody is filled with delight; she and I daydream of our new life with two of our favorites. My pack will grow, and I cannot imagine a better human or dog. I have to admit that even though I didn't pick Winston or Kenner myself, they are both amazing males. *Almost Alphas, but I'm not sure I am ready to give them that title yet.* They have both taught me as much as I have taught them. I am looking forward to everyday adventures with them both, not just being weekend warriors. I fear that I may need more help in the coming months to run the show that is our lives. My hips will probably only get worse, not better. This extra manpower will be a welcome change.

It does not take long for Melody to get a job up north. Before I know it, Kenner and Winston are helping us pack all our things into a large truck. We put a 'for sale' sign in our yard and drive everything up to their house. *We are here to stay.* I smile as I look back on my puppyhood and remember all those years ago when I said that I one day wanted a farm. Now, I live on one. I am a firm believer of having goals and saying them out loud often so you can always be working towards achieving them.

Over the years I have found that once I say something out loud that makes it real, then my mind finds a way to make it happen. It doesn't happen overnight, but in time, I always get what I am after. Some call it luck, but I believe there is no such thing as luck. Life is what you make of it. This world owes us nothing, and I have found that it will not give us anything for free, either. The secret to having luck, if that is what you want to call it, is simply deciding what it is we want and then going after it with a lot of hard work. I learned this from my parents and have seen it firsthand by watching Melody. Now, she writes goals down and checks them off once she achieves them. I smile just as big as she does each time she checks an obtained goal off her list, and then writes down another. As long as one has a goal they will never be lost.

Today is a big day for Melody and me. I get to check a few things of my life's to-do list: I have finally grown my pack, and I have done so with quality individuals that will no doubt be able to carry on and share my Ultimate Alpha Legacy with others. Melody and I have successfully put Kenner and Winston through a long, grueling interview process. Now, it is finally time to live as a pack since they have made the cut. I am excited, but also apprehensive due to the upcoming changes and my slower-than-normal ability to adapt to new houses and kennels. I know, that this is what Melody and I are meant to be doing. The only thing that is holding me back from jumping in headfirst are my worries about leaving Grandma, Grandpa, and Denali behind.

My initial pack members must have sensed my apprehension because they all come to see Melody and I off. Grandma and Grandpa took turns assuring me that they will visit often and that we will do the same. I tell myself that it is going to be the same, only different. Life spins around us and doesn't stop. It is a revolving door of changes, time to step out and embrace another one.

Four hours later, we arrive at Kenner's farm and unload the large truck. *Did I say Kenner's farm?* I guess I can officially call it ours now. We are home, Melody and I are now Driftless Iowa residents. Winston and I stretch our legs from the long ride and start a game of chase while our two human pack-mates do the heavy lifting. Winston is always watching for birds; he has some weird obsession with them, especially the little 'tweeties,' as I like to call them. Personally, I still don't understand it. I think that chasing rabbits is much more fun and far more rewarding. *At least when we catch the little cotton-tails, we get a tasty treat.* I love a good chase, though, and can't turn down a good leg-stretching, as I am quite stiff from our ride. So, rabbits or not, I follow Winston the best I can as he pursues a little black tweety bird.

Winston explodes from his place in the yard he is in hot pursuit the tweety bird. This particular tweety bird is called a Killdeer. *I have no idea why*

350

he chases these birds especially. He never catches them. Killdeers are the oddest members of the avian family I have encountered thus far. They pretend to be hurt, but just as Winston closes the gap, they fly away, taunting him. I have to give him credit for always being optimistic. I doubt that he will actually catch this one, just like all the others he has chased, but there is no way I will squash his hope. Who am I to say that he will never get one? Sometimes, hope is all it takes to tip the scale for a win. No matter how this ends, Winston is in hot pursuit of the bird and I am in pursuit of him. *Let the never-ending fun begin.*

Winston and I run until we are exhausted. I need to rest since my hips are suddenly screaming in agony, so I look back at the yard. Dang, it is about a quarter mile away now. *Maybe I should just rest here.* I am about to lie down in the field when I see Melody and Kenner celebrating not just the move, but the fact that the truck is finally empty. He picks her up and throws her over his shoulder. Melody squeals with what is probably delight, but it throws me into alert mode. I forget my aching hips and bark to tell her I am coming to save her as I run with everything I have left. As I close in on the two, I hear Melody say through laughter, "You'd better put me down. Ludo looks upset!"

Kenner laughs and spins her around faster. "He loves me. We will be fine, you will see. Always worrywarts, you two!" I am now only feet away from them. The laughter pouring from the two only confuses me more. *Does she need saving?* Kenner spins again, his back facing me now. Because I am still unsure of the situation, I give a halfhearted nip to his right hip as a warning. *He needs to know who is in charge.* Kenner drops Melody promptly.

Then, I cower as Melody scolds us both. "See, I told you so! Are you okay?" she first says to Kenner. Then, she turns and says some of my least favorite words: "Bad boy, Ludo! No bite. This is our family now!"

Kenner replies, "I am fine. Sorry, I guess I should have listened." He kneels to pet and reassure me. "I will never hurt your Mama, boy. Your mom as well and you and Winston are my top priorities!" Somehow I willingly accept Kenner's apology more quickly than usual. I think it is because somewhere deep inside me I know without a doubt the words Kenner has just told me are true.

We spend the rest of the day celebrating and unpacking boxes in the house. Not everything is going as I had envisioned though. I face a few upsets as this new adventure unfolds before us. Kenner and I have some pretty major disagreements on sleeping and kenneling arrangements. I will start with kenneling, as this one upsets me the least. Kenner was warned by Grandpa and Melody before we left what it would take to contain me in a kennel. I only hope that Kenner heeds the warning he was given, as I am counting on him to keep me safe during the day so I can take care of them when they are home. I need to be contained and unable to harm myself when my separation anxiety fits rear their ugly heads. I still have not figured out how to fully beat Lucifer. I have more good days than bad now, thanks to Winston, and I am not ashamed to talk about it, which I find also helps tremendously. I have learned over the years that everyone has problems; not one of us is without fault. Watch out for the one's who thinks they are perfect as they are often the worst. *To be Ultimate Alpha-strong, we must admit our problems and work through them.* Melody and I do this daily on our runs, which have turned into walks thanks to my slowly failing backside.

Kenner has seen my previous two fortresses and is just as good an engineer as Grandpa, so I am sure he will amend this problem in no time. Kenner is more than efficient when it comes to problems. He builds a large indoor kennel for Winston and me before the day's end. I am not happy about having to be inside all day long again. I understand his reasoning though. Kenner does not own the farm we live on, so he cannot cement in an inescapable bottom for an outdoor kennel. Our new kennel has a wooden floor that will just have to do. I am sure that with Winston to help pass the time, this will work. It has to!

Winston always does his best to talk sense into me. As my panic tries to set in after Melody leaves for work, he says, "Lu, she always comes back for us. You tell me all the time. She has never, and will never, not come back! Say it with me now!" Between Winston's constant reassurance and playful distractions, I know that I will adapt quickly to our new life at the farm. Melody and Kenner do not think it would be a good idea to try me outside in the kennel Kenner had built for Winston. They talk about moving the one he had just built outside, but are still worried that if I escape up here and go into a frenzy, I will get lost—or worse, hurt. I am not familiar with the area, and it is much too far for me to run to Grandpa's like I used to do when I escaped from

353

Melody's old house.

They are probably right to do things this way. *I hate to admit it, but Kenner could be right, and may finally know me better than I know myself.* He knows Melody and I cannot survive without one another. Kenner has assured us both that this is the best and safest way to contain me during the workday. I decide to take his side on this issue and give him my full support, mainly because he is not only in the right but also because no one wants to see Hurricane Melody if something were to happen to me. *No one could survive her in full force. Mystery Man barely escaped with his life.* What we witnessed that day was a small tropical storm, I can't imagine a full-on Hurricane Melody.

Settling into my new kennel arrangements and adapting to farm life are one thing. Sleeping arrangements, on the other hand, really tighten my collar. I am befuddled when Kenner says "Dogs belong on the floor!" Before we lived together as a family I was a nice guy and always appeased Kenner on weekends. Mainly because it was only two short nights. I was willing to endure two nights on the floor in exchange for amazing adventures and constant playtime with Winston when we visited them. Monday through Thursday though I always sleep in bed next to Melody where I belong. I had assumed things would be the same way here. I would take the bed Monday thru Thursday and Kenner could have it Friday thru Sunday. *It is called sharing.*

Evidently Kenner wants all the Melody snuggle time for himself. The two of them argue for only a few short minutes on the subject. I sit patiently waiting for Melody to politely correct Kenner on this matter and inform him he will have to wait until the next weekend to sleep in bed. *Boy, was I wrong.* I cannot believe my ears when they hear Melody finally concede and then side with Kenner on this matter. What just happened here? *He must have brainwashed her.* Does Melody really expect me to spend the rest of my life on the floor like some dog? Hello, I am the highest-ranking pack member in this house! This is absurd! I decide I cannot allow this to happen so every night I jump in bed with them hoping Kenner will go sleep on the couch.

The next few weeks aren't comfortable for any of us, and Kenner is even more stubborn than me. The three of us crowd into Kenner's queen sized bed. Melody and I had a king-sized bed before and I lay panting between the two at night wondering why we didn't bring it with us until I get so hot I can't stand it. Then I jump down allowing Kenner to have the bed for the night and I go lay on the bathroom tile to cool my body.

Since none of us are enjoying our new sleeping arrangements Melody spends lots of time, and a good deal of money, researching and buying Winston and me nice beds of our own. Mine is very comfortable and made of memory foam. I find that this really helps with my often-achy arthritic body. However, the bed is where I belong. Every night, I still climb into bed between the two, and then I get kicked out shortly after settling in. Winston just lies in his bed, laughing and shaking his head while watching the show unfold. Kenner and I have a comical nightly routine: I jump in bed to kiss Melody, then get comfortable between the two. Kenner waits for me to settle in before looking at Melody, who innocently says, "What? I don't see a dog."

Kenner then snaps his fingers and sternly says, "Lu, get down!" I obey only because I really respect him and I love how happy he makes Melody and me. I even admitted to Winston the other day over breakfast that I love them both. *Old age seems to be making me sappy. It is weird and I don't like it.* Melody then pats me on the head, kisses me, and tells me good night. I slowly wander over to my new bed, grumbling all the way to show my disagreement.

As I finally resign to sleeping in my dog bed, I let out a final groan-growl of disgust—always aimed at Kenner, of course. He then growls back at me. The two of us then play a five-minute game of growling back and forth at one another. Both of us refuse to let the other get the last word in for the night. *It is a dominance thing.* I am the pack Alpha and Melody knows it, so she says, "Enough, you two. Kenner, let him have the last word so we can go to bed already!" I then growl one last time after she says this, and Kenner does not reply.

Okay, okay, so I love to hate our new sleeping arrangements because I get a lot of joy out of our new nightly routine. My dog bed is amazing and I am not crowded or overheated from sleeping between the two of them. I sleep better than I ever have before. I refuse to admit this out loud because Kenner does not need to know he is indeed right. I don't want his head or ego to get any bigger. What is it with him and perfection? I thought Melody was the only perfect human. *Now, it appears I have two of them!*

Chapter 44: Living, Loving, and Growing Together

The end of our first week living together as a family arrives. Kenner loads us all into the car and takes us to the Mississippi River for a fishing and relaxation expedition. I have never swum in big water before. Winston assures me that it is easy. Even though I am a bit nervous, my excitement wins out. I love swimming. It is so much easier on my hips than running these days, and exercise helps to keep me loose. *If only we had a pond or a pool at the farm.* I welcome this new adventure for its lackadaisical and low resistance components. *Big water, here I come!*

Today, Winston and Kenner teach me how to retrieve floating dummies that look like blue-winged teals. *This tops chasing and eating rabbits!* The game starts with Kenner commanding us to sit, which we do while shaking with anticipation. I can hardly contain my excitement for the next command. Then, he launches two of these duck look-a-like dummies high into the air. They soar out above the water and land with a splash, floating on the river's rippling surface. Winston and I mark our dummies as they land in the water. Kenner yells, "Fetch 'em up, boys," and the race begins!

It is hardly fair to call it a race. Winston beats me every time. I am new to this game, but with practice, I'd like to think I will overcome Winston one day. I would like to walk away with at least one victory under my collar. *I hate losing at anything.* Sometimes, Winston paddles lazily along beside me back to shore. I think he is just making sure I am doing okay. Either that, or he is trying to steal the dummy I retrieved to showcase his amazing water dog skills. *Herding dog vs hunting dog. It is hardly fair.*

Winston is like the Blue Angel Planes. They would be his equivalent, only in the sky. He glides along effortlessly on top of the water. Winston's water skills remind me of a story from a holy book I read once, where some man walks on top of the water. I, on the other hand, splash for a while before getting up on step. My swim style is more like that of a rickety old bush plane. *Everyone inside is secretly praying I make it to the destination safely.* In the back of my mind, I have resigned to the fact I may never actually beat Winton in this game. I'm okay with it, but it is always good to have goals and something to work towards.

I am learning a lot from Winston and Kenner. As we ride home together in the back of the truck, soaking wet, I find that I am more relaxed than ever. In fact, I think I may even be enjoying the ride. I watch as Winston sticks his face out the open windows of the topper. His brown, bushy beard and eyebrows blow wildly around in the wind. He does not have a care in the world so long as he is with Kenner. Perplexed and envious of this, I ask why he is so relaxed all the time. He replies, "Kenner is the alpha when I am with him. I get to be just a dog, which means playing games and having fun. If he is not around, I have you to be the alpha. My role is easy. I figure it is best to enjoy it while it lasts. Besides, I see how stressed you are trying to keep us safe all the time. That is no way for a guy to live. You will give yourself an ulcer, Lu."

The first part of comment throws me for a loop. *What, he thinks Kenner is the alpha?* "Winston, I am the Alpha. It is absurd that you think it would be Kenner. Though, he is next in line because you are not yet ready for that role."

"Lu, I am just saying you do not have to be the Alpha all the time," Winston lazily replies as he spins in circles to ready himself for a nap. "Let Kenner take care of Melody, and maybe then you can relax a little more. He takes care of her when you are not with them. Think about it. Doesn't he always bring her home safe?"

I sit, pondering his statement. "Well, yes. He does take good care of her when I am not with them, and she always returns unharmed and happy. I suppose I could let him manage her a little more."

Winston yawns. "I do not think she needs much managing at all. Frankly, I think they both do a good job at taking care of themselves as well as us. We are spoiled rotten. You see that, don't you? Besides, if they truly needed protection from another human, they would be better at fighting them off than we would. We don't have words to use like they do. Only our teeth—and that is a game-ender for us. I know you have heard of several cases, as I have, where if a dog bites a human they take the forever nap! Let Kenner deal with those situations if they ever arise. Human laws are much more forgiving."

I sleep on all Winston and I have talked about for the rest of the ride home. *Giving up some of my responsibilities would make my life a little more carefree.* Melody is who I live for, though, so I need to think this through fully before deciding. Perhaps I need to train Kenner a few more weeks before letting him assume more Alpha duties. The thought of relaxing my achy body more and just being a dog is enticing. Winston makes every day look like the best day ever. *I want to live that way, but can I let go enough to obtain his chill surfer dog lifestyle?*

Chapter 45: Retirement

Our first year living together as pack goes more smoothly than I had expected. We have a few difficulties as we adjust to how everyone lives behind closed doors, but overall, there is nothing we cannot handle or overcome together as a pack. Our downs are the average downs that all people go through when adjusting, you know the basic 'can we at least agree to put our dishes in the sink when we are done with them' type stuff. Another winter is winding down, and we are one big happy family, as people like to say.

Melody and I learned a major lesson this year compliments of Winston and Kenner. We learned how to give up control now and then, and it has made us both stronger and happier. This is a big deal for Melody and I because both of us could probably be called anxious control freaks. Melody transformation was amusing to watch, she happens to be just as resistant to change as me. The only difference between her and I is that she doesn't chew her way out of kennels in protest, but instead uses words. Oh, to have a human tongue. Anyhow, since she started trusting Kenner with driving and a few other things she has been able to relax and enjoy the scenery more. I am glad she isn't missing out on life's beautiful pictures anymore, before she couldn't take her eyes off the road and her heart rate was always sky high when in a vehicle. Thanks to Kenner I don't have to worry about her having a stroke as we drive down the road anymore. I too found that by putting my trust into Kenner and letting him take control now and then I get to just be a dog. *Being 'just' a dog is fabulous!* Winston was an excellent teacher when it comes to all things dog so he was just as big a part of my slow transformation. Who knew by learning to give up control, one actually gains it? My pesky little monster Lucifer has basically become extinct now.

Today is another beautiful day, and Kenner tells us all to load up in the truck. We are going on a family ice fishing adventure. Perhaps it is closer to spring now. *I will call it 'sprinter,' a mixture of late winter and early spring.* I am not sure what the short transition seasons are called. Anyway, during the truck ride over, I give up Alpha control for the afternoon to fully enjoy our adventure.

Once we arrive, Winston and I begin running around and sniffing for old bait, aka minnows, next to previously used fishing holes. Minnows are tasty treats! *I love me some super food omegas!* I find the ultimate pile of frozen, rosy red minnows next to an older, iced-over hole. I, of course, do not let Winston in on the action; he is younger and faster in almost all situations now, so I keep this glorious buffet all to myself. Once he catches wind of them, he will surely come to gobble them up much faster and more efficiently than I am capable of doing.

As I paw at the frozen fish and chomp away on the ones I have finally freed, I commit a cardinal sin

362

on the ice: I stop paying attention to how close I am to the open waters. In previous years, Kenner had taught us about gray ice. More of it appears as winter turns into spring. I realize the error of my ways at the same time that Melody begins yelling. "Ludo, no! Here, boy. Come!" I was so excited about discovering this pile of minnows I failed to realize how close this old ice hole was to the open water. There was a reason it was an old hole, and no one was using it anymore. Open water laps over gray ice in the gentle breeze. I immediately turn to obey Melody's command, but as I head back, I hear the dreaded noise that no fisherman wants to hear when standing out on the ice, a sound like a gargantuan bowl of fresh Rice Krispies with milk being poured over it: *snap, crackle*—sink!

The ice below my paws explodes like the windshield of the Green Machine did years ago. As the once solid ground turns to liquid, I find myself in the dark, icy river. The temperature is shockingly cold, and that alone nearly consumes me. The newly opened water swallows me whole like the tale of Jonah and the whale. I plunge downward, deep into the water's swift current. I fear that I have completely lost my bearings. I have to decide because my life now depends on it. I look around and see a lighter area of water, then propel my body towards it. I finally find the water's surface and gasp to pull air back into my lungs. Melody is yelling for Kenner. I turn my head in their direction and paddle wildly back towards them.

Due to the current, I had drifted a decent distance from them. I finally make it back to where I had fallen in, but I am running out of steam fast.

Every time I try to get back onto the ice, additional pieces break away, and I am forced back under the frigid water. Each time I plunge back into the water, it becomes harder and harder for me to come back up and battle the current to the ice's edge. My monster is back with a vengeance. He has grown into a Tyrannosaurus Rex, vowing to end me once and for all.

Melody runs towards me. I knew this would be bad for us both. If she gets any closer, I will make myself go under and will not rise back up to the surface then she will have to stop because she will not know where to jump in to save me. I cannot risk her safety, I know if I keep my head above water and keep paddling around panicked she will try to jump in and save me. I was put on this earth to protect her; no way will I let anything happen to her. Kenner somehow reads my mind and grabs Melody's arm as she tries to run past him to my aid. I continue to paddle furiously, trying to get back on top of some solid ice. Kenner quickly reasons with Melody and makes her promise not to move from where she is standing. *I can't believe she actually obeyed him.* Gratitude fills me as she stands there, trembling and shouting after us both to be careful. I know that it isn't easy for her to do nothing, but it will benefit us all. *Give up control to gain it. That's my girl!*

Kenner knows what he is doing. He is the greatest outdoor survivalist I have ever met. I fear that Melody would have just jumped in after me, making our situation much worse. *Kenner will come up with a plan. He always has a plan.* With Melody's freshly made promise, Kenner lies down on top of the ice and sets his plan into motion by assuming the position of a giant starfish. Then, he starts to wiggle his way out to me, speaking calmly as he does so.

Kenner's deep, soothing timbre never sounded so good. It settles my ever-increasing nerves. I listen and obey every command he gives me. I tread water and maintain my position near the icy edge. "Hold it, boy. Hold it right there. That's it, stay. I am coming for you, big guy." I put all my energy into my doggy paddle as the current and temperature tries its best to defeat me. *I will not let the water win. I will not let the water win.* I chant this with each stroke. I have Melody to live for, and Kenner on my team. I fill myself with hope. *I—no, wait. WE have got this!*

Kenner reaches the edge of the ice. Melody stands wide-eyed not far behind him. She is doing her best to keep her promise. However, I can see her inching forward like an old dog who thinks its owner's not watching. This next part has to happen without a hitch, or she will watch the two souls she loves most go down the river. I await my next command.

"Okay, Lu, up boy. Up!" Kenner yells. I put every bit of energy I have left into propelling myself from the water's grip and getting my body partially up on the surface of the hard ice. We only have one shot at this. I am wearing out fast, and there is no way I can muster the energy for a second attempt. I shoot up from the water and heave my body to the side, managing to flop my front paws up onto the ice inches from where Kenner's hands await me. *How do sea lions do it?* The ice doesn't break this time, but I have still failed; I didn't make it close enough to Kenner's hands. I start to slide back into the water, my claws dragging along the ice, allowing me one last look at the pack I love with all my heart. I close my eyes, unable to look any longer, as failure and shame squash my hope. I begin to say a silent goodbye to Melody.

Suddenly, I feel my collar tighten around my neck, it gets so tight I can barely breathe. Somehow, Kenner had thrown himself forward a little more when I slid backwards. Now, his strong hands have a firm grip on the scruff of my neck and my collar. Relief floods me, and my body goes limp as my adrenaline levels plummet. I want to vomit, but don't have the energy. Kenner takes care of everything else for the next several minutes. I have nothing left to give besides a tremendous amount of gratitude.

Kenner yanks my body up from the icy water and pulls me closer to him. "I got you, big guy. Now, let's go home! Just relax and let me do the work. We don't need any more ice giving way." *Those words have never sounded better. I relinquish all control!*

Kenner continues to belly crawl and drag my limp and incredibly worn out body back to safety and into the waiting arms of my Melody. Melody sobs with relief, "Oh, my goodness thank you so much for saving him!" She kisses me repeatedly on the top of my head while she rocks me back and forth like an infant.

Kenner leans in to receive the hero's kiss he deserves and then he hands Melody the keys to the truck while saying, "Why don't you take the dogs to the truck and get him warmed up. I will pick up our gear and meet you there shortly. We better take him home, he is going to exhausted the rest of the day and could probably use a warm soak in the tub. I am sure Ludo's hips will make him pay for all that swimming he just did."

On our way home Melody holds me on her lap in the front seat and has me wrapped in an old blanket they keep in the back of the truck for emergencies. Kenner has the heat on full blast and I can see sweat accumulating on his brow. He probably wants to roll his window down and cool himself off but I know he isn't because of me. It suddenly clicks that Kenner really loves me just as much as he loves Melody. I sit replaying the terrible afternoon over again in my mind only this time I can see all the love he has for our pack. I realize that today is more than just the day I defied the Grim Reaper. Today is also the perfect day for me to abandon my role as head Alpha of the house once and for all. Melody's, Winston's, and my safety are in the excellent and more-than-capable hands of Kenner. I know that he loves us as much as we love him. He showed that he would risk everything for Melody, just as I would, and he is far better at it than I could be at this point in my life. *I am finally turning in my resignation papers.* The time has come for me to relax and enjoy being a dog full-time. I finally have my Ultimate Alpha family, and I want to fully enjoy our time together. *You never know when the ice is going to break again. Next time, I may not be so lucky.*

Chapter 46: Smells Rotten

Finally, our two-year anniversary of living together as a pack approaches. I have really enjoyed myself since resigning from the head house Alpha role. I am finally able to grasp all the information that Winston has shared with me over the past few years and put it to use. I had missed out on so much by stressing myself out all the time. *Sometimes, I must let my worry go and just do me.* I guess some of us need a near-death experience to figure that part of life out. *Thankfully, Melody and I survived ours.* We both had bad things happen to us, but we made it through. To be honest, besides being a little more sore and achy some days, we both came out of our accidents better than we were before them.

Over the past two years, Winston and I have turned into excellent farm dogs. Few animals dare to cross our property lines anymore. However, I seem to be slowing down more and more as time progresses. Winton and Kenner's constant adventuring is sometimes hard to keep up with. Melody and I manage most days, and I am sure she could keep up just fine if she wanted to, but she always hangs back with me. *I would do the same for her in a heartbeat if the roles were reversed.*

My hips and back are not what they used to be. My sometimes barley working hips have put pressure on us all to find solutions that allow me to take part in my normal activities. Melody usually carries me up and down the stairs in the mornings so I can use the bathroom, by mid-morning I loosen up a bit more and can manage by myself. Winston too has made several adjustments in his life to better include me and my slowly deteriorating body. He has gone above and beyond and came up with a masterful modification for my favorite hunting game. 'Get that Bunny!' He allows me to still participate in the fun instead of leaving me behind in the dust as he easily could.

Winston showed me how we can use the farm's outbuildings to aid us during our bunny hunts. I can no longer keep up with him; often, if I try running after him, I struggle to make it back home without help. So now when we play our game I only have to make it to the big red barn, then I hide alongside the back of the building closest to the direction our cotton-tailed snack will come from. *Slightly cat-like, I know, and I am not proud of it, but it works like a dream.* Winston and I have decided that we will never tell the farm cats around the property that he learned it from watching them stalk mice one day. I wish we would have tried this months ago. Rabbit hunting is so much easier now, and our success rate has even gone up!

Once I am in position, Winston gets our target on the run. He is like a lion chasing a zebra through the desert plains, fast and ferocious. As the chase heats up, he steers the prey in my direction. I use my sense of smell and the sound of Winston's heavy breathing to tell how close they are. *At least these senses are still in perfect working order unlike my poor back legs.* Then, just as our target bunny clears the corner of the shed, I pounce out of the shadows. As I fly through the air, Winston yells, "Say hello to my little friend!" The poor, unsuspecting creature serves as my landing pad as I crash back down to earth. Winston and I end things quickly and humanely, then thank the circle of life for this nourishment as we dig in.

I can only take a small amount of credit for our success rate. Winston suggested trying the idea in the first place, and he does all the legwork. I feel bad that I can't help more, but I am happy that he has found a way to include me in the fun. I have learned a lot from Winston over the past several years, and I am grateful for all that he has taught me. Finding my true Zen has really enriched not just my life, but Melody's, too. I can see that she has found hers as well. There is no better way to lead than to walk one's talk. An Ultimate Alpha would never worry about such trivial matters; therefore, I have cast those worries away from my life for good.

Winston and Melody are not the only ones who have helped to adapt things to my aging body. Over the past year, Kenner has done a lot to make things easier for me, too. He builds ramps instead of steps so I can go outside with minimal assistance from Melody. In places Kenner can't put a ramp he often helps Melody lift me so that I can still go wherever they go. I think his genius brain helped get Winston in the correct mindset to help me with our hunting issues. I am good with the way things are now, but if my hips and back get much worse... *Well, I'm just not ready to go there yet.*

You're Welcome

Winston and I are resting on the front lawn on a wonderful, warm Sunday evening in May. I used to hate the heat, but now I welcome it. The bitter cold has made me tin man-stiff ever since I was almost claimed by the river. Melody and Kenner are cleaning out the camper not far from us. We have just come home from a fun walleye fishing trip on Mille Lacs Lake in Minnesota. As the twilight settles in and a warm wind blows some leaves off the trees, I sit and reflect as I listen to the soft rustling noises the leaves make as they flutter down around us. This is the life. I have everything I could ever want right in front of me. I am just about to give Winston my sappy 'happy anniversary, I love you, pal' speech when he instead rises and says, "Come on, Lu, you are rested up from our long car ride home. What do you say—want to go for a quick hunt before bed? It's our anniversary. We should celebrate!"

Winston is a party animal. *Have I mentioned that yet?* I yawn. I may be rested, but that does not mean I have the energy to go chasing after rabbits. "I don't know. Can't we just celebrate on the porch and stay close to home?" I like having the three things I love the most right next to each other. It soothes me.

"No way, man. I can smell a funky creature we need to go investigate. Nothing has crossed our property line in weeks! I must know what is brave enough to do so now. We have a reputation to uphold!"

This comment is what suckers me into what will be my last and most memorable hunting adventure. The two of us sneak off while Melody and Kenner are inside the camper. As we reach the back of the barn, I catch a whiff of what has Winston so intrigued: a strong, musky, sulfur-filled scent. "What kind of creature does that belong to?" I ask.

Before I can get an answer, Winston explodes forward, bounding after the smelly creature. He has a visual; the chase is on. I trail behind. Unfortunately for me that is a very bad place to be. We weave in and out of the farm equipment. When the creature zigs, I zag. I have finally caught up, and as I bring up the rear to distract the oddest-looking, most perfectly black-and-white-striped cat I have ever seen, Winston springs from the shadows. He lands directly in front of the smelly cat with his teeth bared and gleaming in the moonlight. This scares the creature so bad, its tail shoots straight up. The most horrific-smelling pepper spray-like juice shoots out of its butt. *And people say some dogs have bad anal gland issues. No dog in history has ever been this bad!*

I take the brunt of the putrid burst of spray directly in my nose and mouth. Unfortunately for me, my mouth is wide open alligator-style due to heavily panting from our hot pursuit. This pungent stuff steals the wind right out of my lungs and blinds me. I cry out for mercy and turn to retreat back to our house, whipping around so fast that I spear myself on the giant raking mechanism that hangs down in front of one of the tractors. One of the root rakes tines plunges deep into my right shoulder.

Winston hears me cry out and shows the smelly cat-like creature no mercy. "I will get him for you, Lu! No one hurts my brother!"

I try to call out to him. I want him to abort our

hunting adventure and help me. I can't breathe, let alone talk. I can't see anything through the burning blackness that has overtaken my eyes, and now I have skewered myself like the pieces of meat that Melody sometimes grills. The only things in working order now are my ears. I can still hear Winston doing battle with the sewer cat. I can't think about him right now, though. I need air. I thrash back and forth, but only manage to dig the metal hook deeper into my shoulder. Pain shoots through me, and I scream loudly one last time before passing out. The last thing I hear is Melody's voice calling out for me.

Winston finally overcomes the smelly cat and trots back home to a worried Melody and Kenner. Clouds have blown in with the soft May breeze to create a dark moonless night on the farm. Kenner scolds Winston for chasing after, and now smelling faintly like, a skunk. Off in the distance as I slowly start regain consciousness I can hear Melody frantically calling my name. "Ludo, where are you boy? Ludo, come!"

Fresh air slowly finds its way to my lungs, *thank goodness I'm not dead*. I am stuck in some sort of unconscious yet slightly aware state now. I try to bark an answer to Melody but no sound leaves my mouth. My eyes are now watering profusely which seems to be helping me gain my vision back. I lay there and assess my situation with very blurry eyes. Finally, I am able to gather myself and see the metal piece that has lodged itself in my shoulder. All I have to do to get it out is back up, so I grit my teeth together and brace for the pain that I know will find me as I do so. Freed from the root rake I start to make my way back to Melody. I can only see things that are very close to me so I rely on my ears to find my way back to Melody. For once I am grateful for her relentless calling.

Melody and Kenner have flashlights and are following Winston towards me. Thank goodness—I don't know if I could have made it much farther. As soon as I can make out Melody's shadow-like figure and feel her body heat, I run and leap into her arms like an eight-week-old puppy. Melody cannot bear the weight of me all at once; we fall to the ground as she dry heaves due to the overpowering skunk smell and I throw up. Melody shrieks at Kenner, "I have him! He got skunked, and he is in bad shape!"

Kenner calls back to us. "I am coming. Don't worry, we will take care of him. He will be okay." He is immediately by our side, helping us over to the side of the house where the garden hose lies. *Some days, I think the man is like Clark Kent and there is some sort of superman cape hidden under his t-shirt.*

Melody is giving in to her panic monster. "He is struggling to breathe. What do we do?" She isn't wrong by any means; I can only manage gasps. Fluids pour out of every orifice of my head due to the dreadfully acidic oil that covers me. At this point my shoulder is the least of my worries and neither Kenner, nor Melody have even noticed that yet. As soon as Melody finds the hole in my shoulder, she will surely succumb to her monsters panicking ways.

"Can you carry him over here?" Kenner is already ten steps ahead of us, getting some concoction ready in the garage.

"I'm right behind you," Melody replies. She picks

up my trembling body like I am as light as a feather. I am amazed by the amount of strength a person can find when fear is involved. On an average day, I doubt she could carry me that far. Today, though, she throws me over her shoulder like a bag of dog food and runs with ease. She lays me down in the grass, and the two begin working on me like a couple of expert surgeons.

"Rub this everywhere except his face. I will take care of that," Kenner says as he gently streams icy cold water from the garden hose over my face and eyes. The water flushes out my eyes, and things start to slowly come back into focus. *Whew, I'm not blind after all.* He opens my mouth and pours water down my throat even slower than he had my eyes. I spit most of it out at first, trying to get the awful taste out of my mouth. Then, I finally start gulping it down as I realize that having something to vomit back up is better than the retching I am currently doing. He flushes out my eyes and mouth three times. It has never felt so good to toss my cookies.

I am lying there like a limp noodle now. All the adrenaline flees my body as exhaustion consumes me. Melody is massaging a thick mixture of baking soda and Dawn dish soap into my mostly dry fur. Kenner told her that the secret to de-skunking a dog is not to use water right away. This way, the baking soda absorbs the oily odor as the Dawn helps to break it down. Once they soak up the stench, water can be used to rinse it away. Melody moves in front of me to apply the mixture to my front legs and shoulders since she has finished my back half. She lets out a soft squeal. "Kenner, look. His shoulder is ripped open. I didn't see this before. This is a huge cut, we have got to take him in!"

"It will be okay. We will get him cleaned up and take him to the vet. They can patch him up the rest the way," Kenner says calmly. *The man is like Winston. The two were made for each other. I don't think they even know what real stress or anxiety is. How do they always keep it together?*

Once I am cleaned up enough to be put in the truck, Kenner and Melody load me into the back and off we go. Yeah, voodoo doctors, here I come. Any other day I would have protested, but not today. I am excited about anything the witch doctor can give me to take away the pain in my shoulder. Melody rides with me in the back of the truck as Kenner drives. Once we arrive at the vet, a man named Dr. Tom who is the vet on call tonight stands waiting for us in the parking lot with a small table on wheels. Dr. Tom doesn't even start with a hello. He is all business. "Let's get him on the gurney, my nurse is on her way in. You two will have to assist until she gets here. Can you do that?"

"We can do anything you ask of us!" Melody says. She isn't wrong. Add a loved one in pain and a little adrenaline to any situation and one would be amazed at what people are capable of doing.

"Alright then," Dr. Tom says, "This way. We will take him to the surgery room. I need to put him under so I can assess him better and get him stitched up after we get some x-rays. Kenner I think I will have you hold him down for me until I get him under. I don't think in his condition he will be happy with a stranger in his face."

"I can do that, but I don't think you need to worry much about him doc. He is a good dog so long as you don't mess with Melody. She is what he lives for," Kenner replies.

I am wheeled into the vet clinics OR suite and Melody holds my head firmly in place while Kenner places the majority of his weight on my middle section so I can't move. I feel the prick of a needle by right back leg and the lights go out for me almost instantly. For once I am grateful for the voodoo doctors and the magic they perform.

Several hours later, I wince in pain as I wake inside our house on the kitchen floor. I try to move my right front shoulder and it painfully protests. Dang, I was hoping I just had some sort of bad dream. When I look down at my shoulder, I notice that my shoulder has been shaved bare and sewn back together. Coarse black threads in large, criss-crossed Xs hold my skin together. It itches terribly. Suddenly, something moves behind me, catching me off guard. Melody says, "Good morning, big guy. How are you feeling? Want some pain meds?"

If by pain meds you mean some of those special cookies you and Grandpa used to give me, then yes. I will take two, please! My heart warms as Melody rises from where she had been lying on the floor next to me. I did not realize until now that she had slept next to me. She must have never left my side all night. I'm not sure why this surprises me. *We are a true pack, a family.* That is what families do. They never waver or stray, even if one gets into a terribly stinky situation. *Always stand by the ones you love.*

A.J. Arentz

Chapter 47: It Happens to Us All

I am nearly healed up after a month. It took longer than I wanted it to. Evidently, as we age, recovery takes longer. *Old age is for the birds.* I say nearly because while the wound on my shoulder is basically healed, my senses have not all returned to normal yet. *I wonder if they ever will.* Melody's family calls often for updates. We may not live near them anymore, but I know that if Melody says we need help, Grandma, Grandpa, and Grandma Great would come running in an instant.

Melody is giving Grandma Great my most recent health update on the phone while she makes dinner this evening. No one in the family is allowed to be hurt or ill without consulting Grandma Great. She says she is only a nurse, but I am sure she is actually a doctor—if not in this life, then in another. Melody has the phone on the speaker setting. *She knows I like to be included.* Grandma Great is chatting away and filling her in on the goings-on farther south. She is a strong, proper woman, so I snort when she says, "Some days are hell when you are getting old, sweetheart." Grandma Great couldn't be more right.

The next few months seem to pass by slowly. I'm not sure if time has slowed down, or if it is just me. *I notice each minute more as they achily pass me by.* Tonight, Melody sits with me in our oversized chair, surfing the internet on her laptop. My head rests comfortably in her lap as I watch her delete e-mails. When she finishes with that, she switches over to Amazon. The UPS guy seems to visit our house almost weekly. Every time he comes, he leaves a brown box that proudly sports Amazon's logo. Lately, the boxes have contained things like Dinovite, glucosamine, and other doggy supplements. Melody is on a quest to rid me of my aches and pains. For the most part, we are managing well, so I don't have to heart to tell her that there is no cure for degenerative hips plagued with arthritis and old age.

My mindset changes as she searches Amazon. In the search bar, Melody types in 'wheelchair for dogs.' *No, she couldn't. She wouldn't. Would she?* A strange cart-like thing with straps and wheels appears on the screen before us. These contraptions hold up the dog's back half so they only have to use their front legs to get around. If I were younger and still had all my senses performing accurately, I may have welcomed this idea. This is not the case, though. I have become old, and my senses feeble. *I am a proud alpha. No, wait—I am a proud Ultimate Alpha!* I refuse to go down in pain with a humiliating wheelchair strapped to my back half. I may allow Melody to pick my crap up in the yard, but I will not allow her to wipe my butt and prolong my life as I fade away into some vegetative state. *That is no life at all.*

I get up with determination, doing my best to hide my pain. I step on Melody's laptop, walk to the front door, and bark. *No way will I allow her to hit the 'buy now' button!* "You want to go out, Ludo?" she asks. I love how she talks to me as if I am human.

380

She asks questions and then waits for me to answer with one of my gestures. I hit the door handle with my nose to signal my reply. I want her to take Winston and me outside so we can frolic around and play. I need to show her I don't need a doggy wheelchair. *I also need to come up with a plan for my shortening future.*

"Okay, then, you want your Frisbee?" she inquires, looking to where it hangs on the key hook by the door. I bark to confirm my 'yes, please.' "Kenner, the boys and I are going out to play, if you want to take a break and join us," Melody calls up the stairs to him. Kenner is working on a duck mount for a friend's son. The three of us head outside for some evening playtime in the yard.

Kenner joins us outside after ten good Frisbee catches on my behalf. Winston has just returned to the yard after giving up on chasing a squirrel that is probably in the next county over by now. Surely, it will never venture into our yard again. He and I lie down underneath the large oak tree in the front yard, and Kenner joins Melody at the picnic table. I gaze at the three of them and realize that I finally have it all. Love and abundance are all around us. *Everything I have ever wanted, and all I have wanted to leave behind, are sitting right here before me.*

As a peacefulness settles around me Winston speaks and pulls me back from my moment of serenity. "How are you feeling after that Frisbee-fetching rampage? I saw you catch the last two as I was heading back to the yard. That darn squirrel eluded me again, but I will bet him next time. Anyhow, I haven't seen you do moves like that in years! You have to be in agony right now. Just whine and get some of those feel-good cookies already. No need to be a tough guy, no one here is judging you Ludo."

I sigh. "A cookie would be amazing right now, but I can't. Melody was looking at doggy wheelchairs before we came outside. I refuse to go down in history as a weak, broken soul who gets carried everywhere and bumps into things with his wheelchair when unassisted. I had to play hard tonight. I needed her to know I am okay." *For now, anyway.* I wonder how long I will physically be able to keep this act up?

"Ah, so that is what you were thinking about so deeply. I have thought a lot about life lately, too. I have a theory. Want to hear it?" Winston asks in an extra excited tone. I know I am in for a treat as his pupils dilate wildly.

"Even if I didn't want to hear it, I know you will tell me anyway," I say through laughter. "But first, what were you doing when you came up with said theory?" I have to ask because Winston's ideas are often born from whatever it is he was doing last. That is the same way most people stumble upon their own ideas. The only problem with Winston's ideas is that he gets sidetracked easily. Mainly by birds—and those are everywhere. This is a common occurrence, which leaves the majority of his ideas incomplete. If this is a good theory, I want to complete it for him as I have so many other times.

Winston looks away from me as he speaks, embarrassment and shame causing his shoulders to slump. "I was binge watching *Lost* while you were sleeping by the back door yesterday. Melody and

Kenner were at work, and you were out cold. I even ran around with your orange alligator, trying to get you fired up. You just kept snoring away, like a grizzly bear in hibernation mode. It was impressive, all that noise you were making. Anyhow, you left me no choice but to binge watch until you woke up."

Winston is embarrassed because I make fun of him on a regular basis for watching too much television. Lately, Melody and Kenner have stopped kenneling us during the day when they go to work, giving us the run of the house. There are several reasons backing our new routine, but two specific ones were the foundation of their recent decision. Number one, I am too tired and sore to do much of anything besides sleep while they are gone. The separation anxiety that used to plague me when my sweet Melody would leave for work only does so briefly now. Shortly after her departure, sleep finds me, and my anxiety dissipates entirely.

It appears that even Lucifer has grown tired and arthritic over the years. *My monster has finally waved his white flag.* This gives way to Melody and Kenner's number two reason for no longer kenneling us. *Personally, I feel that this should have really been their number one reason all along.* My giant size has always been an issue; I am large and cumbersome, making it difficult to carry me up and down the stairs. I have shrunk a lot over the past year due to losing a significant amount of muscle mass in my back half, but I am still big. I welcome our new routine, no matter what reasoning is behind it. At least this way, I am no longer filled with guilt after Melody or Kenner lug me down the stairs to our kennel, grunting as they go. I especially feel bad when they return home after a hard day of work and then have to carry me back up the stairs to go outside and relieve myself.

Winston continues with his theory. "Okay, so here are my thoughts on life. I think that when humans die, they are reincarnated as either dogs or cats."

I snort. "Winston, I think you have lost your marbles this time."

Winston shakes his head. "No, hear me out for a few more minutes. If we are good during our human years, we come back as a dog. If we are bad, we come back as a cat. Our dog or cat life is Purgatory."

"Okay, go on. I am interested now." I coax him to continue and listen with greater enthusiasm. *He may not be off his rocker after all.*

"If we do well in our dog lives and guide our humans appropriately—you know, create a legacy of goodness that follows in our wake—then we go to Heaven. I think this is why we are born with so much knowledge, but none of us dogs can remember where it came from or how we got it. You see, we aren't allowed the full memories we accumulated in our past human lives because we would want to go back and try to fix or relive things. We are only allowed the knowledge from the lessons we learned. What's done is done; we must always move forward. This is a dog's way. So during this purgatory stage of ours, we have to prove to the big man upstairs that we learned from our mistakes. In doing so, we use our knowledge to help others." Winston finishes.

I cock my head as I consider Winston's words.

He had put a lot of thought into this theory. "Okay, I am biting. You have made some good points so far. What I don't understand is the part about the cats. Explain that to me."

Winston sits up and continues with more animation than before. "Alright, so here is how the cats fit in. If one is bad in their human lives—you know, steal, cheat, etcetera—then they become a cat. The big guy upstairs loves us all and realizes that everyone makes mistakes now and then, so he forgives them of their wrongdoing and gives people one more chance with a cat's life. They say cats have nine lives, but that isn't true. What they should call it is their 'second chance life.' But that is another theory for another day. If the soul then lives a good cat life, they earn the opportunity to be a dog. Their dog life is their final shot at getting to go up the golden staircase. If they don't get their act together and continue to be bad—and let's face it, most cats are— then they go down the red staircase. Life is all about forgiving, learning, growing, and then paying it forward. I have learned that through all my years of being together with you."

I smile with pride. I am tickled by Winston's last words, as I have been trying to teach my whole pack this simple way of living all along. Winston is a bit slower than Melody and Kenner, so knowing that he understands it means they do as well. *A job well done for me!* "Winston, I think you have an excellent theory. I hope you're right about it, too. The part about the cats certainly makes sense. Most cats are rotten to the core, but there are some good ones out there. For years, I have wondered where exactly our vast core knowledge comes from. Having been

385

human in a previous life answers that question completely. I also think you are right about why we lack experience to back it up, and the feelings of familiarity we get from time to time throughout life. You know, the ones we can't place, but we insist we have been there before or done that. Finally, a solid theory to explain all the déjà vu moments of our lives."

Winston stands proudly, reveling in his genius moment. Sadly, I am about to let some of the wind out of his sails. "I need your help, buddy. You know I wouldn't ask for it unless I really needed it."

"Yeah, sure. Name the favor. You want me to grab a snack off the counter and take the heat for it when the trouble rolls down the hill?" He is trying to make a joke, but I can tell that he senses my sincerity as he approaches me, a cautious look on his face.

"You know that I am a planner." I struggle with my next words. "I have to formulate my final plan. I can't do the wheelchair thing. Maybe it is cutting off my nose to spite my face, and maybe I have too much pride and it will cost me my golden ticket to the upstairs. But I simply can't do it. I won't. I refuse."

"Ludo, what are you trying to say?" Winston sits beside me now, his mood growing more dismal by the second. He is anticipating what I will say next.

"I am saying that I can't put Melody or myself through the deteriorating part of my life. Melody will kill us both trying to hold me together. It will consume her. She will go back to being stressed and depressed, and I will lose everything I worked for. It will tear this family apart. You know I am right. I know you see it, too. I want to go out on a high note, Winston. I feel that I have earned that. I want to go out with the same pride and dignity I entered this world with. I want to leave with my chest and head held high!"

"But–" Winston tries to interrupt.

I cut him off. "It's time I start to pass the torch. You are ready; you know you have been for a long time." Several minutes of silence follow. I gaze into the distance, scouring for ideas. I don't want to get hit by a car or a tractor. I don't want to go out in anymore pain than I am already in. I could wonder away from the farm and not return, but Melody would never abandon me so I can't abandon her.

"No. You are wrong! Stop thinking over there. I can see the wheels turning in your head and I assure you none of those thoughts are worth pursuing." Winston chokes the words out. He is struggling to keep it together now. His body shivers like it is freezing outside and not the beautiful, warm evening that it is.

"I'm not wrong Winston. You know I am not, and I need your help. Are you going to help me or not?" I ask gruffly. "It's not like this is easy for me. You know the circle of life, this is how it goes."

Winston stands and almost shouts as he speaks, "I don't give a birds-behind about what the rules or laws of the circle of life say. You have always paved your own path in life. Why would you follow some pre-mapped path now? This isn't like you! I can't I won't except this!"

I look up at Winston from where I am laying

with sympathy filled eyes. "This is one part of life we can't change Winston. Death will eventually claim us all, but even with death I will have life through all of you. You, Kenner and Melody will carry with you all I have taught you. You will share that knowledge and experience with others and I will in some way always be there." I pause a moment for him to acknowledge that he is listening and receiving the message I am trying to relay. Winston nods slightly giving me the signal I need to continue. "I am not following a pre-mapped path either. I am still making my own way. I decided when and how to step into this world years ago, and I will decide how I step out of it. All I am asking for is a little help. This part I know I can't do alone. I have to do this right as I have the leave Melody in the best and safest way possible. I know if I do this wrong I could ruin her."

"Okay, then. I am listening now, but I want to go on record. I still don't like this and I still think you are wrong. I just don't know if that is me being selfish or if you truly are wrong? But I will do anything for you. I owe you that much, and if this is how you want to cash in your chip, I will help. But I won't like it, not one bit. And I am going to try to talk you out of whatever it is we are going to do, every chance I get. You have my word, though. I will do it. Now, what's the plan?" Winston sighs.

Chapter 48: The Plan

Winston and I create a solid plan after about a month. I am doing my best not to show any pain as I move slowly about the house. Miraculously, I manage to keep Melody off Amazon and away from doggy wheelchairs. The wheelchair would have made my life easier, and I would have appreciated it. Knowing that it had come from all the love and need Melody has for me would have made it an acceptable gift by any standard, but that is the easy path. That is the path that will only drag Melody backward.

I know that I won't be able to be with her forever; I have the fatal flaw of being mortal, just like all living things in this world. I refuse to leave Melody in a state of darkness. I am her light. Without me, I fear that she may not find her way back. I know that Kenner and Winston will be there for her, but we share an unbreakable, irreplaceable bond. I am going to leave an un-fillable hole in her heart, and I need to do it very carefully. *Once a heart is weakened, it has a higher chance of shattering.*

I have done what I was put here to do. I am an Ultimate Alpha. I have successfully formed a pack of purely good people and another dog to share the lessons I have taught them with others. They will all continue to help others and lift them up when hard times find them, this Ultimate Alpha family of mine will carry on my legacy. All of us make it our mission to help every living creature we meet. Everywhere we go, we do our best to breathe light and positivity into others' lives. We have all seen the darkness of life and felt its torment in various ways. We understand its perils, but we have survived them. This gives us the ability to help others do the same.

I have taken three once broken souls and put them all back together, helping them to achieve better states of mind. This is the way I must leave them. This is the way I must leave Melody. *Always leave things better than you found them.* If I deteriorate into nothing, she will, too. She has too many years left on this earth. If I do that to her, I will be selfish. By leaving her before this happens, I am being selfless. *The way of an Ultimate Alpha.* Winston and Kenner will make sure she understands. *It's better this way. She will see.*

Today, I awake filled with all kinds of mixed emotions. My body aches with each step, and pain radiates farther up my back than it ever had before. Food no longer tastes good, and I can't seem to get over how tired and sleepy I still feel, even though I just finished an eighteen-hour nap. I admit I had a little sleeping help from some special cookies. Kenner gave me an extra last night. That man truly loves me. I have been incredibly tired for several weeks now, but I have managed to hide it more until recently. I am finally declining so rapidly now that I can't hide it anymore. Mentally, I have just as much love, passion, strength, and awareness as the first day I locked eyes with my sweet Melody. Physically, though, it is time. I have been praying every night for the strength to carry out my plan to the very end.

Melody stays home from work today to snuggle and comfort me. I know she is home because I can hear and smell her bustling about out in the kitchen. She has called into work a couple times this week. This is part of the Melody slipping backward that I wanted to avoid. It is hard for me not to be happy about her staying home with me though. I am always elated to get any extra time with her even if she is sick and I just get to lie by her side. *There are no bad moments.* I have learned to love every second of every day. I cherish any family time I get. Life is short, and tomorrow... Well, let's just say that I have finally run out of tomorrows. So I embrace each special moment and see them all as the blessings they truly are.

Over the course of my years, I have learned that moments and time are two of the three things in life one cannot get back if one lets them pass by. The third thing we can't get back is words. You know what I am talking about, the dreadful ones we sometimes let escape our lips without first thinking. The ones that we wish we never said. *Live life with no regrets, Lu. Now, get up and seize the day.* Melody has a book on her nightstand that she has been reading before bed. It is called *Carpe Diem* by Rae Matthews. It is a great book. I finished it the other day when she and Kenner were at work. I am going to take the book's advice and do just that. Time to seize the day! *There are Melody moments to be had and memories to be made out in our kitchen.*

I stretch and shake the sleepiness away, then prepare myself to join her. As I jump down off the bed and land on the floor, pain shoots through my hips, and my back legs slide out from under me. *Dang useless legs. They couldn't support a feather if they tried to.* A loud, helpless yelp escapes me. I do my best to maintain the awkward position that the absence of strength and muscle in my back legs have forced me into by floundering around. I am in a stance that is the exact opposite of Melody's favorite yoga pose, downward dog. About a year ago, Melody switched to working out in the house in the mornings since I could no longer accompany her on her usual runs or walks outside. I know she wanted to go, but she didn't want me to feel bad, and she didn't have the heart to leave me behind. *Love something, set it free. Wait, how does that go again?*

Frustration fills me as I no longer have the strength to pull my legs back underneath myself. I haven't for quite some time now. Kenner has frequently been scooping me up as fast as he can to hide it from Melody. I know deep down she is stronger than we give her credit for. I don't know what Kenner's excuse is for trying to hide my worthless legs from her, but I do know mine. *Denial and fear.* I know what must be done, but I don't really want to do it. *I'm not ready.*

Melody hears my yowling and comes quickly to my rescue. As she runs into the bedroom, I notice that she won't make eye contact with me. She, too, is trying to hide her pain. *Great minds...* I can see the tears welling in her eyes though she tries her best to swallow them back down by opening her eyes wider so they don't spill over her bottom lids. I cast my gaze downward and pretend I hadn't noticed, but as I do, I see two tears escape and streak hotly down her cheeks. *Go ahead, insert two knives into my heart.* This is worse than any physical pain I have ever encountered.

Melody has been hiding her face from me a lot lately. I know that she doesn't want me to know that she is upset, so she keeps putting on this extra happy front. I know that it's all for show. She forgets that I know precisely when tears fill her eyes. I couldn't miss them even if I wanted to. Regardless of whether or not she hides her face from me, I still know they are there. *I can smell them.* My hips and legs may be failing, but my nose is still up to par.

Melody rights her face and bends down next to me. "You are okay, Lu. Let's get your legs back under you, boy." She raises my back half up. "There you go, my big, handsome baby." She comforts me as she lifts and repositions my legs. Then, she places a kiss on top of my head. "Let's go outside and then get you something to eat," she says, leading the way to the front door. She is still avoiding eye contact with me, and I hate it. My heart may as well be a giant stained-glass window, and her tears a baseball bat in Babe Ruth's hand, swinging for a home run. Today, we are both shattering slowly.

Chapter 49: Breaking Point

Melody or Kenner carry me up and down the porch steps so I can relieve myself. I personally find this more than a little embarrassing. I would rather take the help then be reduced to soiling myself or having to go indoors. *That would be humiliating.* I wallowed in self-pity over this same situation last week. It seems that there is nothing I can do to regain the muscles I have lost in my back half. Winston has come up with several theories over the past few weeks and we have tried them all, but none of them worked. *He isn't ready, either.*

I knew I would get old eventually. I just had no idea it would hurt so much. *No one told me that leaving would be so hard.* Last week, I set my great plan into motion. *There's no turning back now.* I took my pain-fueled anger and officially finalized my earth exiting strategy. Unfortunately, as I was working through the final steps of my plan my pain became intolerable as I was processing the part about finally deciding it was time to leave Melody and I took my heartbreak and anger at the world and biology for making me get old and deteriorate out on Winston. This was not part of my original plan, but it yielded the same result. *Everything happens for a reason.*

When Winston passed by me in one the hallways

of our house, jealousy devoured my ability to reason. I could not stand the sight of him, all young and muscular and able. *Able to remain here with her after I go.* He pranced by me proudly. He was just being his usual optimistic, carefree self. I lost my mind and attacked him. *I still don't know why I did it.* It definitely did not make me feel any better, especially after the fact. Jealousy is the only answer I can come up with. Winston had done nothing to provoke me. I fear that I am nearing a threshold on the amount of pain I can tolerate and still stay sane. *Slippery slope.*

I can't say it was much of a fight. I slashed my white fangs across Winston's face in a moment of pain and desperation; all he did was whimper and lie down. Winston wasn't being a coward. He was being respectful by submitting, which made it worse. He didn't challenge me. *He had done nothing wrong.* His only fault that day was slightly brushing against me and my wobbly legs. He knocked me off balance and, in doing so, back into the harsh reality I was struggling with.

Melody was doing her hair just inside the bathroom door by the hallway that I had launched my unplanned attack on Winston in. She quickly separated us from our one sided scuffle. At first I was devastated by what I had just done, then I saw the silver lining in the dark clouds I had just created. This was an inexcusable situation on my part, but it could still work in my favor. I had just given Winston a scar he will now bear for the rest of his life. *This will not be for nothing.* I apologized to Winston and thanked him for everything profusely. I told him that there had been a slight change of plans. *In the end, this way will work better for everyone.* Winston won't have any guilt when it's all over. He had previously fought me every step of the way. *This way, though a bit more painful for his, is absolutely better for all of us.*

Once I finished apologizing and explaining myself to Winston, I went to hide around the corner. Melody was terribly upset by the events I had just caused and had crumbled into a sobbing heap next to the hallway closet. Kenner locked eyes with me as he came running in. His eyes were filled with deep sorrow and empathy. At this very moment, I knew Kenner saw my plan and understood that I needed help to carry the rest of it out. Happiness, relief, and the deepest sadness I have ever felt flooded me all at once.

Kenner had no anger toward me, and I love him deeply for understanding me so well. I know he knew what I needed. I knew he would help me carry the weight of my situation and aid not only me, but also Melody, through the next torturous steps. Kenner knelt and scooped Melody up into his arms, securing her tightly against his strong chest, and initiated a conversation that probably should have happened weeks ago. *Communication is not always easy, but it is always necessary.*

"Ludo is a proud, wonderful dog. He is the best. That is what you always say, and you are right." He hesitated. I knew he too felt the thin ice we were both standing on.

Don't stop. I willed him on, and Kenner continued. "I know that you can see how much pain he is in. By the looks of you lately, you feel it as well." He squeezed her small, trembling frame tighter against his chest and brushed the hair that clung to her tears out of her face.

If someone or something is ever having a panic attack, that is what you do. *Squeeze!* The squeeze activates the sympathetic nervous system, which helps one to relax and breathe again. I don't really understand the science behind it, but I do know it's there and it works. I wanted so badly to be the one squeezing her at that very moment. *If only I had arms...*

Back in our earlier days, I used to lie on Melody's chest when she needed consoling after a bad or stressful day. It was my way of squeezing her. I decided to cling to these delicate memories of a younger version of us. They made me smile. I knew that I would need them to get through the rest of Melody and Kenner's conversation. Winston came and placed his head on my back. He was not only forgiving me, but also trying to apply the much-needed pressure I longed for. He was consoling me. *How did I get so lucky?*

I listened to Kenner as he bravely trudged onward. "I just can't imagine Ludo wanting to live like this. All of his honor and pride is being stripped away from him. He is the proudest dog I have ever had the pleasure of knowing."

Did I mention how much I love Kenner? Alpha to alpha, he knew me, and as the protectors of the world like to say, he always had my six. Melody had her ugly cry going on full force now. You know, the kind that people save for behind closed doors because they can hardly breathe and their face contorts in horrific ways. I got up and walked farther around the corner to give them more privacy. Truth be told, my ugly cry was starting to seep out as well. Winston followed me, offering silent support.

My blood pressure started to skyrocket, and my blood flowed through my vessels like water flows through small, narrow streams after a heavy rain. It was roaring too loudly to hear the words being spoken around the corner. I struggled to gain my composure and hear what I feared, but desperately wanted and needed to be said. *If only I had a tongue that could speak human words...* I felt bad for putting Kenner in that situation, but I will be forever grateful for his help.

Violent sadness stormed through my every cell, numbing my physical pain as Kenner spoke. "You have to ask yourself if you are doing this for him, or if you are doing this for you. Ludo loves and lives for you. I have no doubt that you are both each other's favorite thing in the whole world. He knows that you love him, and he won't leave you until you tell him that it's okay. I just have a feeling that it is also killing him to feel like he can no longer fulfill his duties as the great white protector by your side. He has always been, and always will be, your happiness, your light. Don't let him become your darkness. It will crush him and will ruin everything he has ever been for you."

Melody tried to speak, but nothing was discernable. Loud, gut-wrenching sobs escaped her, with unknown words intertwined. *I hate being the source of her tears. Her sadness.* She has done everything possible to keep me comfortable since my devastatingly fast decline started. I have always brought her joy, happiness, and safety. Kenner was right. If Melody and I continued this way, it would tear us both apart. We would become part of each other's darkness. These were the words I wanted so desperately to say to her. Kenner had done a far better job in relaying the message than I ever could have hoped to do on my own. I wanted to enjoy the time I had left with her. I wanted to go out with my honor and pride. More than anything, though, I wanted to leave this world as her forever light and continue to light her world from afar. Kenner knew this. He understood. It was unspoken between us, and I loved him even more for his ability to see it and put it into words for us both.

I thought I would only ever have a special bond with Melody, but my bond with Kenner runs just as deep in other ways. I know this because I have been sleeping in bed right between Kenner and Melody for several weeks now. *Mr. No-Dogs-Allowed-in-Bed finally caved.* I love the extra snuggles and closeness that this gives me. Their mattress is much more forgiving on my hips and back. I sleep like a rock between the two of them. I am not sure if it is because Melody has her arms wrapped so tightly around me I lack some oxygen during the night, or if it is because Kenner is right next to me, taking care of us all. Kenner's close presence allows me to completely clock out for the hours we spend in bed. I know if anything were to go awry at night, he would see to our safety.

Kenner is a very intuitive man. He senses how awful I feel and how stressed out Melody is by my deterioration. Lately, when we go to sleep and I groan at him as part of our normal nightly routine, he only groans back once. He lets me win quickly because he knows I am exhausted. If he goes to bed first, he lifts me up into bed so I can settle in before they join me. I appreciate these kind gestures, and it warms my heart to know that my Melody is in the good and very capable hands of Kenner and Winston. *Did I mention that I have the best pack on the planet?*

Speaking of Winston, the poor guy still sleeps on his dog bed. At first, he made lots of jealous remarks when our sleeping arrangements changed, but now he says nothing when Melody or Kenner lifts me into bed. *I couldn't make the jump if I tried, not even on a good day.* Winston just gives me a sad look, like he pities me now. I am sure he realizes that his day will come all too soon. *Life is precious, unknown, short.*

Getting back to today, aside from the somber feelings that fill the air, Melody seems determined to make it as pleasant as possible for me as we head back inside. I do not want to disappoint her, so I fully intend to put on a good show and appreciate the spoiling coming my way. "How about a steak, big guy," she says, not asks, as we head into the kitchen. She then pulls the biggest, juiciest T-Bone steak I have ever seen out of the fridge. I can't help but wag my tail until my back aches too much to continue. I halt my tail in action, and it goes limp and hangs like Eeyore's. "Wait here a minute," she says, and quickly leaves the room with idea-filled eyes.

Melody returns a short moment later with my memory foam dog bed from the bedroom. She plops it down on to the kitchen floor so I can lie on it while she prepares my meal. I can hear Winston out in the kennel barking with jealousy. I like that she put him out there. She is making today all about the two of us. *The original duo.*

My mouth waters as my steak rests on the counter, cooling. When she finally decides that it is cool enough for consumption, she cuts it up into bite-sized pieces so I can easily chew them. Then, she serves me right where I lie on my bed. *A guy could certainly get used to this breakfast-in-bed business.* I don't even have to get up. Nothing beats lunch in bed. Judging by the position of the sun in the sky, it is well past breakfast. On a normal day, I wouldn't have been so gluttonous. Generally, I would have worried about the after-effects and digestive distress. Today is different though. I know that it doesn't matter. I won't plague or fog anyone out with my horrible gas later.

I have had some epic gas over the years. On more than a few occasions, I have sent Kenner and Melody running from the room, gasping for fresh air. Winston gives me an "Atta boy" and a high paw of approval when these lovely moments occur. I can't help it; normally, I would walk into another room to do something so vile, but I can't get up fast enough once the urge to launch the dreaded air hits me.

I finish my steak while Melody packs a daypack with my Frisbee, leash, a couple of waters, and a bowl for me. "How about we go have ice cream with Winston, now. Then, we will go on a 'just us' date at the park. Sound good to you, big guy? You up for it?" Her eyes glisten with moisture, which pains me as we head out to get Winston. I wag my tail to confirm my interest in all the above plans. She is making today perfect.

Winston and I lie in our plush, green, grass-covered yard and enjoy our ice cream together. He then ignores our conversation as a rabbit catches his eye. He asks if I want the first attempt at capturing the bustling bunny, but I decline. *I haven't been on a hunt since our skunk incident. That one nearly killed me.* I make Winston promise to bring me back a piece if he catches the rabbit. I am ninety percent positive he won't this time, and I know full well that I no longer stand a chance in being any sort of help to him. Plus, I need to reserve my energy for Melody's and my park date.

I watch with envy as Winston's agile body leaps from side to side until he almost overtakes the rabbit. He would have had it, but Melody realizes what he is up to and calls him off. Then, as she leads him back to the kennel, something indescribable stirs inside me. *Perhaps it is the steak and ice cream I just inhaled.* Indigestion or not, the feelings inside me give me a strong indication that this will be the last time I ever see Winston. I bid him a sappy farewell and make him promise to take care of our humans. He simply says, "I promise, but you are over-reacting. I will see you and smell your horrible gas later this evening. I can't believe she let you eat a whole steak! Enjoy your time at the park. Don't overdo it." *If one can find a way to live life as carefree as Winston does, then they are truly blessed.*

Melody walks over to the passenger side of the Jeep and lifts me in. We then head off for our date at the park. It is a beautiful, sixty-degree, bright and sunny March afternoon. *Normally, March days are not this pleasant.* When we arrive, Melody does not bother leashing me. For one, I am not going anywhere fast, and two, no one is around. I assume there aren't many people around because it is a Thursday. Most people are in school or at work during this time. I have the park and my girl all to myself. Today could not be more perfect. *Time to fill it with light that will last a lifetime.*

Melody pulls out my favorite Frisbee from her daypack. She then launches it into the air for me. I am surprised by the sudden burst of energy I have. *Thank you, sugary ice cream.* I run and catch my Frisbee in a stunning leap. I have not been able to catch midair fliers in quite some time. This is a welcome surprise. I catch ten good tosses of my flying red love, and Melody smiles and claps at each performance as if I am the most amazing Frisbee-catching dog on earth. Finally, I am too exhausted to stand any longer.

I gimp my way over to where Melody stands and lie by her feet. I flip the Frisbee over and around my head. I always do this since there is a hole in the middle of it. *It makes me look like the planet Saturn.* It is also my way of telling her I need a break. I have done this move forever, even when I was younger and could play for hours.

Today is the best playing session I have had in over a year. For a brief moment, it is like I am young all over again. I look up at the sky and say a silent thank you to God and the universe. Melody kneels to join me in the grass. I aim my chest high at the sky and puff it out, proud and full, stud-style. I still have it after all. *At least, I do today.* I rest my head on her

403

lap while she rubs my ears. Kenner had finally given up his secret a couple months ago and showed her the correct way to give a good ear rub. Another gift he had given me. *Four hands are better than two.*

As Melody and I lie there in the grass together, I reflect on how perfect our day has been so far. The sun kisses our cheeks, and I can't help but think of how perfect our life has been altogether. If only I could fall asleep and drift away from this life today, at this moment. If I left today, I would go out on the highest of highs. I could not have created a happier, more magic-filled day for the two of us. If I go today, I will go with all my pride and strength intact. *The way I want to be remembered.* These are the final happy memories I want Melody to have of me. Nothing but the smiles, joyous giggles, and cheering one another on that took place today. This is the light I want to leave behind. She cheered me on as I caught my Frisbees this afternoon, and I cheered her on and prayed for her to be brave and step forward into a future where I no longer physically stand by her. *I will always be by her side in spirit. She will never be alone.*

Exhausted from our perfect day, I drift into sleep on Melody's lap. I don't know how long my nap lasts. I only know I am dreaming of amazing things when Melody's soft voice and stroking hand on my nose pull me from my slumber. "Come on, Ludo. Let's go see Kenner." *Yes, Kenner. I almost forgot. I need him to be a part of this perfect day, too.* Nothing in this world matters more than my pack.

Our next stop is the vet clinic. I am slightly overwhelmed when I see Kenner standing in the parking lot, waiting to help me out of the Jeep. Joy and sadness overtake me as our perfect plan starts to unfold. The day is growing bittersweet now. I know we will soon see Dr. Amy. Dr. Amy started working at the local vet clinic about a year ago, and over the past year I have got to know her well. She requires Melody and I to come in for regular checkups since I have been consuming so many medicinal cookies over the last year. Anyway, Today I know Dr. Amy will give me the gift of sleep and help me drift away from my mortal life on my final, perfect day. Sadness fills me on Melody's behalf, but excitement and relief are all I feel on mine. I am ready to climb the golden staircase and look down on my girl from the other side.

Melody stands at the back of our Jeep with Kenner. He is quizzing us on how our day had gone. I sit next to them in the parking lot without a leash. Truth be told, I have never needed one since my encounter with Mr. Sinister all those years ago. That situation alone was scary enough that I have never wanted nor tried to leave Melody's side again. I sense hesitation in Melody as she recants our day with a smile and glistening blue eyes. Then, she says, "I don't know. This feels all wrong. He has done so well today. You should have been at the park to see him catch Frisbees. It was like he was two years old all over again."

Slight panic starts to fill me. I bark at Melody. "No, don't bail on me now! We must go in, my sweet girl. Today was a gift." I start walking towards the door of the clinic, willing Melody to follow.

Kenner takes the words from my mouth. "Baby,

today was a gift. Look at him. He is ready. He is headed for that door with or without you. You can do this for him. Come on, let's go inside and see the doctor. We can always change our minds in there." Kenner escorts her to the clinic doors where I sit waiting patiently. *I am ready, but my girl is not.*

We enter the clinic's waiting room, and the always friendly staff greets us. It is the end of the workday and we are the last appointment. Appointments like these are filled with very hard, sensitive moments. I am not surprised when the lady at the front desk gets up and walks to the door we had walked through and locks it as she flips the sign to closed. They are giving us as much privacy as they can for our final moments. One of the assistants joins us, and after saying hello and introducing herself, she asks if they can have me step up on the scale. This is normal procedure whenever we come to the vet, so I follow her and do as she asks. Melody is never more than a step behind me.

Shock falls over Melody's face as the scale reads seventy-eight pounds. This is a far cry from my once one hundred-thirty prime. Melody lets out a small gasp as the realization she is doing the right thing falls over her. I have lost nearly half my body weight over the past year. I still have my wonderful mind, but my mortal body is now only skin and bones. Softly, so only I can hear, Melody says, "Oh my, I am so sorry I let this go on for so long."

We follow the assistant to one of the exam rooms. Silence fills the air as we wait for Dr. Amy to join us. Melody continuously rubs and hugs me. Dr. Amy enters the room, greeting Melody and Kenner with a sensitive smile, and me with a special treat. She pats me on the head as she looks at Melody and Kenner with sympathetic eyes and says, "You two are doing the right thing. I know it is hard, but trust me when I say he is grateful to be here right now. Many people wish for the same treatment in the end." I am happy she said those words. I can sense that Melody is about to scoop me up and run with me out of the office.

Groaning, I rub my nose against Melody's limp hands. "I do not want to leave here—not in this body, anyway. Don't fret. I am ready, my girl. I am so tired. It's time." Devastation attempts to take over her face. "I want my perfect ending on this couldn't-be-more-perfect day." *It's okay. I promise.*

Dr. Amy's voice breaks the silence that is settling throughout the room again. "I am going to give him a shot so he can relax and you can enjoy some more time with him. Is that okay with you?" Amy asks.

Melody's reply is a barely there nod. She has not been able to speak since Dr. Amy joined us in the room. Kenner relays Melody's reply with actual words. "Go ahead. We are all ready now."

Yes, we are. I am. The shot Dr. Amy gives me is amazing. Warm, fuzzy feelings and a tremendous amount of love glide through my veins and erase all my pain. I melt into Melody's lap. She moves from the chair down to the floor, clinging tightly to me. Kenner sits behind her. He is acting as her strong base of support. He will now become the rock I have always been to her. He reaches through her arms and strokes my head. I relax knowing Melody will be well taken care of when I am gone and enjoy, reliving the memories of years of adventures we have shared as a family. I smile thinking of the first day Melody and I ever met. I almost peed on her to mark her as mine what a scene that would have been. I remember the first ear rub Kenner ever gave me when he first came over to our house when we lived in Illinois. And then there is Winston. He and I have shared some amazing adventures together. What a hoot it was when Winston and I broke into our house by climbing onto the air-conditioner thinking Melody was in trouble. All that racket we were concerned about was only the sounds of love and passion being shared between two people that were meant for one another. *Ahh, love.*

I am blessed to be surrounded by such a tremendous amount of love. I always have been and I know I always will be where I am going. I know I am leaving Melody, Kenner and Winston in the same state too. Never will any of them search or want for love. I have taught them all how to see it, how to feel it, and how to share it. This magnificent world supplies love in abundance. I have taught my Ultimate Alpha pack to open their eyes, grab it, and share it wherever they go.

Speaking of eyes, mine are now getting heavy. I can feel my heartbeat slowing. I know the times has come to say my goodbyes. I first gaze into Kenner's eyes, I make sure he understands all the responsibility I am now transferring over to him. I can clearly see that my message has been received.

Now for the hardest part, I steer my gaze over towards Melody. My eyes lock with hers and the two of us are instantly transported to a place of love and understanding that only true soulmates will ever know. I ravenously consume all the love that is pouring out of her for me. I know that her letting me go is the hardest thing she has ever done. I also know she is able to do it because she truly loves me. I am astounded by all the love. Melody's and my eyes are still locked on one another, her deep blue irises have captured my chocolate browns and we hold one another for the last time. I can see inside her and her me. We both relive the same memories of our amazing life together. Memories flash through our minds like pictures on one of those old projection players. Flash... Flash.... *Always in sync.* I hear the laughter and remember all the words she spoke and the exact gestures and ways I communicated my replies. *We are running with Paige, talking about boys and relationships. We mow the lawn and play Frisbee, "Great catch Lu. You are the greatest dog ever!" I am swimming in the river with Winston retrieving duck dummies Kenner has thrown for us as Melody cheers me on and calls me back to the beach by her side. "Good job Ludo, look at you go kick those back legs buddy, you got it! Come here my perfect boy!"*

Our peaceful moment is slightly interrupted as Dr. Amy rejoins us. *It's time.* She asks if we are ready, but only receives choked up nods and grunts as a form of consent to continue. Dr. Amy explains what will happen after my next shot. I nudge my nose under Melody's hand. I know she needs more reassurance. *It's okay to let me go now. I'm ready.*

Dr. Amy injects the final, and soon to be fatal, shot in my left rear leg. Then, she slips out of the room to give us privacy. The deepest, most restful

409

and peaceful sleep I have ever felt starts to wrap me up in its arms. It feels like a million warm hugs from Melody all at once.

Melody begins whispering in my ear as I fight to keep my eyes open and locked with hers. "Thank you for everything. Thank you for helping me find myself, for helping me gain confidence and courage. For teaching me how to stand alone when I needed to do what was right. Thank you for being my rock, my safe place. But most of all, more than anything, Ludo, thank you for being you. For being perfect! You will always be my perfect boy. You can go now, I will be okay. I promise. Thank you, Ludo. Thank you!"

You're welcome my sweet Melody. You're Welcome! There is no darkness when I finally close my eyes, bidding my official farewell. A warm glow meets me, which gradually turns into the most brilliant and beautiful sunrise I have ever seen as my eyes gain focus. My body goes limp in Melody's arms. I feel it, too. *I let go.* I am free of my deteriorating earth body.

Incredibly light, and now fully awake on the other side, I stand. I am now one hundred percent pain-free. This is the best I have ever felt. I am now stronger and more powerful than I have ever been. My spirit form and I stand before Melody. *My poor, sweet Melody.* She is still sitting on the floor, holding my body and crumbling into pieces. "I can't leave him. I can't let go," Melody somehow manages to choke out.

Kenner comforts her, holding her tightly as she shakes violently. "It's okay, babe. He is not there anymore. He is happy and pain-free. He is probably

410

catching Frisbees as we speak."

More almost inaudible words escape Melody. "I can't leave him on the floor. I can't put his head on the cold, hard floor."

I am feeling bad for feeling so amazing as I stare at her and Kenner. I wish they could see me. I need to get her to look at me. Then, Melody will know I am okay. She needs to know that she has done the right thing by bringing me to see Dr. Amy today. *Heck, I am better than okay. I am perfect!* Let me tell you, perfect feels more euphoric than words can even describe. Amazing doesn't even begin to cover it.

Kenner solves Melody's predicament by taking off his jacket and propping my body's head upon it. Melody still has her hand on my body as if she can somehow will me to wake back up. She needs my help one last time. *But how?* As I am trying to figure out how to help her, I am overcome by the sudden urge to stretch. My back begins to tingle profusely. I stretch and shiver to quell the odd feeling so I can think clearly. As I stretch again, the most glorious, breathtaking, iridescent wings sprout out from along my spine. *Not only do I feel unstoppable, but now I can fly. So the grass is greener on the other side!*

As my wings finish fully sprouting, Melody looks up. *Can she see me?* Perhaps she feels the soft breeze my flapping wings create. *This is great.* I don't want her to be sad for me, or even miss me. All I have ever wanted is for her to be happy and surrounded by love. I know she is finally at the point in her life where happiness will continue to flow her way, especially now that she has Kenner. The two of them are made for each other. I could never have left her if it

411

weren't for him. *It's true when they say there is someone for everyone in this world.*

The only thing I want now is to take away Melody's current pain. I want to rid her of her feelings of loss and guilt. I need to get her out of this office and away from my old shell of a body. I know that when Melody steps outside, she will see the world differently. Today, the sun will set more brilliantly than it ever has before. She will see the great future that lies before her. She will see in that sunset that we are still together, and that I am still with her. *I will forever be by her side, in some form.* Once Melody is outside, she will feel the weight lift off her shoulders. Freedom will move in, and she will step forward. *Assuming Winston's life theory is correct, Melody will make a great dog one day. She is always moving forward.*

Melody still sits on the clinic floor with her hand over my body's heart. She is still staring up. It seems as if she is looking right at me, however; I know she can't truly see me. If she could, getting her out of the clinic be much easier. I place my nose under her chin, and she inhales deeply. *Can she smell me?* She and I always sniffed one another, a silly daily gesture I will miss dearly in this new life of mine. I flap my brilliant wings, applying gentle pressure with my nose under her chin. As I do, Kenner helps Melody to stand.

Softly Kenner says, "Come on, babe, it's time to go. He's not here anymore. He's up there, smiling down at us."

The three of us exit the clinic together, Melody and Kenner walking hand in hand as I fly along beside my girl. The two of them step out the door and into the most enchanting sunset. I hover next to Melody a moment longer, then say my silent good-bye. I know something Melody doesn't that makes this much easier for me. *Goodbye is not forever.* One day, she will join me up in the clouds with glorious wings of her own. I sniff her one last time. I think she thinks it is a gust of wind blowing her hair back. She looks up. As her eyes find the sunset, Melody again says, "I love you. Thank you."

I inhale hard, wanting to take as much of her scent with me as I can. Then, I spring into the air towards the clouds. I can't wait to explore this new world, my wings propel me gloriously into the bright light of the other side. The leaves on the trees rustle gently above Melody and Kenner, serving as my voice. Just before I cross over, I call out to Melody one last time: "You're welcome!"

Acknowledgement:

First, I want to thank you for taking time out of your busy life to read my book. I hope you enjoyed Ludo's journey in life as much as I did not only living it, but writing it as well. I hope you will consider leaving me a star rating or review on Amazon as it will help me to improve the next story I create for you.

Next I would like to express my gratitude to everyone who saw me through this book; to all those who provided support in not only the real-life story but the creation of this book as well. I want to thank those of you who were there to talk things out with me, read the first-ten drafts, offered comments, and assisted in the editing, proofreading and the cover design.

I would like to thank my family as well as Brea, Paula and of course, my dog Ludo for being the best friends a person could ever ask for, and for getting me through one of the hardest times of my life.

Also, I need to send a massive thank you out to Rae Matthews (Author) for inspiring me to bring this book to life and helping me pay tribute to the best dog ever!

Last but not least, I want to thank my husband, who supported and encouraged me in spite of all the time it took me away from him and our dog children. It was a *long* journey for them.

About the Author:

A.J. Arentz was born and raised in Alaska and now resides in the Driftless area of the Midwest along the Mississippi river. She resides with her husband and three very spoiled dogs. She is an animal lover who can't get enough of the outdoors. Aside from reading and writing she can often be found out hunting and fishing with her husband and their fur

babies.

33031720R00235